LANDLORD/TENANT RIGHTS IN OREGON

Michael H. Marcus, District Court Judge

Self-Counsel Press Inc.
a subsidiary of
International Self-Counsel Press Ltd.
U.S.A.   Canada

Printed in Canada

First edition: February, 1978
Second edition: October, 1980
Third edition: July, 1988
Fourth edition: May, 1992

Cataloging in Publication Data

Marcus, Michael, 1943 -
    Landlord/tenant rights in Oregon

    (Self-counsel legal series)
    First ed. published under title: Landlord/tenant relations for Oregon.
    Includes index.
    ISBN 0-88908-833-0

    1. Landlord and tenant — Oregon — Popular works.
I. Title. II. Series.
KF02517.Z9M37 1992 346.79504'34 C91-091134-7

Self-Counsel Press Inc.
1704 N. State Street
Bellingham, Washington 98225
a subsidiary of
International Self-Counsel Press Ltd.
1481 Charlotte Road
North Vancouver, British Columbia
Canada V7J 1H1

CONTENTS

TABLES

SAMPLES

NOTICE TO READERS

Laws are constantly changing. Every effort is made to keep this publication as current as possible. However, neither the author nor the publisher can accept any responsibility for changes to the law or practice that occur after the printing of this publication. Please be sure that you have the most recent edition of this book.

- -

ORDER FORM

To: Self-Counsel Press
1704 N. State Street
Bellingham, Washington
98225

Please send me _____ Oregon Residential Tenancy Statutes at $5.00 each, (includes $2.50 postage and handling).

Payment enclosed for $_____.
(Prices subject to change without notice.)

Name_____

Address_____

City_____ State_____

Zip Code_____

INTRODUCTION

This book should be useful to landlords as well as to tenants. It is designed to help both lay people and lawyers. I have concentrated on practical problems and solutions in the hope that many landlords and tenants will be able to avoid or to solve problems themselves. But a safe approach to a practical solution requires some understanding of the law, and this book accordingly contains a good deal of explanation of the legal theory involved in landlord/tenant relations.

Chapters 3, 6, and 8 should be particularly useful to lawyers, tenant organizers, and landlords. These chapters discuss, respectively, rental agreements and rules, repairs, and evictions.

The hostility typical of landlord and tenant disputes is equalled in my experience only by that which so often accompanies the agonies of child custody battles in divorce court. This book should enable landlords to give some thought to the law's recognition of tenants' rights and landlords' obligations *before* the emotions of a live dispute intervene, and it should enable them to save everyone involved considerable distress, energy, and money.

Landlords who calmly examine their "rights" to lock out tenants, to discriminate against members of minorities, or to evict "troublemakers" should avoid expense and trouble. In most cases these "rights" are nonexistent. In my experience, landlords frequently make mistakes in the heat of confrontations — to the delight of tenants' attorneys, who would otherwise be without any means to defend an eviction.

Knowing something about the law should also make it easier for landlords to assess the competence of the rental agents and lawyers they select to represent them. Expertise in this area varies immensely. An incompetent rental agent can get a landlord into serious financial trouble by giving tenants grounds for legal action; an incompetent lawyer will only compound the problem for the landlord while running up unnecessary fees.

While I don't expect landlords to subsidize tenants who cannot pay the rent, I do expect that a rational consideration of each party's rights and obligations will, as a simple matter of sound business judgment, avoid costly disputes over which party has the right to do what — disputes that often have nothing to do with the rent.

Landlords should know the practical consequences of ignoring habitability obligations, for there are various remedies available to tenants whose premises are in a state of disrepair. Hopefully, economic self-interest can accomplish some advances in the quality of low-rent housing.

Tenants who can afford to choose among various rental possibilities are in a position to assert their rights as consumers of rental housing. This book will help these people learn what their rights are and, therefore, also equip them to decide what their rights should be. Tenants have a very real opportunity to affect the progress of landlord and tenant law in the Oregon Legislature, which corrected years of landlord-oriented court decisions that had blocked every effort to recognize an "implied warranty of habitability" in residential tenancies when it passed the Landlord and Tenant Act.

The Oregon Legislature is very responsive to citizen input, as landlords have learned quite well. Several associations have lobbyists seeking to assert the interests of landlords at the legislature. Legal aid lobbyists, who were largely responsible for the adoption of the Landlord and Tenant Act in the 1973 session (after six years of unsuccessful efforts), continue to represent tenants each session.

Tenants who are interested in their rights by necessity, and whose ability to take risks is severely limited by the need to survive, should find out from this book what they are entitled to in theory and how to get as much as possible of that theory put into practice with a minimum of risk. You may notice that the tone of many of the letters and notices that appear as examples in this book is so abrupt as to be harsh. They are designed to show the need for the type of information necessary in each type of notice and the need to be unequivocal and unambiguous. By all means, if you get to the point where notices or letters are required, do not hesitate to make them as polite and friendly as you wish. Just be careful, however, to include all of the required information and to make it absolutely clear what you want, why you want it, and, if appropriate, what you intend to do if you don't get it.

Although this book should help lay people solve landlord/tenant problems without going to court, once it appears that the case is likely to end up in court, do not assume that you can safely handle it yourself. There may be situations in which you have no real choice, but the assistance of an attorney may make the difference between success and failure. The principles discussed in this book are general, and any minor variation in the facts of your case could make a critical difference to how these principles apply to your specific situation. If your dispute is likely to reach court, your safest course is to get a lawyer. On the other hand, you have every right to make sure your attorney knows what he or she is doing; this book can equip you to do that.

This book includes changes resulting from the 1991 legislative session and court decisions published through December, 1991. Court decisions have upheld tenants' rights to use repair violations to defend eviction actions (and to have the eviction court order the landlord to make the repairs). The courts have also held that although punitive damages are not available under the Landlord and Tenant Act, emotional distress damages are available for some deliberate violations of the act, particularly those involving unlawful self-help eviction or retaliation. The courts have also recognized the right of redemption in eviction actions based on nonpayment of rent.

Readers who would like a copy of the Oregon Statutes referred to in this book, namely —

- Oregon Residential Landlord and Tenant Act (ORS 90.100 — 90.940)
- Forcible Entry and Unlawful Detainer Statutes (ORS 105.105 — 105.165)
- Oregon Exemption Statutes (ORS 23.160 — 23.305)
- Sale of Abandonded Property (ORS 79.5040(3))

can order them from the publisher by using the order form on page ix, or from either of the addresses below:

Multi-Family Housing Council
545 Union St. N.E.
Salem, OR 97301
Tel: 378-1912 (current price $3.75)

Oregon Legislative Council
Publications
S 101 State Capital
Salem, OR 97310
Tel: 378-8148 ($5.00 per chapter)

1

WHAT YOU SHOULD KNOW ABOUT EACH OTHER

a. INVESTORS vs. SPECULATORS

It is useful for a tenant to know whether a landlord is an investor or speculator. Landlords who are investors usually plan to hold on to their properties for a long time because they make their money by selling property only after it has increased in value ("appreciated") over many years. These landlords have an economic interest that is consistent with their tenants' interest in good housing: they will make repairs when deteriorating conditions are brought to their attention because most repairs are cheaper to deal with before they lead to even worse conditions. Upkeep is simply part of an investor's financial planning; an investor cannot assume that repairs can be left to the next owner. If tenants have trouble with this kind of landlord, it will likely be only in the areas of rent increases, occupancy rules, and the like.

Speculator landlords, on the other hand, count on making a rapid profit by buying and selling their properties on a short-run basis. A speculator might buy one house with a small down payment, hold it for five years, sell it, and reinvest the proceeds in about a 10% down payment in each of three more houses. These, in turn, are sold in five years, and so on.

Besides having little interest in the long-run condition of their properties, speculator landlords have problems with cash flow. Although they typically make a huge profit on paper (often in the neighborhood of 20%), they must turn over most of the incoming rent to banks or other mortgage holders, and they must reinvest the proceeds of sales in new holdings to take full advantage of the tax laws. The system of rapid turnover and reinvestment can often be addictive.

The result is that most speculator landlords rarely respond to requests for repairs without some kind of added incentive. The repairs they do make are often makeshift. After all, they don't care what happens to the property after someone else owns it, and a repair fund has few tax advantages.

Recent federal tax changes limiting deductions for interest on real estate purchases may have a substantial impact on both kinds of landlords; landlords' organizations predicted that those changes would tighten the housing market by discouraging new construction while forcing rents upward.

Almost all landlords have one thing in common: their primary interest in the tenant is collecting the rent. Big landlords are generally more prepared to let tenants "ride" for a few months if their tenants suffer a loss of income. However, they are also least likely to be close enough to their tenants emotionally to have any overwhelming compassion. Small landlords, on the other hand, simply cannot afford to do without the rent because of their own needs, however much compassion they may feel.

b. HOW DO YOU FIND OUT WHAT KIND OF LANDLORD YOU HAVE?

It will take some time and energy to discover whether your landlord is a speculator or an investor. If you're trying to decide whether to take a place, you may have to pay a deposit to the landlord to hold it for a day or two to give you time to decide (see chapter 3).

Take a pencil and paper to the county tax office and ask for help in finding the addresses owned by the same landlord in that county. If you aren't sure of the owner, the same office can give you a name from the address of the rental unit. When you have an idea of how many places the landlord (or owner, if he or she is different from the landlord) owns, you already know something. One of the addresses listed may be the home or place of business of the landlord, but a string of addresses may mean trouble. To find out, make a list of five or ten of these addresses at random, and then try to list some near the place you're interested in. Then ask where you can look up the deeds to the first batch (or to all of them, if you have time). You will find it easier, and the county employees more helpful, than you might expect.

What you're looking for is the average length of time the landlord holds on to property. If most of the deeds are less than five years old, you probably have a speculator landlord on your hands. Another common incident of speculation is delinquent property taxes. Apparently, it is more profitable for speculator landlords to reinvest cash in new holdings than to pay off property taxes — at least until the last minute. On the other hand, if the deeds are generally older, the landlord probably has a long-range interest in the property and, therefore, in its condition.

As a final check, visit the places near the one you are considering and talk to the tenants as you would to a former tenant (see chapter 3). If you find that the landlord holds many units for short periods of time, and if the tenants you talk to have substantial complaints about the landlord, consider your forfeited deposit well worth it and don't move in unless you are willing to sacrifice your peace of mind for many months.

c. TENANTS, RICH AND POOR

Tenants also differ. Of course, rich tenants are more able than poor ones to select decent rental units. However, tight housing markets in some areas put more and more tenants into the same position. The slum lord's slogan, "If you don't like it, why don't you move?" is nothing more than a cruel taunt when there is no real competition among landlords to offer decent housing at low rents.

Paradoxically, in my experience, it is the relatively transient students who are often most insistent on decent housing and most able to devote energy to enforcing their rights. Single parents, whose housing problems often complete the despair of poverty, simply have no strength left to invoke the delicate and tedious tools the law offers for enforcing their rights. A single person with no dependents is usually in a better position to risk eviction, which is the ultimate risk for a tenant in all landlord/tenant disputes.

d. HOW SHOULD A LANDLORD SCREEN TENANTS?

Since the last edition of this book, much attention has focused on "drug houses" and "meth labs" (illegal drug manufacturing operations, a growing and deadly cottage industry) in the landlord/tenant world. A tenant who sells or manufactures drugs can get a landlord into a lot of trouble, thanks to "drug house" and forfeiture legislation which theoretically threatens a landlord's ownership or continued operation of a rental property if it has been used for such purposes (or for prostitution or gambling). If a tenant has turned a rental unit into a drug manufacturing plant, the ingredients are so toxic that there is now legislation requiring the use of certified professionals to make the unit safe for occupancy again, and it is often cheaper to tear down the unit than to restore it to the market safely. But other tenants suffer even more than the property owner, as they are the ones whose quality of life — and safety — is most directly threatened by a neighboring tenant's drug activities.

As police and rental owner-and-manager association trainings stress, the answer to this from a landlord's point of view depends largely on rigorous and intelligent tenant screening. Screening tenants is nothing new, of course, but the risks to all of inadequate screening have increased in the era of the "war on drugs." I endorse the message of the police and association trainings: landlords, screen your tenants, and don't cut corners. Check employment and prior landlord references intelligently and meticulously. Get the number from the telephone book, not the tenant-applicant, and call. Verify that a prior "landlord" is really that, and not a friend who agreed to provide the tenant with a sham reference.

What I have to add to this advice is this:

(a) Owners, screen your *managers* with great care. A poor choice may haunt you in many costly ways, not the least of which may be poor tenant screening.

(b) Do not exaggerate the requirements of the newly enhanced anti-discrimination laws discussed in chapter 15. Those laws correctly prohibit discrimination on the basis of ethnicity, gender, nationality, handicap, and familial status, but it is lawful to discriminate on the basis of income, employment history, criminal history, and — for better or for worse — receipt of public assistance benefits.

Most practical of all is the right to discriminate on the basis of disparity between disclosed income and apparent means. If the applying tenant is on welfare but drives a new luxury car, ask how this is possible, and do not fear the law if you refuse the rental based on an incredible or unverifiable response. As long as your tenant population does not reflect probable unlawful bias against protected classes (those groups mentioned in the anti-discrimination laws), and as long as you apply your screening criteria to all applicants equally, you should not get into trouble with the law for rejecting for a good and lawful reason an applicant who happens to be a member of a protected class.

2

THE RESIDENTIAL LANDLORD AND TENANT ACT

Before the Residential Landlord and Tenant Act was passed, landlords had no obligation to provide decent housing unless they expressly agreed to do so in rental agreements. It should come as no surprise that low-income tenants with virtually no bargaining power rarely extracted such promises. (If you need a copy of the act, see page xiv of the Introduction.)

Before the act, even if a landlord did expressly assume a repair obligation, the doctrine of "independent covenants" prevented the tenant from using the landlord's failure to fulfill that obligation as a defense to an eviction action. The doctrine of "independent covenants" meant, for example, that a landlord could expressly agree to keep a toilet in working order, break that agreement, and evict the tenant for not paying the rent in full — even if the tenant had to use rent money to pay a plumber to fix the toilet. The tenant's only recourse was to bring a separate lawsuit against the landlord; courts simply would not listen to the tenant's complaints as part of the eviction action.

The major significance of the act is that it establishes minimum housing standards, which landlords must meet regardless of the rental agreement, and that it permits careful tenants to use violations of those standards to defend against an eviction. Put another way, the act gives tenants rights to force landlords to make certain repairs, and limits the power of landlords to evict tenants who exercise those rights.

Probably the hardest point for landlords to accept is that the act was intended to enforce basic housing standards for the benefit of the public as well as for just the landlord and the tenant. Instead of greatly expanding code-enforcement bureaucracies, the act turns the desperation of some tenants who can't pay their rent to the public purpose of correcting substandard conditions. If such a tenant has had to endure repair problems that violate the act, but did nothing to force the landlord to fix the problems until that was the only way to avoid being thrown into the street, it is entirely appropriate for the tenant to raise those problems as a defense to an eviction. If the problems are serious and the landlord knew or should have known of them, the tenant may very well get to stay in spite of being behind on the rent.

a. WHAT ARE THE LANDLORD'S OBLIGATIONS?

1. Habitability

Section 90.320 of the act requires landlords to maintain habitable premises. Habitability requirements include the following:

(a) Effective waterproofing and weather protection

(b) A water supply approved under applicable law, capable of producing hot and cold running water, furnished to appropriate fixtures, and connected to a legally approved sewage disposal system, maintained so as to produce safe drinking water to the extent that the system can be controlled by the landlord

(c) Floors, walls, ceilings, stairways, and railings in good repair

(d) Ventilation, air conditioning, and other appliances (including elevators) in good repair, if supplied by the landlord

(e) Safety from fire hazards

(f) Working locks for all outside doors and keys for any locks requiring them

Three items must have conformed to the applicable laws when installed and they must be maintained in good working order:

(a) Plumbing facilities

(b) Heating facilities

(c) Electrical lighting, wiring, and equipment

Separate statutes require landlords to provide smoke detectors and instructions for testing them (ORS 479.250-479.300).

At the beginning of the tenancy, the building and grounds must be "in every part safe for normal and reasonably foreseeable uses, clean, sanitary, and free from all accumulations of debris, filth, rubbish, garbage, rodents and vermin." Thereafter, all areas under the control of the landlord must be kept in that condition.[1]

Similarly, at the beginning of the tenancy, the landlord must provide an adequate number of appropriate receptacles for garbage and rubbish, and these must be in clean condition and in good repair. The landlord must continue to provide and maintain appropriate "serviceable" receptacles. The landlord must arrange for the removal of garbage and rubbish, unless the tenant has agreed in writing to make the arrangements. In cities over 250,000 population (i.e., in Portland), the obligation of providing for removal cannot be shifted to the tenant; the landlord must provide removal at least once a week for containers that allow for 30 gallons accumulation a week.[2]

A landlord must also disclose in writing any utility or service for which the tenant is billed that directly benefits the landlord or other tenants — such as when lighting for a parking lot appears on one tenant's bill when more than one tenant uses the parking area. A violation gives rise to statutory damages of the greater of twice the actual damages or one month's rent.[3]

2. Tenant's privacy

Section 90.335 requires a landlord to give a tenant at least 24 hours' notice of any intent to enter the premises, and a landlord may enter only at reasonable times, unless it is "impracticable to do so," there is an emergency, or the parties agree otherwise. The right to privacy extends to all portions of the rented property over which the tenant has exclusive control, such as the yard of a single family rental, but not to common areas, such as halls in multi-family buildings. Landlords have no other right of access without a court order unless one of the following conditions exists:

(a) The tenants have abandoned the premises. (The tenants have left under circumstances clearly demonstrating that they have no intention of returning.)

(b) The tenants have surrendered the premises. (They have expressly or implicitly given up possession of the premises for good.)

(c) The tenants have been absent for more than seven days.[4]

(d) The landlord is entering on the premises (but not *into* the dwelling unit) for purposes of serving notices required or permitted under the rental agreement, the act, or any provision of applicable law.

(e) The landlord or agent of the landlord is entering to show the premises for sale *and* the landlord and tenant have signed a valid agreement permitting such entries (see text below).

The 1989 legislature directly addressed the dilemma of the landlord who wants to show premises for sale. It is (and remains) unlawful for a landlord to attempt to make the tenant waive privacy rights in the rental agreement, but realtors and property buyers are not likely to await the tenant's presence or convenience to see property for sale.

Owners were often forced to evict tenants to make the property available to be shown.

To solve this problem for tenants willing to put up with unannounced visitors as a lesser evil than eviction, the 1989 legislature provided that landlord and tenant may agree to entries without notice at reasonable times for such purposes. To prevent this provision from being used as a loophole for the wholesale waiver of privacy rights, the law requires that the agreement be made at a time when the landlord is actively engaged in attempts to sell the premises, that it be contained in a writing separate from the rental agreement, and that it is supported by separate "consideration" recited in the agreement. If the tenancy is month to month, the "separate consideration" may simply be that the landlord is withholding the right to evict without cause. In tenancies that require cause to evict (and that do not reserve the right to terminate because the landlord wants to show the premises for sale), the landlord may have to reduce the rent or give the tenant something else of value to make the agreement enforceable.

Landlords cannot abuse the right of access or use it to harass tenants. On the other hand, a tenant cannot unreasonably withhold consent if the landlord wishes to enter to do any of the following:

(a) Conduct inspections

(b) Make agreed or necessary repairs or alterations

(c) Supply necessary or agreed services

(d) Exhibit the premises to prospective or actual purchasers, mortgagees, tenants, workers, or contractors

Generally, a landlord cannot enter in a tenant's absence. Because of the difficulty of scheduling repairs, the legislature added provisions that allow a landlord to use a written 24 hours' notice to enter to make repairs that have been requested by the tenant or that are required for other portions of the premises. This notice must specify —

10

(a) the purpose of the entry (i.e., the repairs to be made),

(b) the persons who will perform the repairs or mainte-nance, and

(c) that those persons may enter on demand and in the tenant's absence.

Once this notice is given, the persons making the repairs may enter repeatedly until the repairs are complete, provided that the entry is for the purpose stated in the notice, the people entering are those specified or acting under their supervision, and the entry is at reasonable times.

The legislature also added a provision for mobile home landlords that allows entry on a mobile home space during reasonable hours of the day and for the purpose of normal maintenance only on less than 24 hours' notice.

3. The duty of owners or managers to identify themselves

The person who enters the rental agreement on behalf of the landlord must disclose to the tenant, in writing, at or before the beginning of the tenancy, the name and address of the person authorized to manage the premises and the name and address of an owner or person authorized to act for the owner for the purposes of receiving and giving receipts for notices and demands. This information must be kept current.[5]

4. The duty of landlords to disclose impending foreclosures

If the premises in which the dwelling unit is located contain no more than four dwelling units "at the time of the execution of the rental agreement" (i.e., soon enough so the tenant can decide not to rent), the landlord must notify the tenant if premises are subject to —

(a) an outstanding notice of default under a trust deed or of trustee's sale,

(b) a pending suit to foreclose a mortgage, trust deed, or vendor's lien under a contract of sale,

(c) a pending declaration of forfeiture or suit for specific performance of a contract of sale, or

(d) a pending proceeding to foreclose a tax lien.[6]

If a tenant has to move as a result of a circumstance the landlord failed to disclose, the tenant is entitled to twice the actual damages or twice the monthly rent, whichever is greater, and all prepaid rent.[7] "Actual damages" include moving expenses if the tenant can demonstrate that they were caused by the landlord's omission. In other words, a tenant who decides to move across the country won't get moving expenses, even if the move was the result of the proceeding the landlord should have told the tenant about when the rental agreement was being negotiated.

These disclosure obligations don't affect a court-appointed receiver[8] or a manager who has complied with the disclosure requirements listed in the last section and who was ignorant of the circumstance that should have been disclosed. In other words, the remedies run against the landlord who should have told the manager to tell the tenant instead of against both the manager and the landlord.[9]

b. WHAT ARE THE TENANT'S OBLIGATIONS?

Tenants must use all portions of the premises and all facilities and appliances "reasonably." They must keep the areas under their control as clean, sanitary, and free of debris, filth, rubbish, and garbage as the condition of the premises permits. They must also dispose of waste in a clean and safe manner and keep plumbing fixtures as clean as their condition permits.

Tenants cannot damage (either deliberately or through negligence) any part of the premises and they cannot disturb

12

their neighbors. (This duty includes controlling the unruly behavior of guests.)[10]

A tenant with a week-to-week tenancy must give the landlord at least 10 days' notice in writing before ending the tenancy; a month-to-month tenant must give 30 days' written notice.[11] In addition, a rental agreement may require that the tenant notify the landlord of any anticipated absence of more than seven days no later than the first day of that absence.[12]

Tenants must test smoke detectors provided by the landlord according to the manufacturer's instructions, but need not do so more often than every six months.

c. WHO IS COVERED BY THE ACT?

The act covers all arrangements between a tenant and someone who seems reasonably authorized to rent a unit as long as the premises are for residential use. Commercial premises are not covered; similarly, statutes intended for commercial tenancies do not apply to residences. Certain residential tenants and arrangements are excluded by section 90.110:

(a) Occupants of institutional residences, such as detention homes, old age homes, and school residences

(b) Transient occupants of hotels and motels

(c) Landlords' employees whose occupancy is conditional upon employment in and about the premises

(d) Condominium owners

(e) Members of cooperatives

(f) Those who rent primarily for agricultural purposes

(g) Buyers occupying premises being purchased under a contract of sale

(h) Members of fraternal organizations in buildings operated for the benefit of the organizations

As a point of interest, off-campus, non-dormitory housing *is* covered by the act. Non-transient occupants in hotels or motels are also covered by the act. An occupant who considers his or her dwelling unit to be a permanent residence is not a transient. The mere fact that a hotel or motel is licensed for transient occupancy has nothing to do with whether a particular occupant is a transient occupant.

The 1989 legislature finally addressed the vague line separating "transient occupancy" in a motel or hotel excluded from the act and relatively permanent occupancy in "residential" hotel or motel rooms. To be excluded as "transient occupancy" a hotel or motel rental must have *all* of the following characteristics:[13]

(a) Occupancy charges must be *charged* on a daily basis and *payable* no less frequently than every two weeks (to avoid the ploy of "charging" what amounts to monthly rent on a "daily basis").

(b) The management must provide maid and linen service daily or every two days.

(c) The period of occupancy must not exceed 30 days.

(d) If the occupancy exceeds five days, the occupant must have a business address or a residence other than at the transient lodging.

Note that the last condition turns on the fact of another address, and not on whether the "guest" has represented or misrepresented that there was such an address. This distinction was part of the bargain because fears expressed by legal aid that desk clerks would be instructed to tell incoming "guests," whose only home would be a low-rent downtown hotel, to insert their *last* address on a registration card which could then be shown to police summoned to lock out the "guest" to prove transiency when the truth was that the person was renting his or her only home in the world. What is at stake here is the ability to circumvent a judicially supervised eviction process.

14

Transients are the only people in our society who can be lawfully locked out of their homes without an opportunity for a hearing.

Public housing tenants and mobile home or floating home (houseboat) dwellers who rent space or moorage are covered by the act. The landlord, of course, is not responsible for maintaining a mobile home or floating home owned by the tenant.

The act *does* apply if —

(a) the tenancy is not excluded by ORS 90.110, and

(b) there is some form of understanding (ORS 90.100(11)) between —

    (i) an owner, lessor, or a manager who fails to disclose in writing the identity of the owner or owner's agent (ORS 90.100(5); 90.305) and

    (ii) a person entitled because of that understanding (ORS 90.100(13)) to occupy a residence or sleeping place (ORS 90.100(3))[14]

The sections of the act just cited are in Appendix 1. If you look carefully at these sections, and understand how I've just used them, you'll have some idea of how complicated the act can be. You will also appreciate how careful you have to be when reading the act, and how important it may be to have the assistance of a good lawyer if things get out of hand.

d. LATE FEES

The 1989 legislature regulated late fees for the first time. ORS 90.260 provides that a landlord may not impose a late payment charge —

(a) on any payment that is received by 5 p.m. on the fourth day after the beginning of the month (or other payment period) for which it is payable,

(b) unless the rental agreement provides for late charges and the tenant has written notice — from the rental agreement or otherwise — of the due dates and the dates on which a late charge becomes payable, and/or

(c) more than once on any single installment.

The new statute also provides that nonpayment of a late fee alone shall not constitute grounds for eviction for *nonpayment of rent*. Note that late payments can be the basis of a 30-day notice without cause for month-to-month tenants or the basis for an eviction notice for cause (depending on the terms of the rental agreement).

3
STARTING A TENANCY

a. FINDING A HOME

1. What can you afford?

The first thing you should do before you even look for a place is to make a careful estimate of your ability to pay for rent and related expenses, and then to assess whether or not it would be cheaper, ultimately, to pay for "extras" or to rent a place without "extras." For example, you should determine how much utilities will cost if they are not included in the rent (by asking a friend if you are new to the area, or even by asking the utility companies), and how much difference it makes to you if certain utilities are provided, while others are not.

If you need a major appliance, check on the availability and prices of used appliances before you put yourself in the position of agreeing to pay a higher rent because a unit coincidentally has just the thing you need. It might be far cheaper in the long run to pay less rent for a completely unfurnished place and to put out $35 to $200 (depending primarily on your tastes) for a stove at a garage sale. Fix a price range and keep to it as long as you can because overestimating your ability to pay may well lead to problems with your landlord or other creditors.

Since landlords vary in their requirements for the last month's rent, deposits, and fees, you should calculate the maximum amount your budget will allow for these expenses. Again, simply exclude places with initial expenses beyond your means as long as possible; spend your energy (and risk repeated disappointment) only on what you can really afford.

2. Where should you live?

After fixing your short- and long-term economic limits, fix your geographical ones. If you have children, find out whether there are schools nearby and check them out. Determine the suitability of various areas for your commuting, shopping, and lifestyle needs. You're going to spend a lot of energy looking, so why waste any of it?

3. How do you begin the search?

The best way to find a place is through a friend who is moving or who knows someone who is. In student communities, this is extremely common; in some urban areas, units pass from tenant to tenant far more frequently than even the landlord is aware of.

A place you find through friends will be one you can really find out about beforehand. This is generally the only reliable way you can learn about the neighborhood and the landlord because you know your friends' values. Of course, competition for friends' places is often great, and most tenants will not have the luxury of avoiding the usually disheartening search for a home among strangers.

In such a search, the two most important rules are to allow yourself as much time as possible and to prepare for disappointments. Unless you do this, you will be more likely to take a place you're not really happy with just to free yourself from the agony of the search. If you can hold out, your chances of finding a good place are greatly improved.

The obvious places to start are the classified section in the newspapers and other free sources of similar listings that may be available in your community. If there's a trick to this process, it is to get up early and chase down the new ads as soon as you can; good deals go fast in most rental markets.

4. Why avoid agencies?

Services that charge prospective tenants a fee for allowing them access to listings are a last resort. Theoretically, these services keep their listings current and promptly remove rentals that are no longer available. Several years ago, a research project by O.S.P.I.R.G. (Oregon State and Student Public Interest Research Group) concluded that, in practice, these agencies often maintain obsolete listings. These services continue to exist, however, and there is no doubt that at least some people find satisfactory housing through them.

The Oregon Real Estate Division (now the "Real Estate Agency") once regulated rental agencies, but the legislature repealed the relevant statute in 1983 and there is no special regulation to protect consumers. If you are stung, the Unlawful Trade Practices Act may be of some use (see chapter 15).

5. What about tenant "blacklisting" services?

There are several tenant screening services that sell information on tenants to landlords who are looking for a good way to predict whether people applying to rent are a good risk. These services vary in their responsibility, accuracy, and the extent of information they provide. Landlords also vary in what they consider to be disqualifying information.

These services usually start by checking court records of eviction actions filed (the records are public information), and simply maintain a list of all tenants whose names appear as eviction defendants. Some services stop there; the better ones follow the cases and remove the names of tenants whose cases have been dismissed or who win the eviction action. Some merely supplement the information when these things happen, but retain the names on the list. The most responsible services remove the names in these cases and rely on other sources of information as well.

The Fair Credit Reporting Act, a federal statute, gives consumers some protection in these cases. It is fairly clear that it applies to tenant screening services. In theory, a tenant has the following rights:

(a) A landlord who relies on a tenant screening service's information to reject a tenant must tell the tenant the source of the information.

(b) The tenant can demand that the service show the tenant the information it has.

(c) The tenant can demand that the service reinvestigate and correct any wrong information it is maintaining about the tenant; if dissatisfied, the tenant may insist that the tenant's side of the dispute is set forth in future disclosures.[1]

The federal law has statutory penalties for sellers and users of such services who do not honor these rights, but the rights are of limited value unless the problem is something like mistaken identity. You may end up getting the record "corrected" to show that you *won* your last eviction action only to find that your prospective landlord is even *less* likely to rent to a tenant who won an eviction action than to someone who lost one. On the other hand, some of the services are quite conscientious in responding to legitimate requests and they correct mistakes, and some will even take your name off the list if you give them a decent argument. Undoubtedly, some are wary of liability for defamation or worry that you may be able to sue under the Fair Credit Reporting Act. The great majority of tenants listed never complain.

If you have a problem with a tenant screening service that you can't remedy with telephone calls and letters citing the Fair Credit Reporting Act, and if you have reason to believe the information being given out is incorrect and making it hard for you to find a place to live, find an attorney familiar with consumers' rights (see chapter 12).

6. Why isn't it wise to "jump right in"?

Once you find a place you want, the temptation is to "jump in," and often you will have no choice. If you plan to live there a long time, and if you can get the landlord to hold it for you for a day or so by paying a nonrefundable deposit *for that purpose only* (this is not prohibited by the Landlord and Tenant Act), here are some things you can do to see if you really want the place.

First, talk to the former tenant, if at all possible, about the pros and cons of the place and of the landlord. Are repairs needed? Does the landlord respond adequately to complaints? Does the landlord respect the tenant's privacy? What is the neighborhood like? Don't forget to ask whether the tenant was happy with the arrangement and why the tenancy is over. You may discover a totally unanticipated problem, such as the coming of a new freeway or the regularity of burglaries in the neighborhood.

Second, talk to neighbors, both about the neighborhood and about the history of the tenants at the house or apartment you are considering. This may be your only source of information if the former tenant has gone and you don't pursue the next step.

Third, take the steps outlined in chapter 1 to find out whether or not the landlord is a speculator.

By the way, a 1989 statute proclaims that a seller or lessor of real property may safely decline to disclose that a death by homicide or suicide occurred on the premises, and prohibits disclosure that an occupant or owner has or has died from the HIV virus or from AIDS.

If you are looking at obviously dilapidated housing because you have little money for rent, there are two more places you might want to check: the building inspector and the police. Although the inspector's office may be wary of giving out information to people who are not owners, you may be able to learn whether the rental unit has been posted as unlawful to occupy. Sometimes a landlord will simply rip the notice off the building and rent to desperate tenants. A victim of this practice who has to move when the law catches up with the landlord is entitled to the greater of two months' rent or twice the actual damages (which may include moving expenses), and is entitled to recover security deposit and prepaid rent.[2] The police may be able to tell you whether a suspiciously vacant rental was a "drug house," which may even pose health hazards if drugs were manufactured there.

b. MAKING A DEAL

Once you have found a place, or at least are seriously interested in one, the next process is to make a deal. Although this entire discussion assumes that you haven't encountered a hard-liner "take it or leave it" landlord, it's really surprising how much can be negotiated to your advantage without really costing the landlord anything.

The question of whether to enter a written or oral rental agreement (if you have a choice) is really quite different from the question of what you can try to get the landlord to accept as part of the bargain. The reason for this is that most of the advantages of a written agreement can be accomplished just by having the landlord sign a written promise or understanding for a particular item, without attempting to reduce all of the terms of your rental agreement to writing.

Section 1 following discusses some topics you should consider getting an agreement on and some tips for making them attractive to the landlord. Section 2 examines the pros and cons of a written rental agreement.

Here are some of the legal requirements concerning all rental agreements:

(a) If the agreement is in writing, the landlord must give a copy to the tenant.[3]

(b) The landlord must identify an owner or manager and provide an address for getting in touch.[4]

(c) The landlord must notify the tenant in writing if any utility paid for directly by the tenant benefits the landlord or other tenants.[5]

(d) The tenant is bound by the landlord's rules, in addition to those in any rental agreement, but only if —

    (i) the tenant has notice of the rule when entering the rental agreement or when the rule is adopted,

    (ii) the purpose of the rule is to promote the convenience, safety, or welfare of tenants; to protect the landlord's property; or to distribute facilities among tenants fairly,

    (iii) the rule is reasonably related to its purpose,

    (iv) the rule applies to all tenants in a fair manner,

    (v) the rule is clear and understandable,

    (vi) the rule is not designed so that the landlord can evade his or her obligations, and

    (vii) if the rule is adopted after the tenant enters into the rental agreement and the rule creates a "substantial modification" of the tenant's rights, the tenant consents to the rule in writing.[6]

Unless the rental agreement fixes a term, the tenancy is month-to-month except in the case of a roomer who pays weekly rent, in which case it is a week-to-week tenancy.

If there is no rental agreement, certain provisions are implied. For example, if the tenancy is month-to-month, the rental is payable at the beginning of each monthly term. (Thus, if the first day of the tenancy falls on the fifteenth of a month, the rent is payable on the fifteenth of every month.) Absent any agreement to the contrary, rent is payable at the dwelling unit and landlords must give 30 days' written notice if they decide to increase the rent.[7]

There are several provisions a rental agreement must not contain:

(a) Provisions that are "unconscionable," that is, so one-sided, harsh, or "shocking" that anyone would have to be desperate to agree to them

(b) Provisions designed to waive tenants' rights under the act

(c) Provisions allowing a landlord to get a court judgment without giving the tenant an opportunity to appear and defend himself or herself

(d) Provisions protecting the landlord from liability for negligence or willful misconduct

All of these provisions are unenforceable if they appear in a rental agreement.[8]

In addition, a landlord is liable to his or her tenant for up to three months' rent in addition to actual damages if he or she —

(a) deliberately uses a rental agreement containing a provision described by (b) or (c) of the list above,

(b) knows that the provision is prohibited, and

(c) attempts to enforce the provision.[9]

1. The agreement: Some terms to consider

There are at least four items you should consider trying to negotiate:

(a) the purpose of deposits or fees,

(b) the specific promises or representations of the landlord concerning repairs or furnishings,

(c) the landlord's ability to raise the rent, and

(d) your security of possession (how long you can stay).

(a) Labeling deposits

The law does not limit the amount of deposit a landlord can require at the beginning of the tenancy, but it does make most deposits refundable and it does limit the purposes for which the landlord can keep all or part of a deposit.[10] A sum of money simply labeled "deposit" or "security deposit" is subject to deductions for a broad class of purposes. It may be used to compensate the landlord for any losses caused by the failure of the tenant to live up to the rental agreement and for any expenses for repairs at the end of the tenancy beyond normal wear and tear.

Yet a "last month's rent" serves the more limited purpose of making sure that the landlord gets the last month's rent; it cannot be used to pay for repairs when the tenant moves out or for any other purpose. Also, in some situations, a landlord cannot serve an eviction notice and ask a court to evict a tenant "before the expiration of any period for which the tenant...has paid the rent...in advance."[11]

Ask your landlord what any additional money is for and try to label the payment accordingly in a receipt. A deposit for property damage should be labeled as such; a "damage" deposit may get confused with the broader legal concept of "damages," which means anything for which a court might award a judgment for money.

The same principles apply to "fees." Try to make the purpose of the payment as narrow as possible to reduce the arguments available to the landlord at the end of the tenancy when you ask for your money back. The next chapter talks about other things you can do at the beginning of the tenancy to protect your rights to deposits, but for purposes of making the deal, remember that no deposits are nonrefundable except a fee clearly designated as such or a sum of money paid before making a deal to keep a place available to you.

Note that many landlords have begun the practice of charging as fees what they used to charge as deposits and designating them as nonrefundable. This is entirely lawful, so be aware that this may happen, try to negotiate, and count on not getting this kind of fee back if you lose the negotiation.

The 1989 legislature added a law that requires professional property managers to keep deposits in interest-bearing accounts unless the parties (including the tenant) agree otherwise, with the interest going to fund low-income housing through the state Housing Agency. The law does not, as yet, require other landlords to keep deposits in interest-bearing accounts, but a landlord may be willing to keep the deposit in a separate savings account that bears interest but remains subject to the landlord's control. This way, the deposit can be returned, with interest, at the end of the tenancy. An offer to split the interest might be more acceptable to a landlord who doesn't want the hassle.

(b) Promises concerning repairs and furnishings

It is common for landlords to make promises at the beginning of a tenancy to perform specific repairs or to supply items like paint, a stove, or a lawn mower to the tenant. Don't be afraid to ask that the promise be put in writing. The back of the rent receipt will do if it is signed by the landlord or the landlord's agent. A landlord who is unwilling to put it in writing is probably unwilling to perform the promise.

If the landlord refuses, carefully consider whether or not you would want the place without the promises. If the request for a promise in writing is honored, make sure it specifies a deadline for performance.

(c) Rent and security of possession

Insecurity of possession is a significant source of anxiety in many tenants' lives. If the tenant does not have a lease for a term of several months or a year or more, a landlord is usually free to evict a tenant for no reason at all or to raise the rent after giving 30 days' notice. It is perfectly permissible, however, for the parties to agree to limit these powers.

26

If you hope to be able to stay put for at least a year, say so and ask if the landlord is willing to agree to a one-year lease (or whatever term you want) rather than leave the agreement on a month-to-month basis. If the landlord is reluctant, see if you can be creative enough to meet specific objections.

For example, a landlord may refuse to sign a lease for fear that expenses will rise and reduce his or her profit. Such an objection should be met by agreeing that the rent will not be increased during the term of the lease except to meet the landlord's actual increases in taxes and specified operating expenses. Such clauses are common in commercial leases and generally function to the mutual advantage of both parties. Again, try to describe the cost increases that can result in an increase in rent as specifically as possible. Generally, you should not agree to pay increased rent as a condition of receiving the same level of maintenance that is required by the Residential Landlord and Tenant Act regardless of your agreement.

A landlord may also be fearful of losing the power to evict a "bad" tenant. Again, get the details about complaints. Have previous tenants thrown loud parties or parked junk cars in the flower beds? Point out that a landlord always has the right to evict for nonpayment of rent, for material violations of a rental agreement, and for abuse of the property (see chapter 8), and that his or her power to evict for cause is not diminished by adding rules of conduct to a rental agreement for a term. For example, if the rental agreement says that no cars may be parked in the flower beds, the landlord can evict for unremedied or repeated violations even if the tenant has a 50-year lease.

If you have reason to believe that the request for a lease for a specified term is hopeless, you might still try to accomplish the same objective a different way: try to limit the circumstances that can give rise to rent increases or eviction notices. For example, my first Oregon landlord was willing to settle for a right to evict without cause only if the property was sold. Yours may have similarly limited interests to protect, and the negotiating process can bring peace of mind to both sides by limiting the tenant's insecurity of possession to the few circumstances that really matter to the landlord.

c. WRITTEN vs. VERBAL AGREEMENTS

There are arguments for and against both written and verbal agreements. To begin with, you may not need a written lease because the Landlord and Tenant Act has included most of the provisions a tenant is likely to get in a rental agreement anyway.

1. Problems you can avoid with oral agreements

If you do not have a written agreement, you are not as likely to be restricted by terms that have to be in writing to be effective and that could well form part of a written agreement. For example, in a written agreement the landlord may —

(a) Shift to the tenant his or her obligation to make certain minor repairs[12]

(b) Escape liability for garbage removal costs (except in Portland)[13]

(c) Permit a rent increase with less than 30 days' notice and specify that the tenant must bring the rent to the landlord[14]

(d) Require the tenant to notify the landlord of any absence of more than seven days[15]

(e) Impose a late fee[16]

(f) Limit the number of people who may occupy the premises[17]

(g) Prohibit pets

28

Note: At least the last two restrictions may be imposed by rules at the time you make the oral agreement. Rules that "work a substantial modification of the bargain" cannot be added to your obligations after you enter an agreement unless you consent to them in writing.[18] On the other hand, it is not unlawful for a landlord to terminate a month-to-month tenancy on the grounds that the tenant would not consent to such a rule change.

Finally, remember that most lease forms are prepared for landlords and heavily favor their interests. In fact, many of the clauses in such forms are invalid under the Landlord and Tenant Act and their inclusion may expose the landlord to liability for attempting to enforce them.[19]

2. The advantages of written agreements

Written rental agreements do have some advantages. A written agreement outlining all the rights and responsibilities of both parties not only informs both parties of their intentions, but may prevent confrontations resulting from poor memories of hasty assessments. Further, a written agreement that follows the provisions of the Landlord and Tenant Act will serve as a useful tool for calling the act's obligations to a landlord's attention. Moreover, a term rental agreement for more than one year may have to be in writing to be enforceable.

Short of such a formal document, you may consider a simple signed letter or memorandum that will serve to establish proof of the things you consider important. At this point you would probably have nothing to lose by giving it a try.

If you do sign a written agreement, you are entitled to a copy.[20] For a few dollars you can have it recorded in the county recorder's office. This will remove any doubt as to whether your interest in the property will be recognized by any later purchaser of the building (unless, under the terms of the agreement, the tenant's rights are in effect only as long as the original landlord owns the property). For this purpose, the agreement should be signed as an original (even if your copy is the carbon), and it should be notarized to satisfy picky recording clerks.

Remember that if you lose your copy, or suspect that your copy is different than the landlord's, you are entitled to inspect the landlord's copy on reasonable notice and to make a copy at a cost not to exceed $.25 per page.[21]

3. Subletting and written agreements

A tenant is free to sublet or assign the premises without the landlord's consent as long as he or she is not prohibited from doing so in a rental agreement. A sublease arrangement makes the subtenant liable to the tenant, and the tenant liable to the landlord for rent, whether the subtenant occupies all or part of the premises. In the case of an assignment, the new tenant simply takes the place of the old and owes the rent directly to the landlord.

As a practical matter, prohibitions against subletting or assignment are almost never part of an oral rental agreement but are often part of written agreements, so this is another consideration if you have a choice between the two.

4

YOU AND THE DEPOSIT

Landlords commonly withhold deposits: often legitimately, but sometimes by making up or exaggerating damage claims after their tenants move out. This practice has led many states to adopt special statutes governing deposits. In Oregon, a landlord must submit an accounting to the tenant in writing for all deductions claimed and must do so within 30 days of the termination of the tenancy. If any portion is wrongfully withheld, the tenant is entitled to recover twice that amount. Any amount withheld without a deposit is wrongfully withheld under the statute, as is any amount withheld in bad faith, including amounts withheld on the basis of a dishonest accounting.[1]

This chapter explains what you can do at the beginning and end of your tenancy to protect your rights to recover refundable deposits and to avoid being held responsible for damage you did not cause. If you follow these suggestions, you may avoid any misunderstanding with the landlord, and you will have evidence you can use in court, if necessary, either as part of an action against your landlord to recover your deposit or to defend an action brought by your landlord against you for damages.

If your landlord does sue you for damages, you may have the right to claim damages against him or her by way of recoupment or counterclaim (see sections **f.** and **g.** of chapter 6 and section **d.** of chapter 8). Note that the landlord may also have counterclaims or recoupments to assert against you.

a. HOW TO PROTECT YOURSELF AGAINST DAMAGE CLAIMS

The only safe way to protect yourself against losing your deposit or against unfounded damage claims is to spend some energy on the problem at the beginning of your tenancy. In addition to trying to label the deposit carefully when you move in as suggested in chapter 3, there are a number of things you can do. As in the case of the repair problems discussed in chapters 5 and 6, you can choose among a variety of approaches which vary considerably in their aggressiveness.

The most aggressive approach possible when protecting yourself against unwarranted damage claims is to demand a building inspection from your local bureau of public works (or an equivalent agency) and have the inspector attach the report to the rental agreement with the landlord's promise to repair all defects. (Good luck!)

It is more common to go through the premises with the landlord before signing or paying for anything to make an exhaustive list of all the defects you can find. Be thorough. Remember that you are trying to protect yourself against damage claims, as well as uncover needed repairs, and your findings will have an important bearing in any later dispute regarding the extent of "normal wear and tear."

"Normal wear and tear" is the deterioration of a dwelling that is to be expected from reasonable use over time; it does not include the results of negligent or deliberate misuse.

Depending on your personality, you might pretend that you're an obsessed inspector, or you might pretend that you're a landlord who desperately needs an excuse to avoid repaying the last tenant's deposit because you just spent it on the horses. Use whatever works to get you in the mood. Note every condition of dirt, wear, and damage and any deterioration of every floor, wall, door, ceiling, fixture, and window. Don't forget to see if everything works. Also, inspect every item of furniture and appliance furnished by the landlord. When you think you're through, the safest proof of the state in which you found the premises is to have the inventory of what you found signed by both you and the landlord.

As a practical matter, you may not have time before taking possession to make an exhaustive inspection, or you may have good reason not to press the landlord for a jointly signed statement. The middle ground approach is to write a letter to the landlord that includes your list of defects (see Sample #1).

SAMPLE #1
LETTER TO LANDLORD DESCRIBING DEFECTS

November 5, 199-

(Make sure it is dated)

Dear Ms. Wolff:

After I moved into the house I rented from you on November 1, 199-, I was able to take the time to inspect carefully the condition it was in when I moved in, so that you will not mistakenly blame me for damages or wear that are not my responsibility. The enclosed list covers everything I found. If you wish to confirm these things for yourself, please call to arrange an inspection. I am usually home after 5:30 in the evenings.

Sincerely,

E.Z. Rect

E.Z. Rect

Enc. list of defects

If you find serious problems you want remedied, it is fairly important that you point them out as soon as possible. Although a landlord should not be able to claim that you waived the right to have him or her make repairs required by the Residential Landlord and Tenant Act, your failure to say anything about them may provide a strong argument that they really didn't bother you much at the time and therefore aren't worth much by way of damages or as a set-off against the rent. To demand repairs, add a paragraph to your inspection letter something like the one in Sample #2. (**Note:** Always keep a carbon copy or a photocopy of everything.)

Of course, demanding repairs involves some risk. (See chapters 5 and 6.) Don't let indecision as to whether to demand repairs delay bringing defects to your landlord's attention. The longer you wait, the more likely it is that the landlord may claim that you caused the defects. If you're in doubt, send a letter like Sample #1 right away. Then, read chapters 5 and 6. If you want to demand repairs, send a demand letter of the sort described in chapter 5.

Particularly if your landlord declines to verify your list, it is safest to get a friend to witness it. Try to get someone who seems credible and who will be around when you move out. Have him or her inspect your place as soon as possible after you move in, and sign a statement at the end of your list something like the one in Sample #3.

SAMPLE #2
PARAGRAPH DEMANDING REPAIRS

```
    You will note that I have placed a check mark
next to some of the items on this list. These
represent conditions that I consider violations of
my rights under the Landlord and Tenant Act, and
I respectfully demand that you remedy these items
immediately. Please call to arrange access to the
house.
```

SAMPLE #3
STATEMENT OF WITNESS REGARDING
CONDITION OF PREMISES

I, Wally Witness, hereby say that on November 7, 199-, I personally inspected the home of T. Tenant, Apt. 3, 101 Knob Hill, and verified the existence of every condition listed above.

Wally Witness

Wally Witness

By the way, notarization may make such a statement look better, but if you take the statement to court the witness will probably have to be there to testify. If you want to be really thorough, take pictures and date them.

You will be glad you went through all this trouble if and when the landlord claims that he or she has to refinish the hardwood floors because of you when it was the former tenant who had the 19 cats!

Although they are less common, disputes occasionally arise over the ownership of appliances and furniture. Sometimes a tenant moves out a stove at the end of a tenancy only to find that the landlord claims it was provided by and belongs to the landlord. The same sort of procedure outlined above can be modified to protect you against such a dispute.

If the items are not listed in a rental agreement, send a list to the landlord with a letter inviting corrections or additions, get a credible witness to sign your list, or both. Of course, if the landlord responds and disagrees, make sure you reply with any corrections promptly. Understand that a former tenant may have removed something that belongs to the landlord or replaced an appliance with a cheaper one. Be sure your list specifies the brand and model of all appliances furnished by the landlord so you don't discover a former tenant's swap for the first time when your landlord accuses you of replacing an electric range with a wood burner when you move out.

b. GETTING BACK DEPOSITS

Earlier in this chapter, I discussed how a tenant can protect his or her rights to recover deposits at the end of tenancy by making some preparations at the beginning of the tenancy. This section discusses when deposits are refundable and how tenants can get them back if their landlords refuse to return them.

1. Is a tenant entitled to a return of the deposit?

The act entitles a tenant to the return of any unused portion of a deposit unless the deposit was paid to secure the signing of the rental agreement, or unless the deposit was a "fee" clearly labeled nonrefundable.[2] A landlord who wrongfully withholds any portion of a deposit, or of any prepaid rent, for more than 30 days after termination of the tenancy and delivery of possession, or who fails to account in writing to the tenant within that period for any deductions, is liable to the tenant for twice the amount wrongfully withheld or withheld in bad faith.[3]

A security deposit is refundable unless the landlord has had to use all or part of it to cover the reasonable expenses of curing a problem caused by the tenant. The problem must be one related to the purposes for which the deposit was paid. Unless the parties have specified a more limited purpose for the deposit at the beginning of the tenancy, a security deposit can be used for the following purposes only:

(a) To remedy the tenant's defaults in the performance of the rental agreement

(b) To repair damages to the premises caused by the tenant, not including ordinary wear and tear[4]

A security deposit may not be used as a penalty for the tenant's failure to stay for any specified term, although a nonrefundable fee may be charged for this purpose.[5] Any portion of the deposit that is not used for the purposes just listed must be returned to the tenant. The landlord has a duty to "mitigate" damages, which means that he or she cannot choose an unnecessarily expensive way in which to cure any problems caused by the tenant.[6]

"Prepaid rent" includes both the regular rent and any sum paid as the last month's rent (or a sum to secure the payment of any last rental payment). Generally, both are returnable to the tenant to the extent that they cover a period of time after the tenant leaves and after the termination of the tenancy.

A tenant who leaves before the expiration of a 30-day notice is not entitled to a refund of the rent covering the rest of the 30 days unless the parties have agreed otherwise or unless the tenant is exercising some special right to terminate the tenancy on an earlier date.

For example, a tenant who terminates a tenancy by serving a "fix or I quit" notice (see chapter 10) is entitled to the return of all unused security and prepaid rent.[7] The same is true of a tenant who terminates because of a landlord's retaliation, lockout, or utility shutoff.[8] A tenant who terminates because of a landlord's abuse of the right of access is entitled to the return of unused security deposits and is also entitled to recover at least one month's rent as damages.[9]

Finally, a tenant who exercises the right to terminate because of a serious and imminent threat to the health or safety of occupants not caused by the tenant (see chapter 10), is entitled to a return of all security deposits (including any last month's rent) and all rent prepaid for the month in which the termination occurs if the condition existed at the outset of the tenancy.[10]

Because a landlord may end a month-to-month tenancy by serving a 30-day notice that terminates the tenancy on a day other than the end of a rent period,[11] situations may arise in which the termination date occurs before the expiration of a period for which the tenant has paid rent. Although the landlord cannot bring an eviction action based on nonpayment of rent before any prepaid rent is used up,[12] if the tenant moves out voluntarily, rent is apportioned day to day, and the tenant is entitled to a refund of any balance.[13]

A landlord apparently cannot terminate a week-to-week tenancy on any date that is not the end of a rent period, so the problem of unused regular rent should not arise in this kind of tenancy.[14]

The purpose of any last month's rent payment (or any similar deposit) is to protect the landlord against a tenant's failure to make the last rent payment. For this reason, it fits the definition of "security deposit" and any portion not used for that purpose must be returned to the tenant.[15]

2. Letting the landlord know your new address

You should let your landlord know where to send your money by leaving a forwarding address, preferably by sending a letter. If you can itemize what is due, do so. If you think there is a reasonable claim for damages beyond normal wear and tear, it is usually safest to get the problem fixed yourself at minimal expense before you leave, rather than allowing the landlord the luxury of spending someone else's money on the repair without the restraints that self-interest would normally impose on spending. Sample #4 is an example of the kind of letter you could send.

If you have good reason to believe that your landlord is in the habit of ripping off tenants for deposits, you can deduct the portion of the deposit you feel you are entitled to from your last rent payment, together with a letter that would read something like Sample #5.

August 30, 199-

Dear Mr. Fullbird:

As I notified you previously, today I am vacating the premises at 7-101 Rotten Row, Anycity.

As you will recall, I paid a last month's rent in the amount of $300, a key deposit in the sum of $10, a cleaning deposit in the sum of $50, and a damage deposit in the sum of $50 at the beginning of my tenancy.

By my calculations, I am entitled to the return of one-third of the prepaid rent, or $100. Since I am returning the keys with this letter, I am also entitled to the $10 key deposit. The place, as you will see for yourself, is cleaner than when I moved in, and I am entitled to the entire cleaning deposit of $50. I fixed the screen door you were worried about, and there is one broken window in the bathroom which I am responsible for. Ace Hardware gave me an estimate of $15, so I would like $35 of the damage deposit back.

Please send a check for the total amount of $195 to me at the following address:

> Penthouse Suite
> Saville Row
> Money City, Nevada

Yours sincerely,

M. Petard

M. Petard

Enc: as stated

The worst that can lawfully happen is that the landlord will serve you with a 72-hour notice for not paying the rent. After receiving the notice, you will have 72 hours to decide whether to pay the difference, contest the eviction, or move

SAMPLE #5
LETTER TO LANDLORD EXPLAINING
DEDUCTION OF DEPOSIT FROM RENT

August 15, 199-

Dear Mr. Fullbird:

As I advised you earlier, my tenancy at 7-101 Rotten Row, Anycity, will end on August 30.

As you will recall, I paid a deposit of $150 at the beginning of my tenancy. I am deducting the portion of the deposit to which I feel entitled from the rent payment which accompanies this letter. I feel justified in doing so for the following reasons:

1. It will save you the trouble of figuring out how much of the deposit to return.

2. The premises are cleaner than when I moved in.

3. The screen door you complained of last month has been repaired.

4. The bathroom window will be repaired by Ace Hardware for $15.

As my normal rent is $175, I am enclosing $40 for this month's rent. If you accept this money as payment in full, I hereby release you from your obligation to return the deposit.

You may inspect my dwelling to determine your need for any further security by coming between 5:00 p.m. and 6:00 p.m. of any weekday this week.

Yours sincerely,

M. Petard

M. Petard

out before the eviction judgment can be enforced against you (see chapter 8).

In any event, if you expect any trouble, get a friend to come look at your place just before you move out in case you need a witness. This can be the same person who saw the premises when you moved in.

3. Small claims court

If all else fails, you will probably have to take your landlord to small claims court to get your deposit back.

The law allows even very small cases to be brought in a regular court if they involve statutes that say the winner can collect attorney's fees as part of the judgment. Since the Landlord and Tenant Act provides for such fees, you may bring your case for a wrongfully withheld deposit in a regular court regardless of how little is at stake.

On the other hand, you will probably find small claims court best suited to claims for relatively small amounts of money for two reasons. First, it will be hard to find an attorney willing to represent you in a regular court when there is little money at stake because a court is unlikely to award a substantial fee. Second, it is unwise to represent yourself in regular court unless you have legal skills; small claims court is, after all, designed for people to represent themselves (although a judge has the power to permit an attorney to appear). Small claims court is relatively speedy and informal. In Multnomah County, and a growing number of other jurisdictions, the court offers a mediation service as part of the small claims process. This may be the most comfortable way to resolve the dispute.

You cannot seek more than $2,500 in small claims court. If you ask for more than $200, your opponent has the option of making you start over in regular court. If your opponent responds to your small claims complaint by filing a claim against you in your case (i.e., by "counterclaiming"), the case will be transferred to regular court if that claim exceeds $2,500.[16] It may be possible for your opponent to elect to remove the case to regular court by filing a counterclaim which exceeds $200 (but which does not exceed $2,500), but this is not yet clear.

If the case stays in small claims court, you will not be able to appeal a judgment that denies your claim. Whether your opponent can appeal, and whether you can appeal a judgment against you on your opponent's counterclaim, depends on whether you live in an area served by a district court or a justice court.

Urban areas and some rural areas are served by district courts. If the small claims court that hears your case is a division of a district court, neither party will be able to appeal. Some rural areas are served by justice courts. If the small claims court that hears your case is a division of a justice court, things get a bit more complicated.[17] Neither side can appeal a judgment for less than $30. Neither side can appeal a judgment denying a claim filed by that side. On the other hand, both sides may appeal a judgment for $30 or more rendered against the side that wants to appeal.

In other words, if you file a claim against your landlord and you win, your landlord can appeal. If you lose, you can't appeal. If the landlord files a counterclaim against you and you lose on that counterclaim, you can appeal that loss. If the landlord loses on that counterclaim, the landlord cannot appeal that loss.

By this point, you should be able to decide whether you are going to file a small claims court case. If so, it is necessary for you to make some attempt to collect the amount you claim before going to court. A letter demanding that the landlord return your money is all that is necessary, but keep a copy. The clerk of the small claims court will ask you to sign an affidavit saying that you tried to collect your money before filing your claim, and the judge may want to see a copy of your letter when the case is heard. A letter like the one in Sample #4 should be sufficient. Of course, if you think you're entitled to all of your deposit back, your letter should say so.

One more thing you should do before actually filing your claim is to decide who you should sue. The person you assume is the owner may only be an agent or manager. You should have been given a written statement about this at the beginning of the tenancy and at any time after that if the information changed. You can find out the name of the owner by asking at the county tax office.

If you were not given a written statement and if you find the landlord was not the person you suspected, you can have the real landlord "served" (given formal notice of the small claims action) by directing the sheriff to hand the summons and complaint to any nondisclosing manager as agent of the landlord for service of process. Also, such a person can be required to perform the landlord's obligations — including returning deposits — so you can sue these people as well as the real landlord.[18] If you are going to try to use these rights, make sure you take a copy of the act with you every time you go to court; you may have to use it to explain to the clerk or the judge what you're up to.

If you have trouble finding a defendant to sue, remember that a lot of people may fit the definition of "landlord" under the act.[19] Also note that anyone who holds the landlord's interest in the property at the time of the termination of the tenancy is liable to you for unreturned deposits.[20]

When you go to court for the hearing, remember to take your evidence and your witnesses. The clerk should assist you with subpoenas if you need them. Hopefully, you will have receipts for everything you paid to the landlord (it's always safest to bring your rent receipts for the entire tenancy); a list, photograph, or other similar evidence of what the place was like when you moved in; a copy of any letters you sent to the landlord about the deposit; and witnesses to the condition of the place when you moved in and when you moved out. Also take a copy of the act. Prepare a short outline of what you have to say. Be brief and to the point.

Your witnesses should be people who personally observed the condition of the premises. To summarize roughly the laws of evidence, a witness who has to rely on the observations of other people isn't worth much unless he or she heard your opponent say something damaging to your opponent's case. Also remember to point out that if the landlord failed to account in writing for any deductions within 30 days after the end of the tenancy, the landlord cannot claim a deduction.[21] On the other hand, if the landlord is entitled to keep some of the deposit, say so.

When deciding whether to go to court, you should realize that the landlord has a right to counterclaim for damages to the premises or for rent due. If you owe rent or damaged the premises, it might be best to leave well enough alone, even if there were no accounting.

5

GETTING REPAIRS: DEMAND LETTERS AND BUILDING INSPECTIONS

This chapter and the next one explain the various ways in which a tenant may try to enforce rights against a landlord who fails to supply decent housing as required by the Landlord and Tenant Act. Repair disputes often start mildly, but some escalate into heated battles as the stakes get higher and higher for both sides. This chapter deals with the relatively low risk devices of demand letters and building inspections. Chapter 6 treats the various rent withholding remedies available under the act and also explains one of the most powerful remedies available to a tenant: a lawsuit against the landlord.

As you read these chapters, bear in mind that each remedy (except suing the landlord) has two functions: to get repairs without ending up in court, and to equip you with proof to defend against an eviction action if you do end up in court. More important, all of these remedies can be used by tenants acting together in a tenants' union; concerted action can be the most effective remedy of all (see chapter 12).

Each discussion of a remedy includes consideration of the risks peculiar to that remedy. Chapter 6 ends with a discussion of the general risks involved in any dispute and with a table summarizing the remedies and the risks.

These chapters assume you want to get the repairs and stay. They omit a provision of the act that appears to assist tenants in getting repairs, but actually amounts to a device where a tenant can terminate a term tenancy before it expires if the landlord refuses to make repairs. Because the device almost never produces repairs, I discuss it in chapter 10, "How Can Tenants Leave?" If you're fed up and ready to leave if the landlord refuses to make repairs, or if the problem is so severe that you have to leave, consult that chapter. Your case may just be the exception to the rule.

Chapters 5 and 6 are designed for tenants who want to enforce their rights to repairs and refuse to accept the retort, "If you don't like it, why don't you move?" When you are through reading these chapters carefully, you should be able to decide which remedy is best suited to your situation and whether the risks involved make it worth pursuing. In addition, the discussion of how to use each remedy should equip you to use the remedy of your choice carefully in order to minimize the risk of being evicted.

Ideally, all tenants should have the assistance of an attorney who is well versed in landlord and tenant law before making this kind of decision. Small factual variations in your situation may critically affect your rights or chances of success, and courts or the legislature may have changed the law since this book was written.

As a practical matter, however, few tenants with repair problems can afford this kind of consultation. Tenants who are eligible for legal aid may find that their local program has its hands full defending evictions — although if you are eligible for legal aid, you should certainly try to get assistance. The eviction statutes contain many provisions, such as those providing parties with form pleadings, which recognize that landlords and tenants may not always have lawyers. You may have to do it yourself.

If you want to be able to use the remedies of the act yourself with a minimum of risk, you will have to read these chapters carefully. Unfortunately, there is nothing simple about the way the law allows you to use a landlord's failure to provide habitable housing as a defense to an eviction; an eviction action is all too often the reaction tenants get when they assert their rights.

46

a. DEMAND LETTERS

1. What are they?

If you choose to take a repair dispute beyond its first informal stages, your next step is usually a demand letter or a building inspection. As you will see in the last section of this chapter, an inspection carries some risk of diverting the landlord's energies from your particular needs, and is probably more likely to anger the landlord than a demand letter, so I will start with demand letters.

A demand letter is simply a written request, usually mailed, preferably by certified mail, stating your request for repairs. It has two functions: first, to make your position known to the landlord in precise terms; and, second, to prove that you have done so. *Keep copies of everything.*

2. Why use them?

As parts of the next chapter will explain, some of the rent-withholding rights under the act require that you give written notice to the landlord of the repairs you need. Even if you use one of the rent-withholding remedies that do not require a prior written notice, the judge or jury will definitely want to know whether or not the landlord actually knew of your complaints. Moreover, a dated demand letter will help you prove whether your complaints to a landlord came before or after any eviction notice in case you must use the retaliatory eviction defense discussed in chapter 8.

(a) Special damages

A demand letter may also be important to a tenant's right to recover what is known as "special damages" — either as a judgment for money or as a court's reduction in the amount of rent owed.

Briefly, "damages" is the label the law uses either to identify the kind of harm that can be reduced to monetary terms or to describe the money a court might award to a party

47

who has suffered that harm. Although there are several kinds of damages in the law, the kinds relevant here are "general damages" and "special damages."

General damages are those that the law assumes always flow from the kind of wrong in question; special damages are those that can, but need not, flow from that wrong. For example, if you are hit by a car in a crosswalk, the law assumes you will suffer general damages by way of pain and suffering, although you may or may not suffer such special damages as medical expenses and lost wages.

In landlord and tenant law, general damages for repair problems include a reduction in the rental value of the premises, while such things as damages to personal possessions caused by a water leak, or theft caused by faulty locks, amount to special damages because they do not accompany every repair problem.

Another difference is that a court may require you to prove that the landlord knew of any risks of special damages before you can recover money (or reduce the landlord's claim for rent) because of those damages. On the other hand, the law assumes a reduction in rental value flows from any substantial failure of the landlord to supply housing that meets the act's standards, and you will not have to prove the landlord knew such general damages would result from the violations. (Of course, you still have to prove the violations occurred.)

Because a court may require proof that the landlord knew of any risks of special damages, you should identify such risks in your demand letter. A strong argument can be made that this proof should not be required,[1] but the best argument is the one that doesn't have to be made.

(b) Emotional distress

A demand letter may also help you recover damages for "emotional distress" (also called "mental suffering" or "mental anguish") if you have suffered substantial anxiety as a result of your landlord's violations of the act.

An Oregon court has awarded emotional distress damages to a plaintiff whose telephone number was erroneously listed as an after-hours number for a flower shop and who suffered the annoyance of many night time calls. The theory of the court was that the calls interfered with the plaintiff's right to "quiet enjoyment" of the property. All tenants are entitled to quiet enjoyment of their premises (i.e., to be free of unreasonable outside interference with their peaceful use of the premises), and substantial violations of the Landlord and Tenant Act may interfere with this right.

I have had clients who suffered severe humiliation because they had to use a gas station rest room while the landlord refused to fix their toilet. Another tenant had to bathe her children while they were partially clothed because the corroded surface of the bathtub would otherwise cause bleeding. In addition, I have had three clients whose deaths were caused or hastened, I am convinced, by anxiety over eviction disputes.

The Oregon Supreme Court has agreed that a tenant may recover emotional distress damages under certain circumstances for violations of provisions of the act that prohibit deliberate misconduct such as lockouts, utility shutoffs, and retaliation. On the other hand, the court has held that emotional distress damages were not available for merely negligent or nonculpable violations of provisions that do not require deliberate misconduct for their violation, such as the habitability section.

The court has said that tenants who suffer severe emotional distress because of a landlord's conduct that is "outrageous in the extreme" may recover emotional distress damages under the common law, which is the body of court decisions outside the Landlord Tenant Act and other statutes.[2] What is not entirely clear, however, is whether a deliberate violation of the habitability section can support emotional distress damages. Logically, and in view of the cases mentioned above, the answer should be yes.

If your situation involves a substantial risk of emotional distress, identify that risk in your demand letter. Hopefully, your letter will prevent the harm you fear. If not, it may help you recover damages (or reduce any rent owed) because of that harm by proving the landlord knew of the risk.

It may also help establish your "general damages," that is, the degree of inconvenience for purposes of assessing the loss of rental value damages.

3. How to use the remedy

If all informal conversations have come to a standstill, and you don't want to distract the landlord by ordering a building inspection, then use a demand letter. It might look like the one shown in Sample #6. Of course, the idea is to give the landlord the impression that rapid compliance will save money. (Remember to keep copies of everything.)

If you've already had the inspection, your letter might look something like the one shown in Sample #7. Or suppose that your front lock does not work properly, and you want to advise the landlord of "special damage" risks. Sample #8 gives an example of the sort of notice you might give the landlord (perhaps by adding this to the letter already shown as Sample #7).

If you or any member of your family are likely to suffer emotional distress, Sample #9 gives an example of the sort of paragraph you might include in your demand letter.

4. Negotiating and compromising

Assuming you get a reply to your demand letter, the next step is to negotiate an acceptable solution to the dispute and to get a settlement in writing. If the landlord is willing to listen, it may be to your advantage to suggest devices to save the landlord some work, while not reducing your rights. For example, you might arrange to have the plumber come, and you might pay for the work out of the next rent check. This way, you may have more control over the timing and over the quality of the work than if you were to force the landlord to find the labor. Don't agree to an expense limit with the landlord without first obtaining a binding estimate. On the other hand, many landlords have maintenance people they use regularly (but many of these people are simply incompetent for some tasks).

SAMPLE #6
LETTER DEMANDING REPAIRS
(Before building inspection)

November 15, 199 -

Dear Ms. Wolff:

Over the past two weeks, we have had several discussions in which I have asked that you do something about the fact that we have no heat and our front door won't lock. Although I have made every attempt to allow you to investigate these complaints, you have not made any of the repairs requested.

Although I have reason to believe a building inspection might disclose problems with which I have no complaint (such as the novel, but apparently, safe, approach to electrical wiring your cousin used to install the stove), I will be forced to call for an inspection to back up my complaints if you do not make repairs voluntarily.

Unless I hear from you by November 22, I will have the premises inspected and will seek the assistance of an attorney to enforce my rights.

Yours sincerely,

Thomas Tenant

Thomas Tenant

SAMPLE #7
LETTER DEMANDING REPAIRS
(After building inspection)

November 30, 199-

Dear Ms. Wolff:

As you can see by the inspection report (of which I enclose a copy), I have had the premises inspected when my efforts to convince you to make repairs produced no results. Although I do not insist that everything on the list be remedied immediately, I am requesting you to remedy the following items right away:

No heating

No front lock

If I do not hear from you by December 15, I will seek the assistance of an attorney to enforce my rights.

Yours sincerely,

Thomas Tenant

Thomas Tenant

Enc: as stated

SAMPLE #8
NOTIFICATION OF "SPECIAL DAMAGE" RISKS

I wish to emphasize that the repairs I am requesting are needed to prevent my suffering damages beyond a mere decrease in rental value. As you know, there have been many burglaries in this area, and I am afraid that your continued failure to fix our locks will result in the theft of two priceless antiques that have been in my family for years: a grandfather clock in the hall and a Lincoln rocker in the living room. Also, I have a stereo system worth upward of $400. I will hold you responsible for damages for the loss of these items if caused by the lack of a working lock.

NOTIFICATION OF RISK OF EMOTIONAL DISTRESS

> As you know, my aged mother lives with us. She has been extremely upset and humiliated by having to use the rest room at the service station while you take your time repairing ours. Her doctor has told me to do what I can to avoid further distress to her, so moving might do her harm as well. Unless you do something immediately, I assure you I will hold you liable for any emotional or medical harm you have caused.

One way to encourage the landlord to do the work quickly is to agree that part of the rent will be withheld until the work has been completed. This is an arrangement the landlord may or may not be willing to accept. Remember that a tenant is entitled to damages and even a court order for substantial violations of the habitability provisions of the act.[3] It is often effective to provide the landlord with copies of the relevant provisions of the act during negotiations. Once you convince your landlord that he or she may be liable for damages for past violations, you might offer to release him or her from the liability if he or she promptly complies with a request that isn't required by the act (like providing paint).

If you come to some agreement (and assuming that things have gone beyond the stage of complete mutual trust), put it in writing. Make sure you cover everything so that the landlord can't argue you waived a complaint. Sample #10 shows an example of a settlement agreement that should give you a good idea of how to cover most topics. Both parties should keep a signed copy of the agreement, as well as copies of any receipts.

5. The risks of demand letters

The major risk of demand letters is that they may lead to an eviction notice. Another risk is that your identification of risks of special damages or of emotional distress may backfire. By

SAMPLE #10
SETTLEMENT AGREEMENT

This agreement between Laverne Landlady (land-lady) and Maria Petard (tenant), is intended to resolve completely a dispute that has existed between them concerning the condition of the premises at 007 Disrepair Way, through the date of this agreement. To this end, the parties agree as follows:

1. The landlady will pay for a front door lock and keys and for the installation of the lock in a sum not to exceed $20, permitting the tenant to deduct the actual cost from the rent due on April 1, provided the tenant furnishes the landlady with a receipt and the balance of the rent. [In other words, the tenant is withholding part of the rent until the repairs are made.]

2. The landlady will have the upstairs toilet fixed by a licensed plumber as soon as possible. The plumber is to be retained and paid by the landlady. Until the first rent payment date after the toilet is fixed, the tenant may reduce the monthly rent due by $30.

3. The landlady will furnish six gallons of paint to the tenant, and the tenant will paint the interior walls of the living room, dining room, kitchen, and master bedroom in a competent manner, in colors chosen by the tenant.

4. The tenant acknowledges that upon completion of this agreement the landlady has fulfilled all obligations of the Landlord and Tenant Act concerning the conditions known to the tenant as of the date of this agreement, and releases the landlady from any and all further liability for such known conditions, provided that this is fully performed by May 30, 199-, including fixing the toilet.

Maria Petard   March 15, 199-
(Tenant)   (Date)

Laverne Landlady   March 15, 199-
(Landlady)   (Date)

identifying valuable pieces of personal property, you may help your landlord enforce a money judgment against you in the future (if the item is not "exempt" from seizure — see chapter 7). Telling the landlord about the presence of an ailing parent may reveal a weakness of which a really unusual landlord will take advantage.

b. BUILDING INSPECTIONS

Cities and counties have various departments and bureaus that employ inspectors whose jobs are to determine whether buildings meet code requirements. Although there are building inspectors, fire inspectors, health inspectors, electrical inspectors, and many more, I use the term "building inspection" here to include inspections by any or all of these officials, except where it is important to distinguish among them.

Building inspections are almost always advisable if a demand letter alone doesn't do the trick and you're not ready to give up. The main reasons for an inspection is to obtain an experienced and neutral expert's statement about the condition of your home. This kind of evidence may be important to any of the rent-withholding defenses discussed later, and the date of the inspector's notification to the landlord may figure critically in any retaliatory eviction defense.

1. Code violations and the act

Not every violation of the building code is necessarily a violation of the Landlord and Tenant Act. Some provisions of the act require that certain items comply with building codes *when installed* and that they continue to function in good working order. For such items, the codes are relevant only to assess "good working order." Also, some code requirements, such as those requiring that ceilings be at least a certain height, often have nothing to do with habitability. On the other hand, safety from fire hazards may reasonably require complete fire code compliance, and water supply systems and sewage disposal systems must comply with the applicable codes to meet the requirements of the act.

2. Code violations may give you additional rights

Some code provisions may be enforceable by a tenant even if they are not covered by the Landlord and Tenant Act. If, under a statute or code provision, a landlord has a duty concerning the premises, the landlord's violation of that duty may form the basis of a lawsuit against the landlord. If a court finds that you were within the class of persons the statute or code provisions was designed to protect, you should recover damages if you can show that the landlord's violations caused you harm through no fault of your own. For example, if a code provision requires landlords to provide fire extinguishers, you should recover damages if you can show that the landlord didn't provide one, and that a fire that you didn't start caused more damage to your belongings than it would have caused if a fire extinguisher had been readily available.

By using the law this way, people who have been injured by violations of code provisions governing the building of party walls or requiring "crash bars" on fire exits have claimed substantial damages in court.

3. How to get an inspection

Although there are usually different inspectors for violations of building, electrical, plumbing, fire, and health codes, the usual procedure is for the building inspector to come first, and then to request electrical and/or plumbing inspections if they appear to be needed. If you are only concerned with an electrical or plumbing problem, or with fire or health code violations, you should ask for an appropriate inspection without going through the building inspector.

To arrange for a building inspection, look in the "government" listings in your telephone book under the city you live in (or the county if you are not within city limits). In Portland, for example, there are listings under "Bureau of Buildings" for building inspections, electrical permits and inspections, and plumbing permits and inspections. Some localities list sewage inspections separately from plumbing inspections. Fire inspections are obtained through the fire bureau, and health inspections through the county health department ("Department of Health Services" in Multnomah County).

Arranging for inspections outside a city or in a city without specific listings for these purposes may take a little more looking. Just remember that it is necessary to get a permit to do anything almost everywhere, and an inspector is at least theoretically available to ensure that the permit is appropriate and that it is complied with.

You should not have to pay for an inspection. It is the public duty of the various agencies to investigate alleged code violations and to enforce the relevant codes. Occasionally, however, you will run into an inspector who is not used to compliance inspections unrelated to a permit application, and who doesn't like the idea of a "mere tenant" getting "something for nothing." Don't take a refusal for an answer; talk to a superior official, and, if necessary, work your way up to the county commissioner or mayor. Sometimes a letter to the newspaper will get results.

On the other hand, it may just be worth a small fee to get the inspection done quickly and without a separate battle. Just make sure you record the name of the inspector and obtain a copy of the inspection report.

4. The risks of building inspections

Like demand letters, building inspections may trigger an eviction action by the landlord. They also have additional risks: if the landlord does nothing to repair the premises after an inspection has revealed violations, the enforcement agency involved may ultimately go to court to get an order that the landlord repair or have the premises vacated. The latter result may make you wonder who the code provisions are supposed to protect! Except in the case of immediate health or fire hazards, however, this risk is usually minimal, because the enforcement process takes a great deal of time, and you should win or lose the repair controversy long before the process threatens your home.

A related risk is that the landlord will be forced to fix something — such as door widths or ceiling heights — that you really don't care about, and then have no money left over to do what you want done. Worse yet, the landlord may decide that compliance with a code provision that means nothing to you is too expensive. If the enforcing agency insists on compliance, the landlord may simply try to evict you. Although the retaliation defense discussed in chapter 8 may help, even retaliatory evictions are permitted if compliance with the codes "requires alteration, remodeling or demolition which would effectively deprive the tenant of the use of the dwelling unit."[4]

6

GETTING REPAIRS: WITHHOLDING RENT AND SUING THE LANDLORD

If you have tried demand letters and building inspections without success (and without receiving an eviction notice),[1] the next step is often some form of rent withholding, which is probably the oldest remedy used by tenants. Long before the adoption of the Landlord and Tenant Act, tenants often simply refused to pay any rent or applied some of the rent to needed repairs as a final act of frustration, moral indignation, desperation, or some combination of these reactions to landlords' refusals to make repairs. Before the act, however, this remedy had two fatal flaws. First, unless the landlord had made a clear and direct promise to the tenant to make the repairs in question, the law imposed no duty on the landlord to make the repairs. Second, even if the landlord had made such a promise, the doctrine of independent covenants (discussed in section **e.** of this chapter) prevented the tenant from defending an eviction action on the basis that the lack of repairs justified the tenant's failure to pay all or part of the rent.

Before the act, then, the argument that seemed so essentially fair to tenants — "If a landlord refuses to uphold his or her part of the bargain, why should I be required to uphold mine?" — fell on deaf ears in court. The Landlord and Tenant Act has set out to change all this, although there are times when it is not obvious in court.

The act imposes repair and maintenance obligations on landlords regardless of any agreement between the parties, and as you will see from reading this chapter, the act at least largely abolishes the doctrine of independent covenants. In some situations, a tenant is not required to pay rent or is authorized to use part of the rent to cure problems caused by the landlord's violations of repair or maintenance obligations. The act also gives a tenant a right to recover money damages for these and most other violations by the landlord.

Each of the remedies discussed in the following pages can help a tenant show either that no rent is due or that the amount due is less than that demanded in an eviction notice. By the same process, a tenant may use these devices to refute a charge that there is a default in rent when asserting a retaliatory eviction defense in any kind of eviction action (see chapter 8, section a.). Similarly, these devices may help a tenant defend an action for back rent after the tenancy is over.

Finally, any of these devices may be used as the basis for a lawsuit for damages and other relief against a landlord. The principle of dependent covenants may defeat a landlord's attempt to offset back rent against the damages you seek. You are entitled to seek damages under most of these remedies, and it may be necessary to use these devices to show there was no default in rent in order to recover damages for the landlord's retaliatory conduct.

All of these remedies can enable a tenant to divert rent money from the landlord to repairs, but they vary in their safety. I discuss the reliability of each in the following pages. Generally, however, interrupting the flow of rent to the landlord is usually your most powerful weapon to obtain repairs (either because the landlord finally gives in or because you free money from rent payments to get the repairs done yourself), but it is also the most likely way to end up in court as a defendant in an eviction action for nonpayment of rent.

One word of caution: although the act contemplates that some tenants can and will do their own repair work, don't undertake anything you can't handle. Not only can some work by physically dangerous, but you also run the risk of giving the landlord a claim for damages on the theory that your work made things worse.[2] Finally, whether or not you do your own work, do not do anything without the landlord's written permission unless it is a needed repair and you have sent a demand letter (or have at least attempted to give oral notice in an emergency).

a. LACK OF ESSENTIAL SERVICES

1. The remedies

If a landlord's violations of the major habitability section of the act (ORS 90.320) or of the rental agreement result in the loss of heat, hot or cold water, electricity, or any other "essential service," section 90.365 may provide useful remedies.

Under certain conditions, the section gives a tenant a choice among four remedies:

(a) The tenant may procure substitute "essential services" and deduct their cost from the rent.

(b) The tenant may procure substitute housing, stop paying the rent, and recover the cost of the substitute housing from the landlord.

(c) The tenant may have the needed repairs made and deduct their cost from the rent. This is the "repair and deduct" remedy.

(d) The tenant may recover damages based on the reduction ("diminution") in rental value of the premises caused by the loss of essential services.

Of these remedies, (a), (b), and (d) are available only if the landlord's violation that caused the loss of services was "deliberate" (on purpose) or "grossly negligent" (reckless rather than merely careless). Remedy (c) is available if the violation was at least "negligent" — it needn't have been deliberate or grossly negligent. Remedy (d) is best ignored because damages are available with less restrictions under another section of the act, as discussed in section **f.** of this chapter.

61

None of the remedies under the essential service section (ORS 90.365) is available until the tenant gives the landlord written notice specifying the problem and allowing a reasonable time in which the landlord can correct the violation. In an emergency, however, a tenant may use the repair and deduct remedy, (c), after attempted verbal notice followed by written notice as soon as circumstances permit.

Note that all of these remedies can be used to justify rent withholding if they are properly used. Each can show that all or part of the rent wasn't due to defeat an eviction action based on nonpayment of rent; each can show that the tenant was not in default as part of a retaliatory eviction defense in any kind of eviction action (see chapter 8).

Most important, all of the remedies (except (d)) can enable the tenant to get the repairs made if the landlord refuses to perform them. The major strength of the essential service remedies is that they take a lot of the risk out of measuring the amount of damages. Unlike the "recoupment and counterclaim" remedy discussed in section **f.**, which requires a rather crude estimate of the cash value of the landlord's violations, the essential service remedies ordinarily enable a tenant to compute precisely the amount of rent that is not due.

The essential service section was designed to assist a tenant, who is without a service because of a landlord's violation, to maintain heating, plumbing, electrical, or other facilities in good repair (e.g., a burned out water heater) or because of nonpayment of a utility bill for which the landlord was responsible. The section applies only when a landlord's violation of the habitability section (ORS 90.320) or of a rental agreement results in the loss of an essential service. A tenant cannot rely on the section if the loss of services was caused by a deliberate or negligent act or omission on the part of the tenant, a member of the tenant's family, or a guest. For example, a tenant cannot use this section when the loss of a utility service was the result of his or her failure to pay a utility bill for which the tenant was responsible under the rental agreement.

2. The risks in general

The essential service remedies have important limitations. The limitations that apply to all of them are as follows.

The first risk is that the term "essential service" is ambiguous. Although it clearly applies to hot and cold water, heat, garbage collection (if the tenant hasn't accepted this responsibility under the rental agreement),[3] gas and electricity, and although fire extinguisher maintenance and vermin extermination are probably included, there is room for doubt beyond that. My view is that any habitability obligation under ORS 90.320 that fairly translates into a maintenance obligation (e.g., "railings maintained in good repair") implies a corresponding duty to provide that maintenance as an "essential service." This problem led the 1985 legislature to specify when and how the repair and deduct remedy (discussed below) applies to stoves and refrigerators, which is probably the most commonly appropriate use of the essential service provisions.

The second risk is that a tenant's rights under the essential service section may stand or fall upon a court's reading of such dangerously ambiguous terms as "grossly negligent" and "reasonable." Of course, both parties may find it advantageous to avoid the risks of ambiguity in court by agreeing beforehand on a repair schedule that may or may not include the same remedies as those listed in the essential service section. Finally, the essential service section says that a tenant cannot use any of its remedies and also use the more general remedies provided by section 90.360: injunction, damages, and/or termination of the tenancy (all of which are discussed later in this chapter). The impact of this limitation may vary. It may mean that a tenant who wishes to use the repair and deduct remedy when a wiring defect causes an electrical failure may have to give up any right to recover special damages for the loss of food spoiled in a freezer because of that failure.

On the other hand, the tenant can recover special damages under the "recoupment and counterclaim" approach without losing the right to the 90.360 remedies (injunction, damages, and/or termination). The only loss is the predictable measure of damages afforded solely by the essential service section.

It is clear, by the way, that a tenant can use essential service section remedies for some breaches while proceeding under 90.360 for other problems. Besides, if the landlord's violation was "willful" (a term that should include "deliberate" violations and may include "grossly negligent" ones) the tenant has the choice of injunction, double damages, and/or termination under another action of the act that is not exclusive of the essential service section. (See chapter 7 on lockouts and utility shutoffs.)[4]

In addition to these general limitations, each of the essential service remedies has its own peculiar risks. These risks, and the details of each of the remedies, are covered in the next three sections of this chapter.

b. SUBSTITUTE SERVICES

1. The remedy

The substitute service remedy of ORS 90.365 permits a tenant to procure "reasonable amounts of the essential service during the period of the landlord's noncompliance and [to] deduct their actual and reasonable cost from the rent."[5] Sometimes this is simple, and sometimes it is not.

If your landlord was supposed to pay the electric bills, but stopped doing so, this remedy permits you to have the utility service upon an account for you in your own name and restore the service. Assuming you give the landlord the appropriate written notice, you should be able to deduct the cost of paying for your own service from the rent. In this context, "actual and reasonable cost" means you can't deduct more than you actually pay for service and that you cannot take advantage of the situation to consume more of the utility service than would normally be consumed by a family of your size.

2. How to use the remedy

Like all essential service remedies, the substitute service remedy requires not only that you give written notice of the problem, but also that you allow the landlord a reasonable time under the circumstances to deal with it before you take matters into your own hands. Sample #11 is an example of the kind of letter you could write. Notice that in this example the landlord was required under the rental agreement to supply electricity and pay for it. Although the landlord must maintain the electrical wiring in good condition, there is no requirement that a rental agreement make the landlord responsible for paying for such utilities; the parties are free to agree on who will be responsible for payment.

SAMPLE #11
LETTER THREATENING SUBSTITUTE
SERVICE REMEDY

October 20, 199-

Dear Ms. Wolff:

As the landlord, you are required to supply and pay for electricity under our rental agreement. I have just learned that you have failed to pay electric bills for my house, located at 123 Dark Street, for over two months.

The electric company says it will turn off my electricity on November 15, 199-, if the bill isn't paid. If you haven't taken care of this by November 14, 199-, I will open an account in my own name and deduct the amount of any required deposit plus each month's electricity charges from the rent.

Yours sincerely,

Thomas Tenant
Thomas Tenant

65

If you use this device and it becomes necessary to procure and pay for substitute services, attach copies of the relevant receipts along with an explanatory note with each rent payment that is reduced by your use of this remedy. Again, keep copies of everything.

3. The risks

One problem with obtaining substitute services is that the utility provider may not cooperate. If the Public Utilities Commission has jurisdiction, you should request its help. If the utility is not subject to the commission (the people there will know), call the agency the commission refers you to. Typically, this will be a governmental agency, such as the Portland Bureau of Water. In any case, always work your way up from subordinate to supervisor as far as possible before giving up.

The general practice is to permit a tenant to open a new account without paying off the landlord's outstanding balance, but problems arise when one utility meter serves more than one dwelling unit. Also, some utilities may demand a substantial deposit, and you may later have a dispute with the landlord concerning whether the deposit is part of the "actual and reasonable cost" of getting a substitute service. Of course, if everybody read the statute with a view to its purpose, the tenant would be permitted to deduct the cost of the deposit *and* the cost of the service from the rent.

This remedy can get even more complicated when your problem can't be solved by opening a new account with a utility company. For example, when a heating system becomes unworkable, a tenant may have no effective way of "procuring" the essential service of heat (assuming the problem is not lack of fuel). Although this remedy would seem to permit a tenant to purchase or rent an electric heater for each major room, electric heaters draw an enormous amount of electric current and often lead to blown fuses. They are extremely dangerous if someone uses oversized fuses and they can cause a fire by overloading the electrical circuits and by igniting flammable material that is placed too close to the heating element. If you want to try this route, your electric company or an electrical inspector may be able to advise you on the capabilities of your wiring. Also, shop around for heaters, and compare the cost of renting to buying. The landlord may argue that the more expensive approach was not "reasonable," and it helps to be in a position to prove there was no choice or that the cost differences were not significant. To this end, make and keep notes of your conversations with stores, inspectors, and the utility service.

c. SUBSTITUTE HOUSING

1. The remedy

The substitute housing remedy for loss of an essential service permits a tenant to move out temporarily, to stop paying the rent, and to recover the "fair and reasonable value of reasonably comparable substitute housing."[6] The former limitation that the amount recovered cannot exceed the "periodic rent" was replaced by the requirement that the substitute housing be "reasonably comparable," as the legislature recognized that temporary substitute housing may cost a bit more than the longer-term housing rented by the tenant. On the other hand, if a modest motel is available to a tenant whose family was living at a low rent, the law does not require the landlord to pick up the bill for a fancy hotel. Factors such as available transportation, location, and availability of choices are all relevant to determining when substitute housing is "reasonably comparable" to the tenant's usual rented home.

The "fair and reasonable value" alternative is undoubtedly designed to benefit a tenant who receives free temporary housing from a friend or relative; the landlord is still liable to the tenant for the value of the substitute housing up to the amount of the periodic rent.

Example

You move into your great-aunt's apartment because your furnace broke down in January during a cold spell. She may not have demanded any rent from you, but the court would be entitled to award you an amount that is representative of the fair and reasonable value of your substitute housing. If, for example, your aunt normally paid $300 per month for rent, and you shared the apartment for a month, you might receive an award of $150, for this would be the fair and reasonable value of your substitute housing.

The double recovery (because a tenant can both stop paying the rent and recover the cost or value of the substitute housing) is necessary to give landlords an incentive to make repairs. If they were not in danger of having to pay the cost of substitute housing, landlords might be better off doing nothing, rather than making the repairs. For example, if you moved in with your great-aunt, the landlord might just treat your tenancy as if it has ended, when, of course, it hasn't.

2. How to use the remedy

In the unlikely event that you find this remedy attractive (probably only if you have a long-term rental agreement), Sample #12 is an example of an appropriate note to send to your landlord. If your landlord does not respond, make sure that it is clear you are not abandoning the premises when you move out. (An abandonment would allow the landlord to treat the lease as ended.) Sample #13 shows how to make your position clear.

3. The risks

The main problem with this remedy is that the tenant has to move, which is a burden that is rarely worth it, especially when suing the landlord would probably accomplish as much or more. (See section **g.** of this chapter.) If substitute housing is ever useful, it is probably best suited for tenants with long-term rental agreements.

SAMPLE #12
LETTER THREATENING SUBSTITUTE
HOUSING REMEDY

November 3, 199-

Dear Ms. Wolff:

I have been asking you to do something about the failing water heater at my house at 123 Dry Street for weeks without success.

Things are so bad now that I can't get enough hot water at any one time to bathe. If you don't fix it within one week, I will find substitute housing, stop paying rent, hold you liable for the cost of my substitute housing, and retain my rights under our lease.

Yours sincerely,

Thomas Tenant

Thomas Tenant

SAMPLE #13
NOTIFICATION OF SUBSTITUTE HOUSING REMEDY

November 11, 199-

Dear Ms. Wolff:

Because you did not fix the water heater as I requested in my letter of November 3, 199-, I am finding substitute housing until you do so. Furthermore, I am withholding rent and demanding that you reimburse me for the costs of the substitute housing.

This action does not mean that I am giving up my possession of your house.

Yours sincerely,

Thomas Tenant

Thomas Tenant

69

d. REPAIR AND DEDUCT

1. The remedy

This essential service remedy allows a tenant to pay for the necessary repairs and to deduct the cost from the rent. Note that repair and deduct remedies are only available for essential service problems, as discussed in section a. of this chapter. Also remember that this is the one essential service remedy for which mere negligence on the part of the landlord is sufficient; "gross negligence" or a deliberate act on the part of the landlord is not necessary.

The 1985 legislature made it clear that repair and deduct remedies extend to stoves and refrigerators (but not air conditioning equipment).[7]

After giving the landlord the appropriate written notice, the tenant may have the necessary work done in a competent manner and, after submitting to the landlord receipts or an agreed upon itemized statement, deduct from his or her rent the actual and reasonable cost or the fair and reasonable value of the work not exceeding $200.[8] Be sure to get and keep receipts.

"Appropriate written notice" for these purposes is notice that gives the landlord a reasonable time within which to provide the essential service without your resorting to "repair and deduct."[9] What is reasonable for these purposes will depend on the circumstances; you may have to use the remedy in an emergency immediately after trying without success to reach the landlord by telephone (you must follow up with written notice as soon as possible anyway).[10] In the case of a faulty cooking appliance or refrigerator, "reasonable notice" is to be "determined in light of the degree to which the tenant has been deprived of cooking or refrigeration facilities."[11] In other words, a landlord should have more time to respond in the case of one faulty burner than when a tenant's stove is not working at all.

You can exceed $200 if both parties agree.[12] Get it in writing to be on the safe side. "Actual and reasonable cost" means that you cannot solve your problem in an unnecessarily expensive way just because you expect it to come out of your rent. The term "fair and reasonable value" is designed to permit you to do the work yourself, or to have a friend or relative do it without charge, and to recover the reasonable value of labor and materials from the landlord even if they are donated to you.

2. How to use the remedy

Samples #14, #15, and #16 are examples of notices designed for a typical repair and deduct situation. By comparing them carefully with section 90.365, you will see how the process should work. Remember that any deviation from the statutory conditions can prevent you from successfully using this remedy as a defense to an eviction action. (If you need a copy of the act, see page xiv of the Introduction.)

You should try to deliver the written notice to the landlord's home or place of business personally and make a note of the time and place of delivery. Keep a copy of the letter for your files. Cases that aren't so serious would require a greater period of notice. Always calculate the notice period by weighing your present inconvenience against the future consequences of a judge or jury ultimately deciding that the landlord should have had more time to comply.

If the landlord does not respond, pay to have the work done and pay the balance left out of the next month's rent in the usual manner, but enclose a letter similar to the one in Sample #15 with your rent payment.

The reason for the last paragraph in Sample #15 is to limit the time during which the landlord can sit around and think up excuses. Unless objections are stated promptly in a return letter, it will be hard for the landlord to convince anyone that any of the complaints are not merely afterthoughts.

SAMPLE #14
NOTICE OF REPAIR AND DEDUCT REMEDY

May 15, 199-

Dear Mr. Fullbird:

I called your office and home telephone numbers today to notify you that the water heater, which you know has been leaking, has now failed altogether. I have no hot water at all and need to bathe my children.

The law permits me to have a new water heater installed and to deduct the expense (not to exceed $200) from the rent. You may, of course, agree to let me exceed the $200 limit. You are entitled to a period of time, reasonable under the circumstances, either to fix it by your own means or to specify who you want to do the work, provided that my rights to have the work done in a workman-like manner and within a reasonable time under the circumstances are not lessened.

If you had to do without hot water, I think you would agree that 48 hours is a reasonable deadline. Therefore, I hereby give notice that unless you install a new water heater or specify someone who is a licensed plumber to do so within 48 hours, I will buy a water heater, have it installed, and deduct the total cost, not to exceed $200, from next month's rent.

You can reach me at one of the following telephone numbers:

Home: 555-9999

Work: 555-1111

Yours sincerely,

M. Petard

M. Petard

Enc: Copy of ORS 90.365

REPAIR AND DEDUCT NOTICE
(After you have had repairs made)

June 1, 199-

Dear Mr. Fullbird:

Enclosed are a check for $150 and a copy of a $150 receipt from Act Plumbing, reflecting the cost of a water heater and its installation.

As I notified you in my letter of May 15, 199-, the water heater had been leaking all along, as you knew, and stopped working altogether on that date. You did not replace it or specify the person you wanted to do so within the 48 hours from the time I left the notice at 1234 Broke Street, so I hired Ace Plumbing to do the work. (Section 90.365 of the Landlord and Tenant Act lets me do this.) This month's rent of $300 is, therefore, paid in full.

If for any reason you dispute the amount of the deduction or my rights to have proceeded in this manner, please state your objections promptly and in writing.

Yours sincerely,

M. Petard

M. Petard

Enc. Copy of ORS 90.365

You should say only that the landlord knew of the problem beforehand if it is true, of course. In the examples shown, by establishing that the landlord had prior notice, the tenant can show negligence. If the landlord specifies the person who is to do the work, your letter should state that the repairs were done by the specified person.

If you have to spend more than one month's rent, your notice might look like Sample #16. Similarly, if you exceed the $200 limit by mutual agreement, you should state this as well,

SAMPLE #16
REPAIR AND DEDUCT NOTICE
(When expense exceeds the rent)

June 1, 199-

Dear Mr. Fullbird:

As I notified you on May 15, 199-, my water heater went out. You neither replaced it nor specified the person to replace it within the 48 hours specified in my notice. As you can see from the enclosed Ace Plumbing receipt, the total expense was $189.95, an amount which exceeds my monthly rent of $175.00 by $14.95. Section 90.365 of the Landlord and Tenant Act allows me to deduct the cost from my rent. So, my rent for June is paid in full, and I will pay $160.05 for my rent next month.

Please state any objections promptly and in writing.

Yours sincerely,

M. Petard

M. Petard

Enc. As stated.

---

although you should obtain a written authorization to exceed $200 before doing so. Your reliance on an oral agreement when spending more than $200 will preclude any objection by the landlord, assuming you are believed. However, it is safer to get the landlord's signature on a statement (see Sample #17).

In an emergency, the repair and deduct remedy permits you to attempt to give the landlord verbal notice if you follow it up as promptly as conditions permit with written notice (see Sample #18).

3.   The risks

There are two major risks involved with the repair and deduct remedy. First, it seems so practical that many tenants

SAMPLE #17
WRITTEN PERMISSION TO EXCEED $200 LIMIT

I, J. Fullbird, landlord of the premises at 100 Erosion Boulevard, hereby authorize M. Petard, the tenant at those premises, to spend as much as $210 to obtain the following repairs to the premises, and to deduct the actual cost of such repairs, not exceeding that sum, from future rent payments:

Repairing hot water tank, kitchen water taps, and bathroom taps.

Dated July 30, 199-

J. Fullbird

(Landlord)

SAMPLE #18
REPAIR AND DEDUCT NOTICE
(In an emergency)

June 1, 199-

Dear Mr. Fullbird:

This morning, a water supply pipe in my house burst and water rushed all over the basement. I was unable to turn off the main valve (the handle was missing), so I called your office immediately. There was no answer, so I called a plumber. I will deduct the amount I paid the plumber from the next month's rent. I am enclosing a copy of the receipt for $78.85. See ORS 90.365.

Please state any objections promptly and in writing.

Sincerely,

M. Petard

M. Petard

Enc. As stated

use it too hastily and carelessly. This risk can be minimized by weighing carefully the likelihood that a judge or jury might think a problem was not substantial, or that the landlord should have had more time than you allowed to deal with the problem. The risk can also be minimized by carefully following the sample letters shown here.

Second, if you use this remedy, you will make some substantial modification or repair of the landlord's property. There is always the risk that the work will not be done properly or that the landlord will claim that the property has been damaged by poor repairs. For this reason, it is safest to encourage the landlord to exercise the right to specify a repair person, rather than letting him or her defer to your choice. On the other hand, the identity of the repair person may determine whether or not the necessary work can be done within the $200 limit, so weigh this factor in your choice.

Ideally, you should get several estimates and try to get the landlord to agree to your choice in writing. Most professional repair people are bonded, so the landlord should be satisfied that a responsible party stands behind the work.

If you have to have an amateur do the work, again try to get the landlord to agree to your choice in writing, so that the landlord can't later claim that your choice was negligent.

e. DEPENDENT COVENANTS

1. The remedy

As mentioned earlier, a major significance of the Landlord and Tenant Act is that it abolished the doctrine of independent covenants. That doctrine made any covenant (promise) of the landlord independent of the tenant's covenant (promise) to pay rent. This means that even if a landlord promises to make repairs and then breaks that promise, that landlord could still evict a tenant who responded to the broken promise by refusing to pay rent.

The act fundamentally altered centuries of landlord and tenant law by adopting a principle of dependent covenants in ORS 90.250:

> A rental agreement...may not permit the receipt of rent free of the obligation to comply with subsection (1) of ORS 90.320.

This section also reflects the other major change accomplished by the act: landlords have obligations to supply decent housing whether or not they agree to do so; that obligation is imposed by ORS 90.320 regardless of the terms of any rental agreement (see chapter 2).

Section 90.250 means that any tenant who can demonstrate that the landlord has "substantially" violated the habitability requirements of section 90.320 should be able to establish that the landlord was not entitled to rent for the period of that violation. If accepted, this defense means that the tenant cannot be evicted for not paying the rent during that period; it also means that the tenant is not "in default in rent" for purposes of any retaliatory eviction defense.

Note that this "dependent covenant" remedy should mean that no rent at all is due during the period of the landlord's violation of ORS 90.320. The remedies discussed in section f. of this chapter are different in that they cover a broader range of problems (most violations of the act and all violations of the rental agreement); they are also different in that the amount that is not due depends on the seriousness of the landlord's violations.

2. How to use the remedy

Assuming that a judge agrees that the dependent covenant defense exists, your only problem will be proving that the landlord was in substantial violation of section 90.320 during the period for which he or she claims rent is in default. Therefore, to use this remedy, a tenant would normally start with a demand letter and a building inspection (see chapter

5). If the repairs are not made, the next step would be letters and rent withholding just as in the case of the recoupment and counterclaim remedies discussed in section **f.** of this chapter. With any of these three remedies, it may be useful to take pictures of visible repair problems and to have friends view them in case you need witnesses besides the building inspector if you ever find yourself in court. Also, it is important to be careful spending any of your rent money for repairs for the same reasons as in the case of recoupment and counterclaim remedies (see section **f.**).

3. The risks

There are two major limitations to the dependent covenant remedy. First, section 90.250 makes the right to receive rent dependent only on the obligations imposed by section 90.320(1). Violations of other sections of the act or of the rental agreement are not expressly covered. Therefore, a landlord's failure to provide working locks (an obligation imposed by a section other than ORS 90.320) or to comply with the provisions of the rental agreement may not excuse a tenant's failure to pay rent under the dependent covenant remedy.

Of course, they may excuse nonpayment of rent under one of the essential services remedies discussed above or under the recoupment and counterclaim remedies discussed below.

A second major limitation of the dependent covenant remedy is that judges hostile to the purposes of the act or unfamiliar with its place in the development of landlord and tenant law may simply not accept the existence of this remedy. Such judges may be unwilling to "give the tenant something for nothing," and may read section 90.250 as merely governing the language of rental agreements. In a nonpayment of rent eviction, a tenant who relies entirely on section 90.250 will be evicted if the judge takes this view.

Because of these limitations, it is almost always important to use a recoupment or counterclaim remedy in addition to the dependent covenant remedy. Your problem may not be covered by section 90.320, and you may need a second line of defense even if it is covered.

f. RECOUPMENT AND COUNTERCLAIM

These remedies are probably the most useful devices a tenant has under the act for dealing with repair problems. They both may justify a tenant's refusal to pay at least part of the rent when a landlord violates obligations under the act or under the rental agreement. They both can help a tenant show there was no default in rent to prevent a nonpayment of rent eviction, or to entitle the tenant to a retaliatory eviction defense in any kind of eviction action.

Both remedies work on the principle that the landlord may owe the tenant "damages" for violation of the landlord's obligations under the act or under the rental agreement.

1. Damages

Section 90.320(2) entitles a tenant to "damages" for a landlord's violation of the rental agreement or of the habitability section of the act (ORS 90.320). Section 90.125 entitles either party to "appropriate damages" for almost any violation of the act.

"Damages" simply amount to the monetary equivalent of the harm caused by a wrong even if it's hard to assess the amount. I have already discussed "general" and "special" damages in chapter 5, but it's worth repeating here that "general damages" for a landlord's violation of habitability obligations are measured by the reduction in rental value of the premises caused by that violation. From a landlord's point of view, general damages caused by a tenant's violations may be measured by decrease in rental value or by decrease in the fair market value (sale value) of the premises. "Special damages" are peculiar to each situation, as when a tenant's furniture is harmed by a water leak. Usually, the cost of repairing the furniture or the fair market value of the furniture at the time of the harm (whichever is smaller) would be special damages that might be added to the general damages (reduced rental value) caused by the leak.

The act also specifies some "statutory damages." These are minimum amounts that must or may be awarded for certain kinds of violations. The purposes of such provisions are to ensure that an injured party will recover something even when it's hard to prove or to measure damages and to deter others from committing violations that the legislature deems particularly common or serious. For example, one statutory damage provision permits an award of up to twice the actual damages or twice the monthly rent (whichever is greater) as a sanction against retaliatory evictions.[13]

If a tenant has a right to any kind of damages because of a landlord's violations of the act or of the rental agreement, the act provides that the tenant may bring an "action."[14] Although this generally means filing a lawsuit in court (as discussed in section **g.** of this chapter), the act defines "action" as also including recoupment and counterclaim.[15]

2. The remedies

"Recoupment" is the process by which the mutual debts of two parties cancel each other out, in whole or in part, if the debts arose out of the same transaction. For example, when a contractor sues for payment on a building job, the defendant might defeat all or part of the claim by proving that the contractor's performance was defective and that the value of the building suffered as a result.

In the context of the landlord and tenant relationship, recoupment is a process where a tenant can use the landlord's violations of the act or of the rental agreement to show that the unpaid rent was not really due. If the tenant stops paying rent, regardless of the reason, the tenant may show that all or part of the rent wasn't due by recoupment whenever he or she is entitled to damages for the landlord's failure, for

80

example, to fix a toilet. The major question is the amount of damages to which the tenant is entitled.

"Same transaction" in the context of the landlord and tenant relationship covers all of the relations between the landlord and the tenant that arise because of the tenancy.[16]

The great advantage of recoupment is that it is a remedy that applies whenever the landlord's violations of the act or of the rental agreement entitle the tenant to damages. As long as the right is one of the great majority for which damages are appropriate, and as long as the violation was not the tenant's fault, recoupment should be available. There are no complicated notice requirements or waiting periods, although a notice of some kind is always advisable (see chapter 5). Of course, you must always act in good faith and "mitigate" (minimize) your damages.[17]

Another advantage of recoupment is that you can use it to defend an eviction for nonpayment of rent without having applied your rent money to repairs or services. If things work out so badly that you choose to move, you can spend your money on moving expenses and defend any action for back rent by using the recoupment defense.

Example

You pay rent for many months even though your landlord hasn't responded to your requests for heat and for repairs to a leaky roof. As the weather gets colder and wetter, you finally stop paying rent and the landlord tries to evict you. You can defend the eviction action by claiming that the damages to which you are entitled for the landlord's violations equal or exceed any amount the landlord claims as rent. You don't have to show that you applied any of the rent to repairs or services. If you move out before the landlord tries to evict you, and the landlord sues you for unpaid rent, you can use the same approach to show that all or part of the rent claimed is not due.

A counterclaim differs from recoupment because it seeks more than the defeat of the landlord's claim. In monetary terms, a recoupment can show that all or part of the rent claimed by a landlord is not really due, but only a counterclaim can permit a court to award a judgment for damages against a landlord in an eviction action. More generally, any request for relief above and beyond finding that the landlord isn't entitled to evict the tenant can be called a counterclaim. For example, a tenant can respond to an eviction action by "counterclaiming" for the same kinds of affirmative relief that a tenant can seek as a plaintiff, including an order that repairs be made.[18]

Example

Assume that you stop paying rent and your landlord serves you with a 24-hour notice and brings an eviction action. If you defend by arguing that all of the rent claimed is offset by the damages the landlord owes you because the toilet hasn't worked for six weeks, you are asserting a recoupment. If you claim that the damages exceed the rent claimed and ask that the court award you a judgment for the difference (and/or an order that the landlord fix the toilet), you are asserting a counterclaim.

It is important to understand that if you assert that your landlord's violations of the habitability obligations of the act excuse your nonpayment of rent regardless of how much harm those violations have caused, you are relying on the dependent covenant remedy with its associated risks. To use the recoupment or counterclaim remedies, you may have to show that the amount of damages to which you are entitled equals or exceeds the amount claimed as rent by the landlord.[19] This requires that you be prepared to show the extent of the hardship imposed by the landlord's violations. For example, lack of heat undoubtedly reduces rental value more in winter than in summer; your general damages for lack of heat in January should be much greater than those for lack of heat in August.

It is common for a tenant to defend an eviction action by attempting to use all three devices (i.e., dependent covenants, recoupment, and counterclaim) based on the same violations. Although this approach does not permit a tenant to have the benefit of the cumulative effect of all three remedies, it does mean the tenant will have the benefit of the most useful device of the three which the court allows under the circumstances.

If you counterclaim in an eviction action that is based on nonpayment of rent, you may not seek a greater amount of money than the court has power to award: $10,000 in a district court; $2,500 in a justice court.[20] These limitations, coupled with the advantages of being a plaintiff (discussed in the next section), generally mean that a tenant who wants to rely on a court order as a means of getting repairs should go to court as a plaintiff instead of waiting to become a defendant in an eviction action. The remainder of this discussion of recoupment and counterclaims assumes that you hope to accomplish your objectives by withholding rent while making sure that you have a strong defense if things don't work out and the landlord tries to evict you.

3. How to use the remedies

If you are going to withhold rent on the recoupment and counterclaim theory, here's how to go about it.

First, give the landlord notice of your intentions. Decide whether you are going to withhold all or part of the rent, depending on how disgusted you are with the landlord's failure to respond to more reasonable requests, the nature and extent of the landlord's breaches, and the hardship you are suffering. Something like the letter in Sample #19 will do.

Second, open a special savings account in your name and deposit every cent of the withheld rent into that account as the rent becomes due. You might make an exception if you need the money for expenses that are absolutely necessary

SAMPLE #19
NOTICE THAT YOU ARE WITHHOLDING RENT
DUE TO LANDLORD'S BREACHES

January 15, 199-

Dear J. Fullbird, landlord:

Although I have made every effort to accommodate your needs, you have failed completely to respond to mine or to fulfill your duties under the law to remedy the following conditions at my house:

leaking roof
blocked toilet
broken furnace
faulty kitchen wiring
inoperative oven

I have had numerous telephone conversations with you in which you have come up with one or another reason to delay or evade repairs. On December 1, 199-, I sent you a formal request for repairs and a copy of an inspection report listing code violations on the premises. *(This paragraph should continue in this manner to list all of your efforts at achieving compliance to date.)*

I have simply and completely had it; if you had to face the terrible choice of living here or moving, you would undoubtedly feel the same.

This will give you notice that I will not pay one more cent toward the rent until you have promised in writing to make all of the repairs by March 15, 199-, and until you have demonstrated a sincere intention of fulfilling that promise by completing at least the following repairs:

fixing the toilet
fixing the furnace

If you don't comply, I will pursue all my available remedies under the Landlord and Tenant Act.

Yours sincerely,

M. Petard

M. Petard

Enc. as stated

and caused by the landlord's breaches. For such expenses, keep meticulous records and all receipts.

What is at stake here is whether or not you will be able to persuade a judge to allow you to pay only part of the rent into court as the price of asserting your counterclaim and having a second chance to pay the rent and stay on the premises under the "payment of rent into court" provision. Other reasons to avoid spending the withheld rent on unessential repairs are the difficulties in relating the amount of damages you suffered as a result of the landlord's breach to the costs of the repair under ORS 90.360 and the possibility that you will end up moving after having spent your hard-earned money fixing someone else's property.

By paying rent into a savings account (as it becomes due), you will be demonstrating your good faith and dispelling any notion that you are withholding rent because you simply don't have the money. You will also be accumulating a sum of money that may encourage the landlord to settle. The money will also provide you with funds necessary to support a counterclaim if you have to pay rent into court. It may also pay your moving expenses if you lose, settle, or quit. Of course, once you pay the money into court, you lose control of it until and unless the court orders it returned to you. This choice is discussed in chapter 8, section **d**.

The third step in using the recoupment or counterclaim remedies is to keep track of every added expense and inconvenience caused by the landlord's violations of the act or of the rental agreement. This record will be useful in negotiating with the landlord or in presenting your case in court. If the landlord agrees to make repairs, write up a settlement agreement as discussed in chapter 5. If the landlord doesn't give in, consider going to court first (as discussed in the next section of this chapter) and read chapter 8 on evictions.

4. The risks

(a) Recoupment

The major limitation of the recoupment approach is that you cannot measure the damages exactly. Suppose you stop paying all or part of the rent and use the money to have a plumber fix the toilet. Using the defense of recoupment, you will show that no rent was due only if a court agrees that the amount of damages you suffered (which would probably be measured by the decrease in rental value caused by lack of a working toilet, plus any special damages you suffered) at least equals the total amount of unpaid rent.

Unlike the essential service remedies of substitution and repair and deduct discussed earlier, a recoupment approach does not ensure that the measure of damages will be the cost of repairs. With an essential service remedy, proof that the actual and reasonable cost of fixing the heater was $179.50 will show that $179.50 was not due as rent, assuming all other requirements for using the essential service remedies are met. With recoupment, the amount of rent not due depends on the assessment by the judge or jury of how much you should be awarded as damages for the landlord's violations. If the only damages you claim are for lack of heat, whether or not you are evicted may depend on how the judge or jury feels rental value is affected by lack of heat for one month in the middle of winter.

In an eviction action based on nonpayment of rent, a court may rule that the 24-hour notice must demand the correct amount of rent before the tenant can be evicted for nonpayment. Under these circumstances, all that is necessary with the recoupment defense is to convince the judge or jury that the damages suffered by the tenant reduce the amount of rent due below the sum demanded in the notice. On the other hand, if the judge is of the view that the critical question is only whether there is a default in payment of rent (regardless of whether the 24-hour notice asked the correct amount), things may get very risky.

Example

You may pay $150 monthly rent for a long time, even though your landlord has continually refused to repair the heater. Unwilling to run the risks associated with the essential services remedies, you simply stop paying rent and spend $179.50 to have someone fix the heater. The landlord gives you a 24-hour notice demanding the rent, you don't pay, and the landlord brings an eviction action based on nonpayment of rent. You argue to the jury that you are entitled to at least $150 in damages for doing without heat all those months and, therefore, that the $150 claimed by the landlord is really not due. The landlord argues that most of those months were warm, so the rental value was not affected that much. The amount you spent on repairs is not necessarily the same as the amount of damages you should recover. If the jury fixes your damages below $150, you will be evicted if you rely only on recoupment. Moreover, any retaliation defense will be useless because the jury has found you "in default in rent."[21]

Of course, the dependent covenant defense would solve both problems by showing that no rent was due regardless of the harm you have suffered if the violation in question was covered by the habitability section (ORS 90.320) and if the judge accepts the defense. (See section e. on dependent covenants.) Otherwise, a counterclaim may save the day.

(b) Counterclaims and the right of redemption

One of the most unusual provisions of the Landlord and Tenant Act is the section that allows a judge to order a tenant to pay all or part of the rent claimed by the landlord into court as a condition of being allowed to assert a counterclaim. This is often referred to as the "rent-into-court" or "redemption"[22] provision. It does not apply to recoupment or to other defenses; it does not apply in actions for rent when the tenant has moved out; and it should not apply to eviction actions that are not based on nonpayment of rent.[23]

The rent-into-court provision permits (but does not require) a judge to make the tenant pay less than all of the rent claimed into court because the judge feels the tenant will probably show at trial that less than the amount claimed is really due.

Although the rent-into-court provision is objectionable because it effectively charges the tenant for a day in court, it also has a positive side which, if you can afford it, is well worth the price. If you pay rent into court, you are entitled to an opportunity to pay any amount still owing to the landlord (if the court finds that the amount paid into court is not enough to cover the rent that is in default). If the amount paid into court is enough to cover any rent found due, or if you make up any difference after the trial, "judgment shall be entered for the tenant in the action for possession."[24]

The effect of this "second chance" or "redemption" provision is to take the risk out of estimating damages. Even if the court decides you are entitled to a smaller amount of damages for the landlord's violations than you had estimated, the rent-into-court provision will give you a second chance to prevent eviction for nonpayment of rent.

This is discussed again in chapter 8, but the safety of paying rent into court is an important consideration in selecting among the various repair remedies long before anyone ends up in court.

Example

Just as in the last illustration, you have paid $150 monthly rent for a long time, the landlord has refused to fix the heater, you have stopped paying rent, and the landlord has brought an eviction action for nonpayment of rent after you get fed up and spent $179.50 to have the heater fixed instead of paying the rent. This time, instead of merely relying on the recoupment defense, you file a counterclaim in the eviction action. You ask for $179.50 for fixing the heater and $400 for the reduction in rental value of the premises over the entire period of time for which you had to go without heat. The landlord then asks the court to make you pay all of the $150 he or she claims as rent into court. You argue that you will probably win your counterclaim and show the judge the receipt. The judge makes you pay $100 into court. At the trial, if the jury decides you are entitled to only $30 damages for your lack of heat, the result will be that the landlord will get the $100 paid into court, but you will have the choice of paying an additional $20 to make up the entire balance due. If you pay the $20, you should win the eviction action and you can stay.

As you will see in chapter 8, the ability to "win" the case by paying the $20 in this illustration may determine whether the court awards attorneys' fees and court costs to you or against you. It may be worth it to pay the $20 even if you have decided to move anyway.

By the way, in this illustration the tenant would also win if the amount paid into court was equal to or greater than the amount of rent the court found due to the landlord. Also, if the tenant wins the counterclaim so that the landlord owes the money, the court will release the money paid into court as part of the money the landlord owes to the tenant. Finally, if the court finds that the damages suffered by the tenant equal the amount of rent paid into court, that money will also be paid to the tenant.

Attorneys who regularly represent tenants often have their clients pay rent into court without waiting for the landlord to ask for an order, and landlords' attorneys are beginning to learn *not* to ask for rent to be paid into court for fear of losing the case on the basis of the redemption provision.

You will see by reading chapter 8 that a tenant may also be required to pay rent into court to get a delay in the trial date. It is not clear whether rent paid into court for such a delay will give the tenant the same rights to a "second chance" as does rent paid into court to support a counterclaim. Therefore, if you are going to have to request any delay in the trial date, you should generally counterclaim if you have grounds to make sure that you will get the benefit of the "second chance" provision of the counterclaim section of the act.

g. SUING THE LANDLORD

1. The remedy

Everyone has heard the contention that the best defense is a strong offense. This certainly states my position on whether a tenant is better off as a defendant in an eviction action or as a plaintiff in a lawsuit against a landlord. It is now perfectly clear that a tenant with substantial complaints concerning a landlord's violations of a rental agreement or of the act may file a complaint in circuit court and seek the following kinds of relief:

(a) Protection against eviction until your case is over

(b) Protection against any retaliatory eviction

(c) Damages for the landlord's violations of the act or of the rental agreement

(d) An order that the landlord make repairs, and, where appropriate, an order that the landlord refrain from making unlawful entries or from attempting to evict the tenant through lockouts and utility shutoffs (see chapter 7)

(e) A declaration fixing the rent due in the future at a reduced amount until repairs are completed

(f) Damages under the Unlawful Trade and Unlawful Debt Collection Practices Acts (see chapter 15)

(g) A finding that the landlord is liable to you for your attorney's fees and court costs

(h) Any other relief the court deems appropriate

Of course, what you ask for and what you get will not necessarily be the same, but all of these forms of relief should be available in appropriate cases.

For a tenant, the advantages of being a plaintiff are many. If you go to court first, there is less chance that you will end up on a tenant screening list, or that the court will believe that you made things up as an excuse for not paying the rent. Also, the landlord and his or her attorney are more likely to have a realistic discussion of the possible outcome and expense of the case than if they are free to assume they are dealing with a routine eviction. If you go to court as an eviction defendant, the landlord's attorney may spend a great deal of energy assailing your motives and those of your attorney to cover up for misjudging the case in initial discussions with the landlord. This interferes with the landlord's rational consideration of any advantages of settlement.

Moreover, for a variety of reasons, things go more slowly when the tenant is the plaintiff, so there is more time for adequate preparation than in the speedy procedure envisioned by the eviction statutes. In addition, you are not restricted by the monetary limits of district or justice court if you have brought the case in circuit court. As plaintiff, you can sue for any relief you are entitled to, while counterclaims in an eviction action are limited to claims arising under the act, the rental agreement, or certain consumer protection laws (see chapter 8). (If you need a copy of the eviction statutes referred to in this book, see page xiv of the Introduction.)

If you ask the court to order the landlord not to bring a separate eviction action or not to engage in unlawful "self-help" eviction attempts, the landlord will probably ask that the court require you to put up an "undertaking." An undertaking is a device for protecting your opponent from any loss caused by the court's order if it turns out at trial that the court shouldn't have made the order before trial. The undertaking is usually in the form of a promise by a bonding company or a financially solvent individual to pay the landlord all losses if and when it is determined that the court's order should not have been made. On the other hand, there are statutes which permit the court to require the payment of money into court instead of an undertaking.[25]

Using these statutes, and by making an analogy to the rent-into-court provisions of the Landlord and Tenant Act, your attorney may be able to convince the court to allow you to pay rent into court as an undertaking for the court's order restraining the landlord. The Oregon Supreme Court has made such an order.

Most such court orders are not effective unless there is an undertaking or its equivalent, and the result of the rent-into-court equivalent is a perfectly proper, court-sanctioned rent strike with obvious financial implications for the landlord. An exception is that no undertaking should be necessary if the tenant is seeking an order that the landlord refrain from violating the act's prohibitions against lockouts, utility shut-offs, and invasions of privacy (see chapter 7).

If the court awards you an order after the trial that the landlord make repairs or refrain from bringing a retaliatory eviction, there is also no need for an undertaking. Undertakings of this sort are only necessary to support orders before trial because the court may decide that the orders shouldn't have been made. If the trial results in an order, there is no longer any doubt whether the order should be granted, at least as far as the trial court is concerned.

2. How to use the remedy

If your landlord has really "done you wrong," if you have tried everything else, and if you are ready for a long fight to enforce your rights to decent housing, an affirmative action is probably the way to go. Keep all your records, estimate your damages accurately (being very specific), find an attorney as discussed in chapter 12, and see your landlord in court!

3. The risks

There are, however, disadvantages. Suing your landlord rather than defending an eviction action requires much more energy on the part of your attorney. It is, therefore, more difficult to get a legal aid attorney to do it and more expensive to hire your own attorney to do it.

An affirmative action (suing) takes a lot of time. If you are like many tenants, you will run out of energy long before the case can be tried, and you will settle for a period of free rent, perhaps some cash, and adequate time to move, when you had originally hoped for an order for repairs and a long-term lease in return for past damages. You will do better than most tenants, but unless you have exceptional endurance, you will settle for something quite different from what you had originally wanted. Don't be alarmed by this; it happens in almost all civil litigation: well over 90% of all cases are settled before trial on terms that neither side would have accepted when the case was first filed.

h. THE RISKS IN GENERAL

Now that you have read about each of the repair remedies available under the act and the limitations of each, it is important that you consider the risks involved in any landlord and tenant dispute.

The major risk you run in asserting your rights to repair is that the landlord will try to evict you either to avoid the expense of repair or to vindicate the principle that a property owner can do as he or she pleases regardless of the Landlord and Tenant Act. This risk is worsened by the likelihood that your name will end up on a list distributed by a tenant screening service to landlords. In other words, you may find landlords refusing to rent to you in the future if you end up in eviction court now, even if you are in the right.

Your risks tend to increase as a repair controversy escalates. In most cases, an informal exchange between you and the landlord may leave you with evasions or excuses rather than the requested repairs, but if you give up at this stage, you are probably safe from eviction. This safety will usually continue as long as you pay the rent and otherwise "behave," but if you become assertive by writing a demand letter, for example, the landlord may give you an eviction notice. Even if the landlord simply ignores you, you will have to choose between giving up and taking the risk that the next step — perhaps a building inspection — will push the landlord over the edge. Again, if nothing happens, you will either have to give up or raise the stakes by withholding rent or going to court yourself. If you withhold rent, the chances are that the landlord will bring an eviction action for nonpayment of rent. Your primary alternative is to bring an action of your own.

Although a court fight is always a burden, it does not follow that you must avoid court at all costs. The ultimate risk, of course, is that you will lose. If so, you may be evicted from your home and be held liable for the landlord's court costs, attorney's fees, and any back rent. But tenants win court fights too, and the great majority of court cases are settled before trial. The critical test (assuming you're willing to take any risks) is the likelihood that you will win — a likelihood that also has a direct bearing on pretrial settlement possibilities.

To assess your chances of success in court, you must start by discarding the myth that judicial proceedings are reliably predictable. In fact, anything can happen in court, especially to a tenant who is relying on the relatively new Landlord and Tenant Act, which is unpopular with some judges. For example, one judge has ruled that a stove is not an "appliance" within the meaning of the provision requiring landlords to maintain appliances furnished to the tenant in good working order. In such a case, vehement disagreement is no substitute for an appeal, and an appeal may be financially impossible (see chapter 8, section f.).

On the other hand, there are many things about your chances of success that are predictable. Although you can

94

never be certain of the result, your chances of winning should depend heavily on how clearly your situation comes under one of the remedies discussed. This depends on the strengths, limitations, and ambiguities of those remedies, and on the care with which you use them.

For example, if you send a demand letter or request a building inspection only to have your landlord give you an eviction notice, you may be able to use the retaliatory eviction defense discussed in chapter 8 by presenting copies of letters and other proof to the court. This defense, however, is not available to a tenant who is "in default in rent." If you have not paid the rent, you will have to show that it was not due by proving that you properly used one of the rent withholding remedies discussed in this chapter.

Except for "suing the landlord," all of the remedies discussed have two functions: first, to obtain repairs without a court fight, and second, to help you win a court fight if it cannot be avoided. Every repair remedy must be selected with the understanding that it may later be critical in a court fight.

Table #1 compares the coverage and limitations of each of the remedies, but make sure you read chapters 5 and 6 to understand them fully. For example, repair and deduct is only available for "essential services," but the discussion of this remedy shows how essential services may include many conditions that also violate the provisions of the habitability section (ORS 90.320).

Finally, remember that concerted action through a tenants' union can increase your chances of success, while raising the stakes for both sides (see chapter 12). All of the remedies discussed in chapters 5 and 6 are available to tenants acting together as well as to a tenant struggling alone.

TABLE #1
REPAIR REMEDIES AND THEIR LIMITATIONS

	Demand letters	Building inspections	Substitute services	Substitute housing	Repair and deduct	Dependent covenants	Recoupment	Counterclaims	Suing the landlord
KINDS OF PROBLEMS									
Habitability violations ORS 91.320	x	x				x	x	x	x
Essential services	x	x	x	x	x	x	x	x	x
Other violations of the act	x						x	x	x
Violations of the rental agreement	x						x	x	x
LIMITATIONS									
Written notice to landlord required	x		x	x	x				
Landlord's act must be negligent					x				
Landlord's act must be deliberate or grossly negligent			x	x					
Remedy is complicated to use			x	x	x				x
Measure of damages is imprecise							x	x	x
Tenant may have to pay rent into court								x	x

7

LOCKOUTS, UTILITY SHUTOFFS, INVASIONS OF PRIVACY, AND SEIZURES OF TENANTS' BELONGINGS

This chapter deals with lockouts, utility shutoffs, invasions of a tenant's privacy, and seizures of a tenant's belongings during the course of a tenancy. Chapter 11 deals with belongings left behind at the end of a tenancy.

The problems discussed in this chapter have three things in common: they involve illegal conduct on the part of the landlord, the police probably won't help, and you will need a lawyer if the landlord doesn't back down. I will discuss the things you can do to protect yourself before you get to a lawyer. Chapter 9, written for landlords who need an emergency court order, may be helpful if you insist on being your own lawyer or have no choice. If you do go to a lawyer, it may be that the landlord will back down after one phone call. If so, you will have to decide whether to bother suing the landlord for any damages to which you may be entitled, including your lawyer's fee. If the landlord doesn't back down, your lawyer will probably have to ask a court to order the landlord to comply with the law, as discussed in chapter 6.

a. LOCKOUTS AND UTILITY SHUTOFFS

A lockout occurs when your landlord changes the locks or otherwise removes or excludes you from the premises by force; a utility shutoff occurs when a landlord "willfully diminishes services to the tenant." Both are equally unlawful means of attempting to get rid of you without judicial intervention. A landlord simply has no right to do such things if you refuse to leave voluntarily.[1]

Police rarely help tenants who have been locked out, believing such disputes to be "civil" rather than "criminal" in nature. In Portland, at least, the police recognize that tenants may have the right to break back into the premises from which they have been wrongfully excluded. The police are obliged to protect all parties from assault or battery, which are criminal offenses.

Occasionally, a landlord may attempt to convince the police that there was never a rental agreement and that the tenant is a trespasser, even though a holdover tenant with no defense is not a trespasser for these purposes. If this should happen to you, it should be enough to show the police a rent receipt or any other evidence of your tenancy such as utility bills addressed to you or correspondence from the landlord. You might even describe the contents of the middle drawer of the bedroom dresser if things get tight.

If you expect a dispute, prepare a "proof packet" of items to show to the police, and get in touch with a lawyer.

If your landlord removes or excludes you, seriously attempts or threatens unlawfully to do so, or "willfully" diminishes or interrupts your utility services to get rid of you, the act gives you the option of terminating the tenancy or permitting you to ask a court for an order that the landlord stop violating your rights and for "statutory damages" (see chapter 6). Statutory damages, in this case, are up to twice your actual damages or twice the monthly rent, whichever is greater.[2] Since emotional distress is often a legitimate and substantial portion of "actual damages" under such circumstances, the economic consequences may be disastrous for a landlord who violates these provisions. A tenant need not terminate the tenancy or ask for a court order to be entitled to damages.

Even if a landlord's behavior in causing a loss of utility service is not quite so serious as to be deemed willful, you may have self-help remedies under the essential service section of the act if the behavior is at least "negligent." In any event, you may have rights to a court order and damages under the general provisions of the act even if the landlord wasn't even negligent (see chapter 6, sections **f.** and **g.**).

If the provider of the utilities, such as the electric company, shuts off your service because you haven't paid bills that are your responsibility, you won't have any rights against the landlord unless a habitability violation caused your bills to be unusually high. Sometimes a defective electric water heater causes an abnormally high consumption of electricity; a running toilet will greatly inflate your water bill. If the landlord is responsible, it may take a court order to deal with the problem. If it's your fault (or if a court order is taking too long), you may be able to convince the utility company to restore service by making some kind of payment arrangement. If the utility is covered by the Public Utilities Commission (PUC), its Complaints-Utilities division may help negotiate with the provider.

PUC rules require utilities covered by the PUC (municipal utilities, such as city-run water bureaus are not covered) to give detailed notice rights to customers prior to termination in most situations.[3] Residential gas and electric utilities must advise customers of the right to make a repayment plan in lieu of disconnection.[4] A major reform is the provision that a utility cannot terminate, even for nonpayment, if the customer can provide appropriate certification that termination would significantly endanger the "physical health" of a member of the customer's family. The utility may, however, require the customer to enter a time payment plan; if that plan is not honored, the company can disconnect only after a hearing and if the PUC agrees to allow the disconnection.[5]

The rules also require attempted notice at the premises.[6] Hopefully, if the problem is a landlord who isn't paying for utilities as agreed, this will give the tenants notice so that they can pay the bill to avoid a shutoff. The tenants may be able to deduct the cost from the rent if they follow the statute carefully (see chapter 6).

If the utility isn't covered by the PUC, try to work up the chain of command just as you would when trying to arrange for substitute services. Always examine the back of any utility bill for instructions for handling disputed bills; ask for a hearing if you can't work things out on the telephone. Remember, the landlord may be liable for damages if he or she failed to disclose in writing that you are paying for a utility service that reaches other dwellings.[7]

b. ABUSE OF ACCESS

Landlords' and tenants' rights concerning inspections of the premises and other landlord entries are discussed in chapter 2. In this chapter, I merely list the remedies available to a tenant whose landlord violates rights of privacy by making unlawful entries, lawful entries in an unreasonable manner, or repeated demands for entries that are otherwise lawful but have the effect of unreasonably harassing the tenant. The remedies are as follows:

(a) The tenant is entitled to an order that the landlord stop making such entries or demands.

(b) The tenant may terminate the rental agreement if he or she chooses.

(c) The tenant may recover actual damages (which can include emotional distress) of not less than one month's rent.[8]

Again, see an attorney if you can't work out a solution.

Sometimes changing the lock or adding a chain lock does the trick, and there is nothing in the Landlord and Tenant Act that says your landlord must have a key to your lock. On the other hand, there is nothing to prohibit a clause in a rental agreement requiring your landlord to have a key for emergencies. As a practical matter, the risk here is that the landlord will have a legitimate need to get into your home in a real emergency while you're gone. Under some circumstances, you may be held responsible for the cost of repairing damage done to get in without a key.

c. WRONGFUL SEIZURE OF PERSONAL BELONGINGS

A landlord may not seize a tenant's belongings to enforce a claim for unpaid rent; a "security interest" in such goods on behalf of a landlord is not enforceable.[9] A landlord who wrongfully seizes and retains property to enforce a rent claim is in double trouble: not only is the tenant entitled to recover up to twice the actual damages, but the tenant is relieved of any responsibility for any rent that was unpaid at the time of the seizure.[10]

Since your goods may be virtually worthless to your landlord, once he or she understands that there is no lawful basis for holding your belongings to make you pay rent or damages, he or she may back down. It is a drastic mistake for a landlord to try to coerce a settlement in return for release of the goods. This would only increase the chances of the tenant recovering damages, and a release given just to stop a clearly illegal seizure won't hold up in court.

If the landlord does agree to return the goods, don't sign a receipt for the goods unless you are sure you are getting everything back in satisfactory condition.

8

EVICTIONS AND DEFENSES

If for any reason a landlord wants a tenant to move, but the tenant refuses to leave voluntarily, the landlord may not force the tenant to leave by any means other than a court order. Self-help evictions are illegal in Oregon, and a landlord who attempts to throw out a tenant without going to court is taking a big risk: the tenant should be able to get a judgment against the landlord for a substantial amount of money, and the landlord may even be guilty of a crime.

This chapter discusses the various eviction actions a landlord may use and the defenses that may be available to a tenant.

A landlord considering an eviction action should be able to tell from this chapter which type of eviction action is appropriate, how to use it, and how likely it is that the tenant will succeed with any defense or counterclaim.

A tenant facing an eviction must decide quickly whether and how to defend against that action. If the tenant does nothing, the landlord will get an eviction judgment by default, but there should be no award of attorney's fees.

Forcible entry and detainer (FED) statutes provide court forms for both parties. (If you need a copy of the statutes, see page xiv of the Introduction.) I have provided samples of additional forms here that a tenant might use if no attorney is available to represent the tenant. I have also included a model settlement agreement that may be useful to both parties to an eviction dispute.

a. STARTING AN EVICTION ACTION

Except in unusual cases, a landlord who wants to evict a tenant must start by giving the tenant some kind of notice. The various notices are discussed in later sections of this chapter. If the tenant does not move, the landlord's next step is to go to the clerk of the nearest court and file a forcible entry and detainer action (an FED) by filling out the form of complaint specified by ORS 105.125(2)(a).

The complaint form requires that the landlord check a box or line indicating what kind of notice was served (or that no notice was served), and that the landlord attach to the complaint a copy of any notice relied on. The clerk then fills out a summons (a cover sheet telling the defendant when and where to appear), collects all applicable fees, and forwards the summons and a copy of the complaint to the sheriff, civil process deputy, or anyone else authorized to give the summons and complaint to the defendant. Filing fees are currently $39.30 (the district court small claims amount), but the plaintiff will later have to pay the remainder of the full fee (currently $41.40) if the tenant asks for a trial.[1]

After the initial filing fee is paid, the clerk mails (by first class mail) another copy of the summons and complaint to the defendant at the premises. Mailing alone, however, is not enough. Anyone who is a resident of Oregon, over the age of 18, and neither a party to nor an attorney in the action, may serve the papers on the tenant. There are two ways in which the summons and complaint may be properly served on the defendant:

(a) If the tenant can be found anywhere, the papers may be handed to him or her.

(b) If the process server cannot find the defendant, the papers can be attached securely to the main entrance to the dwelling unit.[2]

103

The summons must specify a time for the tenant to go to court. This time must be seven days after the judicial day next following payment of filing fees unless the landlord requests a longer period or no judge is available until a later date.[3] The court date is called "first appearance."

On the other hand, if the landlord sues for rent in the eviction action (not just eviction for nonpayment of rent), the tenant must have the same time in which to respond to the summons as in other actions. This is now 30 days from service in both district and justice courts.[4]

An attorney can file the complaint for the landlord and may appear for him or her in court, but no attorney fees may be awarded if the tenant does not contest the action.[5]

If the tenant does not appear in court, the landlord will be able to get a judgment by default at the time and place indicated on the summons. If the tenant appears, whether or not the landlord can get a judgment will depend on whether the tenant can successfully assert a defense to the eviction action.

If both parties appear in court at "first appearance" and have not reached a settlement, the court should set the case for trial — typically in about a week. ORS 105.137(5) provides that the trial shall be scheduled no later than 15 days from first appearance. If the case is not tried that soon, and the delay is not attributable to the landlord, the tenant will be required to pay rent "that is accruing" into court "if the court finds after [a] hearing that entry of such an order is just and equitable." Note that some counties, including Multnomah County, are experimenting with mediation: parties in cases that are to be set for trial are sent to a trained volunteer mediator (often an attorney) to see if a settlement can be reached. If so, the case may be resolved by an agreed order; if not, the case will return to the scheduling judge or a clerk for setting the trial date.

b. EVICTION DEFENSES IN GENERAL

As you can see in Table #2, there are eight types of eviction action. As the table also shows, some defenses apply to all types of evictions, while others apply only to some of them. This table is a useful guide, but be sure to read the text as well. Tenants in any form of federally assisted housing should also read chapter 13; mobile home tenants should also read chapter 14.

1. The retaliatory eviction defense

The retaliatory eviction section of the Landlord and Tenant Act is designed to protect tenants against evictions that are motivated by a landlord's desire to get back at a tenant for asserting his or her rights or to get rid of a tenant to avoid responsibilities imposed on the landlord by the act.

Section 90.385 provides that a landlord may not retaliate by increasing rent, decreasing services, or by bringing or threatening to bring an eviction action (which includes serving an eviction notice) after a tenant has —

(a) complained to, or expressed to the landlord in writing an intention to complain to, an agency charged with building or housing code enforcement about a violation materially affecting health and safety,

(b) complained to the landlord of a violation under ORS 90.320 (habitability), 90.335 (abuse of access), 90.435 (utility shutoffs and lockouts), 90.305 (disclosure of manager or owner), or 90.315 (disclosure of utility payments that benefit other tenants or the landlord),

(c) complained to the landlord of a violation of a written rental agreement or, only if there is no written agreement, of an oral one,

(d) organized or joined a tenants' union or similar organization,

(e) complained to the landlord of a failure to give 30 days' written notice of a rent increase (ORS 90.240(4)),

105

TABLE #2
EVICTIONS AND DEFENSES

DEFENSES AVAILABLE	No notice	No cause	For cause	Nonpayment of rent	Substantial injury	Pet violation	Illegal subtenant	Resident manager
Retaliation	x	x	x	x	x	x	x	
Equity	x	x	x	x	x	x	x	x
Terms of the rental agreement	x	x	x	x	x	x	x	
Waiver or new tenancy	x	x	x	x	x	x	x	x
Prepaid rent period	x		x	x				
Defective notice			x	x	x	x	x	x
Breach did not occur or was not material				x	x	x		
Breach cured or offered cure refused				x	x	x		
Breach was of void term or rule				x		x		
Rent not due or subject to recoupment or counterclaim				x				
Rent offered but rejected				x				
Injury not substantial or threat not serious					x			
Wrong kind of tenancy	x	x						x
Access was not unlawfully refused	x							
Defective service of notice			x	x	x	x	x	
Mobile home tenancy		x				x		
Pet incapable of damage						x		
No written rental agreement							x	
Original tenant still there							x	
Occupancy not conditional on employment								x

106

(f) testified against the landlord in any judicial, administrative, or legislative proceeding, or

(g) successfully defended an eviction action brought by the landlord within the previous six months.

Subject to the limitations discussed below, if your landlord violates this section you have a right to recover up to twice your actual damages or twice your monthly rent, whichever is greater.[6] You can seek this kind of recovery either in the eviction action or in a separate action. Your damages may include emotional distress. In an eviction action based on nonpayment of rent, or an action to recover the rent, these damages may be useful in showing that the rent was not due by "recoupment" or "counterclaim." (These topics are discussed in chapters 5 and 6.)

For purposes of this chapter, the most important effect of the retaliatory eviction statute is that it gives a tenant a defense in any retaliatory action against him or her for possession.[7] This means that if you convince the court that the landlord's real motive for bringing the eviction was to retaliate against you in violation of this section, you should win the case unless one of the limitations discussed below applies. (Note that this defense is available in any kind of eviction action.)

Whether the retaliation claim is raised as an eviction defense or in an affirmative lawsuit by the tenant, it is up to the tenant to present evidence, usually circumstantial, that the eviction is retaliatory. That evidence usually amounts to the sequence of events. For example, you might show that the landlord's eviction notice was prepared soon after you asked for repairs. You might also convince the judge or jury that the eviction is retaliatory by showing that the eviction notice was served the day after you and other tenants picketed the landlord's house. Sometimes a landlord will do a tenant the favor of starting an eviction notice with words like "since you asked for repairs..."

Note that it is only unlawful *to retaliate* after the tenant has performed one of the protected acts listed in the retaliation statute. In other words, there is not a defense just because, for example, the tenant won an eviction action within six months before this eviction action. To prevail, the tenant must show that the landlord is bringing this eviction action at least in part *because* the tenant won last time. Likewise, unless the court (judge or jury) is convinced that the landlord brought the eviction action at least in part *because* the tenant joined a tenant's union, that the tenant joined a tenant's union will not be a successful defense to the eviction action.

There are additional important limitations to the retaliatory eviction defense:

(a) The defense is unavailable if you are in default in rent, which means that you will have to show, by using one of the rent withholding devices discussed in chapter 6, that any unpaid rent was not due.

(b) The defense cannot be based on a complaint that related to a condition that was caused by you, your family, or a guest.

(c) The defense won't work if the landlord convinces the court that compliance with applicable codes "requires alteration, remodeling or demolition which would effectively deprive the tenant of use of the dwelling unit."[8]

Also, note that the statute stops short of protecting all good faith complaints — a protection only available to mobile and floating home tenants under ORS 90.765. This may mean, for example, that a tenant who complains of a violation of the rental agreement or of a code violation that does not materially affect health and safety is not protected against retaliatory eviction. These limitations are intentional. For example, a month-to-month tenant who is unwilling to consent in writing to a rule change may lawfully be evicted for that reason. The thinking is that the ability of each side to make a new bargain each month is what month-to-month tenancies are all about. But if the same tenant could be evicted for asking for repairs, landlords could avoid most of the act's provisions by threatening eviction.

Finally, there is always the risk that the trial judge will interpret the statute narrowly by ruling that the defense will fail if it turns out that the condition complained of wasn't as serious as the tenant thought it was, and that it did not materially affect health or safety.

Because of the complexities, it is important to have the assistance of an attorney when the defense of retaliation is critical to your case.

2. Equitable defenses

Equity is the branch of law that deals with the power of courts to make orders instead of or in addition to judgments awarding a party money as damages. Perhaps the most common form of "equitable relief" is the injunction, which is an order that a party behave in a certain way. It is through injunctions that an attorney can get an unlawfully evicted tenant back into his or her home or force the landlord to turn on utilities shut off illegally. Under rare circumstances, a landlord may obtain an injunction to solve an immediate problem with a tenant (see chapter 9).

Equity has always been concerned with fairness, and judges hearing a case for equitable relief have a lot of discretion in deciding whether to grant an injunction, for example, on grounds that it would or would not be fair to do so.

Because eviction actions award something other than, or in addition to, damages, courts have long recognized that the principles of fairness and discretion of equity law are available in defense to an eviction action.

Although equitable defenses are rarely used in eviction actions, there are some common situations in which they should work. For example, assume that your landlord intentionally leads you to believe that your month-to-month tenancy will last indefinitely and encourages you to paint the house, clean up the yard, and plant a garden. As soon as you're finished, the landlord serves an eviction notice. If you can persuade the court that the landlord's plan all along was to get free labor from you, you should win the eviction action by asserting these circumstances as an equitable defense.

Of course, if your landlord expressly agrees that you may stay for a certain time in return for your work, you may have an enforceable rental agreement for a term and that will give you a defense to an eviction action commenced in violation of that agreement. If this is your situation, you may not need an equitable defense at all.

Extreme hardship alone has never, to my knowledge, enabled a tenant to win an eviction action. It has however, frequently convinced courts to delay the enforcement of an eviction action for a time to reduce the hardship on the tenant. Short delays are almost routinely granted if requested by a low-income family who needs a few days to move. This kind of relief can be justified by equitable principles.

For historical reasons, issues raised by an equitable defense are usually tried before the rest of the case and without a jury.

3. Discrimination

Regardless of the landlord's theory of eviction, if the tenant can prove that the real motive for the eviction was to discriminate against the tenant for one of the reasons prohibited under state or federal law, the tenant should prevail in the eviction action. Discrimination is discussed in chapter 15.

4. Federal law

If the tenancy somehow involves one of the several federally financed programs that assist landlords in providing rental housing, or that assist tenants in paying for it, federal law may provide the tenant with defenses that would otherwise be unavailable.

Federal law may restrict the reasons for which landlords can evict tenants and may impose some procedural prerequisites on landlords before they can begin eviction actions. Federal housing programs are discussed in chapter 13.

5. Provisions in the rental agreement

The rental agreement between the parties may restrict the landlord's ability to bring an eviction action and may provide the tenant with additional defenses in several ways. If, for example, the terms of the rental agreement require more than 30 days' notice to evict, a 30-day notice won't do. If the terms of a rental agreement provide for automatic renewal, then the landlord will not be able to use the theory that the rental agreement terminated by its own terms in a no-notice eviction. If the terms allow the tenant to behave in a certain way, the landlord will not be able to use that behavior as a ground to evict for cause. If the rent isn't due until the fifteenth, the landlord can't claim that the tenant was late in paying it on the tenth.

6. Waiver or new tenancy

The Landlord and Tenant Act provides in general that a landlord waives the right to terminate a rental agreement for a breach by the tenant if the landlord —

(a) accepts rent knowing about the default by the tenant, or

(b) accepts performance by a tenant that varies from the terms of the rental agreement.[9]

This means that if the eviction action is based on cause, you have a defense if the landlord accepted rent knowing about that cause. For example, if your landlord complains of loud parties but accepts rent from you, he or she cannot evict you because of parties that he or she knew about when the rent was accepted. On the other hand, the landlord can evict you for a cause that existed after the last rent was accepted.

111

Note that evictions without cause generally cannot be defended on grounds that the landlord accepted rent from you after deciding to evict you. It is clear, for example, that the landlord is free to accept rent covering the period of the no-cause notice. You should be able to convince a court, however, that a new rental agreement was created (or the notice nullified) if the landlord accepts rent for a period extending beyond the period of a prior eviction notice. Note, however, that ORS 105.120(3)(d) gives a landlord four days to refund the excess when a tenant pays beyond a termination date specified in a notice.

A landlord who has served a notice to terminate for cause other than nonpayment of rent does not waive the right to evict by accepting rent prorated to the termination date under the notice. A landlord who has *brought an FED* (forcible entry and detainer) based on a notice of termination *for cause* does not waive the right to evict by accepting rent for any period beyond the termination date specified in the notice if the tenant remains in possession and if the landlord notifies the tenant in writing that accepting rent will not waive the right to evict on that notice *and* the rent does not cover a period past the date on which the landlord accepts it. Such a landlord may also serve a notice terminating the tenancy for nonpayment of rent without waiving the right to evict on a previously served notice of termination for cause.

Also, landlords who receive a portion of the rent from public source under a state or federal housing program for low-income tenants does not waive the right to evict for nonpayment of rent by accepting the portion of the rent that comes from that public source.

A landlord has no obligation to accept late rent after the period of a nonpayment of rent eviction notice. A landlord who does accept rent waives the right to evict *for nonpayment of rent*. To make it safe for a landlord to accept partial rent, the legislature provided two important exceptions, which are discussed below in section c.

112

Finally, your landlord can waive any kind of eviction notice by simply telling you that you can stay beyond the termination date specified in the notice. If you both agree that you will stay for awhile, you have probably created a new tenancy, most likely on a month-to-month basis, unless you agree otherwise.[10] Once your landlord waives an eviction notice or enters into a new rental agreement, he or she cannot rely on the old notice to evict you.

7. Prepaid rent period

The eviction statutes provide the following:

> The service of a notice to quit upon a tenant...does not authorize an action to be maintained against him for the possession of premises before the expiration of any period for which the tenant...has paid the rent of the premises in advance...[11]

There are important exceptions. A landlord does not have to wait until any prepaid rent period expires when —

(a) the only unused rent was a last month's rent deposit;

(b) the eviction is based on a 24-hour notice for personal injury, property damage, outrageous conduct, or illegal subtenancy;

(c) the eviction is based on the pet violation provision; or

(d) the only unused rent was paid for a rental period extending beyond a termination date specified in the eviction notice, but the landlord refunded the unused rent within four days.

8. Defective notice

The requirements for each kind of eviction notice are discussed below, but all eviction notices must satisfy some general requirements:

113

(a) The premises must be described (an address is sufficient).

(b) The termination date must be indicated (e.g., 24 hours from your receipt of the notice).

(c) The notice must be signed by the landlord or an authorized agent.

(d) The notice must be in writing.

(e) If the notice is served by mail alone, the notice must state that the time for compliance or termination is extended by three days (see ORS 90.910(2)).

If the notice does not meet these requirements, or if it is equivocal (e.g., "Get out or pay twice your normal rent"), you may have a defense to the eviction for this reason alone. Of course, the notice must meet the specific requirements peculiar to each kind of eviction action. If no notice is required, this defense won't help.

9. Defective service of notice

If the eviction in question requires some kind of notice, that notice must be served on the tenant in some fashion. In general, all notices under the act (including notices from the tenant to the landlord) may be served in person or by first class mail. Certified mail has been deliberately excluded because it so often was left unclaimed. If the notice is important enough, pay the post office for a proof of mailing, or use both first class and certified mail.[12]

If a notice is mailed, the time for compliance or termination of the tenancy is increased by three days, and the notice must say so, but there are some special rules for nonpayment of rent notices and most 24-hour notices (see section c., below).

For most purposes, time is counted by excluding the first day and including the last. For example, to count the ten days of a ten-day notice served on a Monday, Tuesday would be the first day, and the tenth day would be a Thursday. The tenant has until midnight of the last day to comply.

Incidentally, when a party in a court case has a period in which to file something with the court, the process changes a bit: although weekends or holidays count, if the last day falls on a weekend or holiday, the party has until the next "judicial day" in which to comply. Also, the deadline is the time the clerk's office closes, not midnight.

c. TYPES OF EVICTIONS AND DEFENSES TO EACH

1. Evictions without notice

A landlord may start an eviction action without first serving a notice in only two situations:

(a) When a tenancy has expired by its own terms and has not been renewed[13]

(b) When a tenant unlawfully refuses to permit the land-lord access to the premises[14]

A typical example of the first situation is when a rental agreement for a term comes to an end, such as at the end of a one-year agreement, and does not provide for automatic renewal. Month-to-month and week-to-week tenancies do not fit this situation.

There is considerable room for doubt as to whether a landlord may bring an eviction action without notice in the second situation, so it is safest to treat a tenant's refusal to permit access after 24 hours' notice (or in an emergency) as the basis for an eviction for cause.[15] See chapter 2 for the rules regarding access to the premises.

(a) Variations on the general defenses

A landlord's refusal to renew a lease can be retaliatory; if so, the tenant can use the retaliation defense discussed earlier. Under the requirements of some, but not all, federal housing programs, a landlord cannot refuse to renew a lease without good cause. The provisions of a rental agreement may require notice even though the statute does not. The rental agreement may also provide for automatic renewal. Accepting rent for a period after the end of a term probably amounts to the creation of a new tenancy and a waiver of the right to evict on the grounds that the "old" lease or tenancy expired.

(b) Specific defenses

In addition to the general defenses, a no-notice eviction may be defended on the grounds that the tenancy was not the kind that expired by its own terms. If the landlord uses a tenant's refusal to allow him or her access to the premises to support a no-notice eviction, the tenant can defend by showing that access was not unlawfully refused either because the landlord did not give 24 hours' notice or because he or she abused the right of access.[16]

2. No-cause evictions

The remarkable thing about this power of termination is that a landlord doesn't have to give, or even have, a reason to ask you to leave. Tenants in many other countries, and in a handful of other states, have "security of possession," which requires that the landlord at least have some good reason for terminating the tenancy. In Oregon, tenants do not yet have this unless they live in federal housing (see chapter 13) or in a mobile home (see chapter 14).

(a) How to terminate

A landlord may terminate a week-to-week tenancy by serving a written notice at least 10 days before the termination date specified in the notice. A landlord may terminate a month-to-month tenancy by serving a written notice at least 30 days prior to the termination date specified in the notice.[17]

A typical no-cause eviction notice looks something like the one shown in Sample #20.

March 1, 199-

M. Petard
123 Green Street
Portland, Oregon

Dear Ms. Petard:

   I hereby give you notice that your tenancy at
123 Green Street, Portland, Oregon, will terminate
on April 1, 199-.

Sincerely,

J. Fullbird

J. Fullbird
Landlord

The notice can terminate the tenancy on any date at least 30 days after its receipt in the case of a month-to-month tenancy, although in a week-to-week tenancy the termination date apparently must coincide with the end of a rent period.[18]

(b) Variations on the general defenses

Although most landlords may terminate for almost any reason, or even for no reason at all, there are exceptions. If the real reason for the eviction is retaliatory, the tenant may have a defense. If the landlord's motive is unlawfully discriminatory, the tenant should also have a defense. Federal housing tenants generally cannot be evicted without cause (see chapter 13).

The 1989 legislature modified the prepaid rent period defense to protect periodic tenants who pay their landlord several months' rent in advance, only to learn in a few weeks that a new owner is now the landlord and knows nothing of the months paid in advance. An FED (forcible entry and detainer) cannot be brought before the prepaid rent is used up (subject to the exceptions discussed above for the defense in general).

Also, your rental agreement may give you a defense by requiring a longer period of notice than does the act. If so, the landlord must comply with the agreement.[19]

(c) Specific defenses

The major defense specific to a no-cause eviction is that the terms of the rental agreement do not permit termination without cause. A tenancy for a specific term usually cannot be terminated without cause, and it is entirely permissible for the parties to any kind of rental agreement to agree to limit the circumstances under which the landlord may evict the tenant. Mobile home tenancies may not be terminated without cause (see chapter 14).

3. Evictions for cause

ORS 90.400(1)(a) permits a landlord to terminate a rental agreement if there is a material noncompliance with the rental agreement or a noncompliance with ORS 90.325 materially affecting health and safety. ORS 90.325, of course, is the section spelling out the tenant's obligations to use the premises reasonably.

A "material" noncompliance is one that is important to the landlord, rather than just a technical, minor, or unimportant noncompliance. Similarly, a violation of section 90.325 materially affects health and safety only if it does so substantially; a minimal or merely technical violation will not suffice. Even a major violation of this section that does not threaten health or safety cannot be used as a ground for this kind of eviction if it does not also constitute a violation of the rental agreement. If it is really serious, however, it may permit the landlord to use the "personal injury/property damage/outrageous conduct" eviction discussed later in this chapter.

The termination for cause eviction is rarely used by landlords who have the right to terminate without cause because

118

the no-cause approach is much simpler and is subject to fewer defenses. However, if the rental agreement is for a term that has not yet expired, the only ways in which a landlord can terminate are for some form of cause, although the time periods vary from 24 hours' notice for illegal sub-tenants, personal injury, property damage, or outrageous conduct, to 10 days' notice for a pet violation, to 30 days' notice under this general for-cause eviction option. The same is true of any rental agreement that provides that it cannot be terminated without cause.

(a) How to terminate

To terminate for cause, the landlord must deliver a notice to the tenant specifying the acts or omissions that the landlord claims as cause to evict, and stating that the tenancy will terminate on a specified date at least 30 days after the tenant receives the notice. If the problems can be remedied "by repairs or the payment of damages or otherwise," the notice must state that the tenant can avoid termination by remedying the problem within 14 days.[20] If the tenant actually remedies the breach by paying damages or making repairs, or if the tenant offers money damages or repairs as a remedy, then the agreement shall not be terminated, even if the landlord refuses the offer. Otherwise, the tenancy terminates as provided in the notice.

The notice does not have to give the tenant an opportunity to take care of the breach if it is not "remedial by repairs or the payment of damages or otherwise," although anything but extensive damages to the premises should be considered capable of being remedied. Sample #21 shows an eviction notice for a cause.

If a landlord gives such a notice and the tenant takes care of the problem or stops committing the violation but does the same thing again within six months, the landlord may terminate by giving ten days' written notice specifying the breach and the termination date.[21]

119

SAMPLE #21
NOTICE OF EVICTION FOR CAUSE

```
                                    March 1, 199-

M. Petard
#107-123 Green Street
Portland, Oregon

Dear Ms. Petard:

    You have breached clause 22a of your rental
agreement by removing a portion of the hedge that
separates your yard from the yard of the tenant
in unit #108. This constitutes a material breach
of your rental agreement. For that reason, your
tenancy will terminate as of April 1, 199-.
However, you can avoid this termination by restor-
ing the hedge to the condition it was in immedi-
ately before you altered it, and by doing so no
later than March 15, 199-.

                                    Sincerely,

                                    J. Fullbird

                                    J. Fullbird
                                    Landlord
```

In mobile home situations, the notice period, the opportunity to remedy any breach, and termination after a repeated violation may vary (see chapter 14).

(b) Variations on the general defenses

A tenant who can convince a court that the cause stated in the notice was merely a pretext for a retaliatory or unlawfully discriminatory eviction may defeat the landlord's claim for possession. Equitable principles disfavor a "forfeiture" (a major loss in the nature of a penalty); they also disfavor allowing one party to get a windfall. These principles may help a tenant show that any noncompliance wasn't serious enough to warrant eviction.

A defense based on the insufficiency of the eviction notice is particularly likely to work in this case because eviction notices for cause tend to be complicated, and there are greater opportunities for error than in the other kinds of notice.

Remember that a landlord who has brought an FED (forcible entry and detainer) based on an eviction notice for cause does not waive the right to evict on that notice by accepting rent under some circumstances or by serving a new termination notice based on nonpayment of rent. See the general discussion of the waiver defense above.

(c) Specific defenses

The defenses specifically applicable to evictions for cause naturally deal with the existence and severity of the alleged breaches. If you are a tenant, you may argue that an alleged breach did not occur, or if it did take place, that it was immaterial. You may show that the trouble was taken care of or that a remedy or damages were offered but refused by the landlord. Finally, you may show that the term or rule that was violated was an unenforceable provision. Provisions in rental agreements are unenforceable if —

(a) they are "unconscionable" (i.e., so one-sided, harsh, or "shocking" that no one would agree to such terms unless he or she were desperate),[22]

(b) their purpose is to waive tenants' rights under the act,[23]

(c) they authorize anyone to agree to permit the landlord to get a judgment against the tenant without giving the tenant an opportunity to assert a defense in court,[24]

(d) they are designed to protect the landlord from the landlord's willful misconduct or negligence.[25]

A rule is unenforceable if any of the following situations apply:

(a) The tenant didn't know about it.

(b) The rule is not reasonably related to its purpose.

121

(c) The purpose of the rule is not to promote the convenience, safety, or welfare of tenants, to protect the landlord's property, or to fairly distribute facilities among tenants.

(d) The rule does not apply to all tenants in a fair manner.

(e) The rule is not clear and understandable.

(f) It was adopted after the beginning of the rental agreement, it substantially modified the tenant's rights, and the tenant did not consent to the rule in writing.[26]

Mobile home tenants have added protection: violation of a rule cannot be grounds for eviction unless a written rental agreement specifies that the rule is one which, if violated, may be grounds for eviction (see chapter 14).

4. Evictions for pet violations

ORS 90.405 permits a landlord to terminate on at least ten day's written notice if the tenant has a pet "capable of causing damage to persons or property" in violation of the rental agreement and the tenant fails to remove the pet from the premises within the period of the notice. If the tenant commits a second similar violation within six months of the first notice, the landlord may terminate on ten days' notice without giving the tenant an opportunity to remove the pet.

(a) How to terminate

The written termination notice must specify the violation and state that the tenancy will end on a date not less than ten days after receipt of notice unless the tenant removes the pet prior to the date specified. Sample #22 is an example.

(b) Variations on the general defenses

As with evictions for cause, a tenant who can show that the pet violation was only a pretext for a retaliatory eviction should win. For example, if nearly all of the landlord's other tenants have similar pets, and your pet has neither done any damage nor frightened anyone, the court might accept a

SAMPLE #22
NOTICE OF TERMINATION FOR PET VIOLATION

March 1, 199-

M. Petard
123 Green Street
Portland, Oregon

Dear Ms. Petard:

   Although your rental agreement specified that
you may not keep a dog on the premises, you are
now keeping a dog in your apartment. Your tenancy
will terminate on March 13, 199- unless you remove
the dog from the premises before that date.

Sincerely,

J. Fullbird

J. Fullbird
Landlord

---

retaliation defense if you are the only tenant being evicted and you are also the only tenant who called in an inspector.

Equitable principles or the waiver defense might help a tenant whose landlord knew of the pet when the tenancy began and indicated there would be no problem with the "no pet" clause as long as the pet caused no problems. The prepaid rent period defense is not available.

State law expressly prohibits discrimination against persons with seeing-eye or hearing-ear dogs or other "assistance animals."[27]

(c) Specific defenses

A tenant can defend this kind of eviction by convincing the court that the pet was not capable of causing damage to persons or property, that there was no pet, or that the pet was removed within the time allowed (unless this is the second pet violation notice within six months.) I would expect any argument that a dog or cat wasn't capable of causing damage to fail; this clause was added to avoid deciding whether tropical fish or goldfish were "capable of causing damage."

As with evictions for cause, if the landlord is relying on a rule rather than the language of the rental agreement, the tenant can defend by showing that the rule is unenforceable. If adopted after the tenant entered into the rental agreement, a no-pet clause probably requires the tenant's written consent to be enforceable.

This type of eviction does not apply to mobile home or floating home tenants.

5. Evictions for nonpayment of rent

(a) How to terminate

If a tenant is at least seven days late in paying the rent, the landlord may serve a notice stating that he or she will terminate the rental agreement if the rent is not paid within 72 hours of the notice.[28] Although the law is not clear on this, it is probably best to state the precise amount of rent due and that the rental agreement will terminate unless the rent is paid. Sample #23 is an example.

The contrary argument is that the notice will be found void if the net rent (after deducting any damages due to the tenant under the act or the rental agreement) found due is less than that stated in the notice; I still think it's safest from the landlord's point of view to state the amount of rent that is unpaid. It is clear to me that a notice that fails to inform the tenant of the opportunity to cure the default is fatally defective.

As I mentioned in discussing eviction defenses in general, the 1985 legislature clarified rules for service of notices under the act and made special provisions for service of a nonpayment of rent notice. A rental agreement may provide that a nonpayment of rent notice is deemed served (as if it were personally delivered) on the day on which it is both mailed

124

March 8, 199-

M. Petard
123 Green Street
Portland, Oregon

Dear Ms. Petard:

Your rent for 123 Green Street, Portland, in the amount of $165, was due on March 1, 199-, but has not yet been paid. Unless you pay your rent within 72 hours of receiving this notice, I will terminate your rental agreement and start an eviction action.

Sincerely,

J. Fullbird

J. Fullbird
Landlord

by first class mail and attached in a secure manner to the tenant's front door.

In any event, the notice may not be served until rent has been unpaid for seven days, including the first day rent is due. This means that a 72-hour notice may be first served on the eighth if rent is payable on the first of the month.

A tenant may mail the rent within the period of a 72-hour nonpayment of rent notice, unless all of the following are true:

(a) the notice is personally served;

(b) a written rental agreement and the notice specify a place for payment;

(c) the specified place is either on the premises or, unless the tenant has become unable to make rent payments in person since the last rent payment ("unable"

125

doesn't mean the tenant is broke, it means the tenant can't get there), at a place where the tenant has made all previous rent payments in person; *and*

(d) the specified place is available to the tenant throughout the period of the notice (this means 24 hours a day — such as a manager's mail slot).[29]

(b) Variations on the general defenses

Although the retaliation defense is unavailable to a tenant who is in default in rent,[30] if the tenant can show that the unpaid rent is not due because he or she is exercising one or more of the rent-withholding remedies discussed in chapter 6 (including recoupment), then the tenant is still entitled to use the retaliation defense because there is no default. Note, however, that there is at this point no need to use retaliation as a defense because by demonstrating that there was no default a tenant should win any eviction action based on nonpayment of rent. Retaliation would then be relevant only if the tenant counterclaimed for damages or a declaration as to what amount of rent is lawfully due.

Some landlords make the mistake of serving the notice on the seventh day of default. Because the tenant must first fail "to pay rent within seven days," a notice served before the eighth day is premature and should not support an eviction judgment.

Tenants are often required to pay the "last month's rent" in advance. Although the prepaid rent period defense expressly does not apply when the only unpaid rent is a last month's rent deposit, there *may* be an argument that the rent is not due because of the last month's rent deposit. This is tricky. The landlord need not wait for the expiration of the "last month" before *bringing* an eviction action — but that does not mean that the landlord *has a right to evict*. If you have responded to a 72-hour notice for nonpayment of rent by writing the landlord and saying "this is my last month — use the last month's rent," the rent is arguably not past due, so the landlord arguably should have no right to evict *for non-payment*. Individual cases will probably turn on the language of the rental agreement and the communications between the parties.

The general waiver defense also applies to nonpayment of rent cases. Although a landlord has no obligation to accept rent after the 24-hour period of an eviction notice based on nonpayment of rent, acceptance of the rent after that period constitutes a waiver of the landlord's right to evict.

As mentioned earlier, there are two important exceptions to the waiver defense in nonpayment of rent cases:

(a) A landlord who accepts partial rent before serving a nonpayment of rent eviction notice and based on the tenant's promise to pay the balance by "a time certain" does not waive the right to evict if the tenant fails to pay as agreed. The landlord can serve a non-payment notice and proceed to eviction court if necessary. The notice cannot be served sooner than it could have been served had no rent been paid, and the tenant must have 72 hours from the notice or until the "time certain" (whichever is later) to cure the default (avoid eviction on the notice). This permits a cautious landlord to accept partial rent and serve a 72-hour notice that will expire when the balance is due.[31]

(b) A landlord who accepts partial rent after serving a 72-hour notice for nonpayment of rent can avoid the waiver if the parties sign a written agreement to that effect. The agreement may provide that the landlord may proceed to evict without serving a new notice if the tenant fails to pay by a "time certain."[32] Also, remember that accepting rent from a public source under a federal or state low-income housing program cannot be the basis of a waiver defense.

(c) Specific defenses

The most important defenses to an eviction for not paying rent are those that show the rent was not due. If you, as a tenant, can show that no rent was due because of the dependent covenant defense, because of a successful recoupment or counterclaim, or because of any other device discussed in chapter 6, you should win any eviction action based on nonpayment of rent. You may also win even if your defense merely establishes that the 24-hour notice to pay overstated the amount actually "due" (as opposed to correctly stating the amount merely "unpaid"), although the law on this is not yet clear.

The "dependent covenant" defense, in particular, should establish that you owe no rent for any period during which your landlord deliberately and substantially violates the habitability requirements of the act (assuming, of course, that you did not cause the violation).[33] You might use a recoupment or counterclaim based on habitability violations or other breaches of the act or rental agreement to show that any amount claimed as rent for the last month or so of the tenancy is more than offset by damages that your landlord owes you for those violations. A landlord's violations that last as long as one year before the eviction action may be used this way, although older claims for damages may be barred by the statute of limitations.

Habitability violations that support this kind of defense are listed in chapter 2 and discussed in chapter 6. Other violations are the same as those that support a counterclaim and are listed in section **d.** of the chapter.

Note that asserting a counterclaim and paying rent into court entitles you to a second chance to avoid eviction by paying the landlord any balance of rent found due at trial (see chapter 6).

You should also win if you convince the judge or jury that you paid the rent or offered it to the landlord unconditionally within the time allowed by the notice and under the rules discussed above.

Finally, if your landlord raises the rent and tries to evict you for not paying the increase, you should win by showing that the attempt to raise the rent was invalid.

There are at least three situations in which a rent increase is ineffective:

(a) When the rental agreement does not permit a rent increase

(b) When the landlord fails to give 30 days' written notice of the increase[34] (or, for mobile or floating home tenants, the landlord fails to follow the 90-day notice and "discussion" requirements of the statute[35])

(c) When the increase in rent is motivated by a desire to retaliate against the tenant[36]

Generally speaking, a rental agreement for a term such as six months or a year does not allow a landlord to raise the rent during the term unless it expressly provides otherwise. On the other hand, a month-to-month or week-to-week rental can be increased with 30 days' notice unless the rental agreement expressly provides otherwise. As noted in the general discussion of the retaliatory eviction defense, a retaliatory rent increase is invalid in any kind of tenancy assuming that the situation is covered by section 90.385.

6. Evictions for personal injury/property damage/outrageous conduct

ORS 90.400(3)(a), (b), and (d) identify the circumstances that permit a landlord to bring an eviction action after only 24 hours' written notice. The landlord may serve such a notice if the tenant or someone in the tenant's control or the tenant's pet —

(a) seriously threatens immediately to inflict personal injury on the landlord or other tenants,

(b) intentionally inflicts any substantial damage to the premises, or...

(c) commits any act that is outrageous in the extreme.

The first category also applies to the behavior of a tenant's pet. The last category covers one example landlords have given me that does not fit in either of the first two categories: two drunk tenants defecated off the balcony of a singles' apartment.

In response to rising concerns with "drug houses," the 1989 legislature enacted statutes permitting local governments to threaten property owners with loss of their rented property (or its use) if they knowingly allow tenants to use it for drug manufacturing or dealing (or prostitution or gambling).[37] The statutes contain protections to ensure that a reasonably alert owner or manager will act in good faith when public officials notify them of such problems. The primary "drug house" law requires that the landlord be served a written notice if the locality intends to insist that the landlord stop illegal activity in a rental unit.

The legislature also amended the "outrageous conduct" eviction statute (ORS 90.400(3)(d)) to specify that "outrageous conduct" includes an act that the tenant, or a person in the tenant's control, has committed and that has resulted in written notice to the landlord under a state or local law, of drug manufacturing or delivery, gambling, or prostitution activity, or has resulted in a judgment against the property under ORS chapter 465 because of such activities. The qualifications that the tenant or person in the tenant's control must have "in fact committed" the conduct, and that the landlord must have received a written notice of the activity, are designed to protect the tenant whose suspicious neighbor mistook a Tupperware party for drug activity, or whose landlord was the source of anonymous and unfounded complaints to police that will trigger such a written notice.

From the perspective of the landlord, and from that of other tenants and residents burdened by a tenant's illegal activities, remember that the standard of proof in an eviction action is quite different from that in a criminal trial. A landlord need not prove drug activity beyond a reasonable doubt ("to a moral certainty"); all that is required is that the judge or jury deciding the facts be persuaded that it is more likely than not that the allegations are true. Therefore, it should be much easier to deal with drug activity as a basis for eviction than as a basis for a criminal conviction, and this is a factor that partially explains the current popularity of compelling landlords to evict drug dealers.

Also note that a landlord who acts in good faith to bring an eviction based on this kind of activity need not worry about libel or slander. As long as the accusations are made solely in the legal papers filed by the landlord (including the eviction notice) and in the actual court proceedings, a "privilege" applies which offers strong protection against civil liability even if the landlord is incorrect.

(a) How to terminate

The notice must specify the causes for the eviction and state that the tenancy will terminate in 24 hours. Sample #24 is an example.

(b) Emergencies, the police, and temporary restraining orders

If a landlord is facing the kind of extreme problem that this kind of eviction notice was designed to address, waiting for the 24-hour notice, service of the eviction summons and complaint, first appearance, and (if the tenant fights eviction) the trial may seem far too long a time, even though the eviction process is extremely fast when compared to almost any other judicial proceeding.

Chapter 9 deals with other options. I suggest that landlords with this kind of problem read this section and sections **e.** and **f.** of this chapter first, as they provide some familiarity with the

March 1, 199-

M. Petard
123 Green Street
Portland, Oregon

Dear Ms. Petard:

Last night you intentionally inflicted substantial damage to your apartment by knocking down a wall with a sledge hammer. Accordingly, your rental agreement will terminate 24 hours from your receipt of this notice. If you are not out of possession by then, I will commence an eviction action to recover possession.

Sincerely,

J. Fullbird

J. Fullbird
Landlord

judicial process, and because landlords will probably want to serve a 24-hour notice in addition to any other options.

(c) Variations on the general defenses

Because this type of eviction was designed to cover serious problems, a landlord's abuse of the provision by using it for a trivial incident may help a tenant convince a court that the real motive was to retaliate against the tenant. The law of equity favors a strict reading of "substantial" for the same reason that it favors a narrow reading of "materially" in cases of eviction for cause.

Federal housing tenants are probably not subject to this type of eviction action unless their lease so provides either directly or by permitting eviction for any cause allowed under state law.

(d) Specific defenses

A tenant should win an eviction action under this provision if he or she can convince the court that a threat was not serious or that the tenant did not threaten immediate personal injury, that any injury or damage inflicted was not "substantial," or that any conduct specified in the notice was not "outrageous in the extreme." The "in the tenant's control" qualification is intended to recognize that a tenant should not be evicted on 24 hours' notice for conduct of others beyond the tenant's control. Note, however, that there is a case that says that this qualification does not prevent eviction because of the conduct of a *co-tenant* even if the defending tenant had no power to control that conduct (e.g., a mother evicted because of the conduct of her teenage son).

If the eviction is based on alleged drug, gambling, or prostitution activity, the implication of the requirement that the landlord receive a written notice under a state or local nuisance abatement or "drug house" law implies that the eviction cannot be used without such a notice. If the activity is otherwise "outrageous in the extreme" (e.g., acts of prostitution visible to the public), a notice would probably not be required. When a notice is required, it may well be that what the landlord has received is not a notice "under" such a law, but a notice earlier in the process than the formal notice required by the statute. For example, the Portland Police Bureau has notices they send to property owners that are generally precursors to the formal notice required under Portland's "drug house" ordinance. In any event, mere receipt of a notice does not entitle a landlord to evict; the court must be persuaded that the tenant or person in the tenant's control was actually guilty of the allegations and, if not the tenant, that the actor was under the tenant's control.

7. Evictions of illegal subtenants

If a person occupies premises by consent of a former tenant who vacated and sublet or assigned the premises to the new tenant in violation of a clause of a written rental agreement with the landlord, the new tenant can be evicted on a 24-hour notice where —

(a) the real tenant has vacated the premises,

(b) the occupant is in possession in violation of a written rental agreement that prohibits subleasing the premises to another or allowing another person to occupy the premises without the written permission of the landlord, and

(c) the landlord has not knowingly accepted rent from the new occupant.[38]

(a) How to terminate

As usual, the process must begin with a written notice, in this case one for 24 hours. The notice must specify the cause (see Sample #25).

Note the last sentence in Sample #25, which is, of course, optional. It represents the trade-off between landlords and tenants available under the act. Landlords sometimes want a way to get such occupants to sign a written rental agreement and to screen the occasional undesirable tenant, while tenants have an interest in making sure that landlords cannot treat new occupants in these cases as trespassers. After all, the new occupant may have been told that there was no clause prohibiting assignments and that the landlord always allowed tenants to pass possession of the unit in this manner. In any event, the new occupant may be perfectly acceptable as a tenant as long as the landlord has an opportunity to perform whatever screening is appropriate. On the other hand, it is important to the landlord that any invitation to apply to rent not be readable as an equivocation about the intent to evict; equivocal notices may be ineffective.

(b) Variations on the general defenses

The difficult part about this kind of eviction action is that it presumes that the person occupying does not meet the definition

March 1, 199-

J. Lately
123 Green Street
Portland, Oregon

Dear Mr. Lately:

My tenant of the premises of 123 Green Street signed a lease that expressly prohibits subletting, assigning, or allowing another to occupy without my written permission. I understand that the tenant moved out and purported to sublet the premises to you. At no time, however, did anyone ask my permission. It is my practice to screen tenants before renting to them, and I have not accepted you as a tenant.

As is my right under the law, I hereby give you notice that if you are not out of possession within 24 hours from your receipt of this notice, I will commence an eviction action to recover possession.

Feel free to apply to rent the premises at once, but until and unless I accept your application, I do not consent in any manner to your continued occupancy, and it is my intention to proceed with an eviction action if you do not vacate within 24 hours.

Sincerely,

J. Fullbird

J. Fullbird
Landlord

of a tenant: someone "*entitled* under a rental agreement to occupy a dwelling unit to the exclusion of others."[39] The retaliation provision generally protects tenants, so a defense based on retaliation might fail unless the tenant could prove a right to occupy under the rental agreement, in which case the eviction would be defeated anyway.

On the other hand, rights and remedies under the act extend to third persons under appropriate circumstances, and a court might well agree that retaliation is a defense if the judge or jury found that the only reason the landlord brought the eviction was that the "illegal" subtenant asked for repairs, for example, when the landlord has a history of accepting "illegal subtenants" as new tenants as long as they don't ask for repairs. The prepaid rent notice defense does not apply to evictions under ORS 90.400(3), and this is one of those evictions.

The other general defenses could work in appropriate circumstances. For example, the terms of the rental agreement may fail to prohibit subletting (in the absence of such a prohibition, the tenant is free to sublet); the notice may fail to specify the reason for the eviction; the notice may be improperly served. Note that the waiver/new tenancy defense is partially built into the requirements for this kind of eviction. It is unavailable if the landlord has knowingly accepted rent from the new occupant, which would create a new tenancy.

(c) Specific defenses

As usual, specific defenses include disputing the existence of the requirements for this kind of eviction, that is, that the agreement was in writing, that it prohibited this occupancy, that the landlord did not consent in writing, and that the landlord hasn't knowingly accepted rent from the new occupant. Disproving these contentions should defeat eviction. Likewise, and perhaps most easily overlooked, if the original tenant is still in possession, this eviction cannot be used. If the landlord wants the new occupant out and the tenant refuses to comply, the remedy is to evict both, assuming that the landlord can properly do so under any of the other eviction devices.

136

Note, however, that if the occupant claims as a defense that the tenant is still in possession, the tenant has the burden of proof on this issue in the eviction action.[40] This is because the new occupant is obviously in a better position to prove the presence of the tenant than the landlord is in to prove the absence of the tenant.

8. Evictions of resident managers

Under *some* circumstances, a person who manages property for a landlord and receives reduced or free rent in return is excluded from the Landlord and Tenant Act. This is true *only* where that person is an employee of the landlord and his or her right to occupancy is conditional upon employment in and about the premises. A resident manager who answers an ad for such a job, signs an employment contract with a written provision that the manager's right to occupy the dwelling unit is conditional upon the employment and terminates with the employment, and who moves into a unit specialized for a manager is clearly likely to be excluded by this provision. On the other hand, an existing tenant who accepts a rent reduction in return for assuming managerial duties without any express discussion of the impact on their right to occupy is quite clearly *not* excluded from the act.

To evict a resident manager who *is* excluded from the act, a landlord must use the eviction process (if the manager does not vacate voluntarily). The eviction may be brought after 24 hours following written notice of the termination of employment or as set forth in a written employment contract, whichever is longer.[41]

(a) How to terminate

Again, this type of eviction is only available if the person is excluded from the act by the nature of his or her right to occupy the unit. For this reason, and because the length of the notice of termination depends on the employment contract, it is difficult to give an example. Sample #26 assumes that

137

there is a written employment contract that provides for written termination of the employment relationship on 24 hours' written notice in the employer's sole discretion and that expressly renders the employee's right to occupy the unit conditional on employment in and about the premises.

SAMPLE #26
NOTICE TERMINATING EMPLOYMENT AND TO VACATE MANAGER'S UNIT

March 1, 199-

George Toiler
123 Green Street
Portland, Oregon

Dear Mr. Toiler:

For reasons of which I am sure you are aware from our repeated discussions, I hereby exercise my right under your employment contract to terminate your employment as manager of the premises at 123 Green Street, effective 24 hours following your receipt of this notice. As also provided in the contract, this will also serve as a demand that you vacate the manager's apartment at the premises within the same 24 hours. If you fail to do so, I will commence an eviction proceeding to have you removed.

Sincerely,

J. Fullbird

J. Fullbird
Landlord

(b) Variations on the general defenses

If this eviction action is appropriate, the manager is not a tenant under the act and cannot use the retaliation defense as a tenant might under appropriate circumstances. On the other hand, the slowly developing law of wrongful discharge from employment might recognize a defense based on public policy where, for example, the manager was fired because the manager called life-threatening fire hazards to the attention of the fire marshal after the landlord made it clear nothing would be done otherwise. The most likely relevant anti-discrimination law is employment rather than housing related, although a manager should win by showing that the firing was based on a desire not to allow persons of the manager's ethnic background, for example, to occupy the premises. Note that housing anti-discrimination laws are not avoided just because the tenant is excluded from the Landlord and Tenant Act.

Notice defenses are likely to be determined by employment law rather than landlord tenant law, particularly because the wording of the relevant statute speaks of notice of "termination of employment" rather than of a "tenancy" or "right to occupy." In general, I would expect this kind of issue to depend entirely on the terms of the employment contract, except that the notice must be written to support this kind of eviction.

If the landlord accepts rent for a period after termination of the employment, a court would probably find that the acceptance of rent started a new tenancy between the parties.

(c) Specific defenses

The most likely defense is that the tenant is not properly excluded from the act by the terms of any employment contract or by the circumstances of the arrangement with the landlord. Usually, this will reduce itself to a debate over whether the parties understood when entering the arrangement that the right to occupy was conditioned on employment in and about the premises or was merely payment for managerial work *without* being reduced in value by such a condition.

d. WILL COUNTERCLAIMS DEFEAT EVICTIONS?

As discussed in section **f.** of chapter 6, a counterclaim is a device whereby a defendant asks that the court award him or her relief instead of or in addition to the relief sought by the plaintiff. A landlord contemplating an eviction action (or an action for back rent) should give some thought to whether the tenant can and will counterclaim. A tenant facing an eviction action should decide whether a counterclaim is available or advisable. (Should a landlord bring an action for rent or damages after the tenant has moved out, it is almost always advisable for the tenant to assert any available counterclaim in that action.)

This section explains when counterclaims are available, how they affect a landlord's right to recover possession of the premises, and how a tenant should decide whether to assert a counterclaim in an eviction action.

1. When can a tenant counterclaim?

A tenant can counterclaim in any kind of eviction action, as well as in an action for back rent or damages.[42] You can use a counterclaim in an eviction action to seek an order requiring the landlord to make repairs just as if you had filed a separate lawsuit. You can also use a counterclaim (or separate lawsuit) to recover damages. Generally, you can seek damages if you have suffered harm as a result of your landlord's violations of the rental agreement or of the Landlord and Tenant Act.

A few provisions of the act, however, are apparently intended only to have a limited effect and would not support an award of damages. An example is the section making improperly adopted rules unenforceable.[43] On the other hand, several provisions carry "statutory damages" so that a tenant may recover a monetary award even if the tenant cannot prove that the violation of the provision caused harm. Statutory damages

140

are designed to ensure some recovery even when harm may be difficult to prove in order to deter future violations.

In addition to violations of the act or of the rental agreement, a violation of the Unlawful Trade Practices Act or Unlawful Debt Collection Practices Act may support a counterclaim (see chapter 15), but counterclaims other than these are not allowed in an eviction action.

Here is a list that includes most of the bases for counterclaims by a tenant in an eviction action. Statutory damage provisions are shown in parentheses.

(a) The landlord has been guilty of bad faith.[44]

(b) The landlord has deliberately attempted to enforce a rental agreement term that the landlord knows is prohibited by the act. (The tenant is entitled to actual damages plus up to three months' rent.)[45]

(c) The landlord has violated any provision of the rental agreement.[46]

(d) The landlord has violated the habitability section or almost any other provision of the act.[47]

(e) The landlord has knowingly failed to disclose in writing that the tenant is paying a utility provided for services that benefit another tenant or the landlord. (The tenant is entitled to the greater of twice the actual damages or one month's rent.)[48]

(f) The landlord has deliberately or with gross negligence failed to provide an essential service. (Damages are limited to reduction in rental value.)[49]

(g) The landlord has locked the tenant out or shut off utilities to try to get the tenant to leave. (The tenant is entitled to up to twice the actual damages or twice the monthly rent, whichever is greater.)[50]

(h) The landlord has abused the right of access. (The tenant is entitled to at least one month's rent.)[51]

(i) The landlord has retaliated against the tenant by increasing rent, decreasing services, threatening to bring an eviction action, or bringing an eviction action. (The tenant is entitled to up to twice the actual damages or twice the monthly rent, whichever is greater.)[52]

(j) The landlord has wrongfully seized and retained a tenant's belongings. (The tenant is relieved of any obligations for unpaid rent and is entitled to recover up to twice any actual damages.)[53]

(k) The landlord has violated the Unlawful Trade Practices Act with conduct that is not covered by the Landlord and Tenant Act. (The tenant is entitled to at least $200.)[54]

(l) The landlord has violated the Unlawful Debt Collection Practices Act. (The tenant is entitled to at least $200.)[55]

Note that a counterclaim is not available for every violation. The tenant must be able to show that the violation caused some kind of harm, unless the section in question has a statutory damage provision permitting a recovery without proof of harm. Of course, most violations of the act necessarily involve a loss in the rental value of the premises, and this kind of harm is enough to support a counterclaim.

In addition to statutory damages and damages for any reduction in rental value of the premises, a tenant may recover damages through a counterclaim for personal injuries, lost or damaged personal belongings, and any financial loss or expense caused by any of these violations.

Although emotional distress damages are not available for "nonculpable" habitability violations, the Supreme Court of Oregon has held that a tenant may recover damages for emotional distress caused by deliberate violation of the lockout, utility shutoff, and retaliation provisions. It remains to be seen whether emotional distress damages can be recovered for deliberate habitability violations.

If the tenant wins on the counterclaim the court can make the landlord pay for the tenant's attorney's fees in an amount set by the court. With the exception of unlawful trade practices counterclaims, the court can award attorney's fee against the tenant if the landlord wins.[56]

2. When can a counterclaim allow a tenant to stay?

Whether or not a counterclaim can defeat the landlord's attempt to recover possession in an eviction action depends on the nature of the eviction action and of the counterclaim.

Counterclaims are most useful in nonpayment of rent eviction actions. If the counterclaim offsets all rent claimed, the tenant should win. It may be that merely reducing the amount owed below the amount demanded in the 24-hour notice will defeat the eviction action.

Equally important, a tenant who pays rent into court to support a counterclaim in a nonpayment of rent eviction action will have the benefit of the "second chance" provision discussed in section f. of chapter 6. This provision allows a tenant to win the eviction case even if the court finds the counterclaim damages insufficient to eliminate all default in rent. If the rent paid into court covers the net amount owing, or if the tenant adds enough to the money paid into court to pay all rent that the court finds due, judgment will be entered for the tenant in the action for possession.[57] The Oregon Supreme Court has recognized that, absent bad faith, a tenant who pays rent into court to support a counterclaim cannot lose possession if the rent paid into court covers any balance found due, and the court of appeals has applied this to protect a tenant who *failed to recover anything on the counterclaim*, but filed it in good faith.[58] The legislature has made it clear that if the tenant has to pay a balance because the money paid into court won't cover the rent found due to the landlord, but the tenant still retains possession under this provision, the landlord won't have to pay the tenant's attorney fees.[59]

In other kinds of eviction actions, a counterclaim may defeat the landlord's claim for possession only if the basis for the counterclaim has something to do with the landlord's right to evict. For example, suppose that your landlord has attempted to enforce a term of your rental agreement that is prohibited by the act, and you have refused to obey that term. If the landlord uses your violation of that term of the rental agreement as the basis for an eviction for cause, you should win the eviction action if you win a counterclaim based on the landlord's knowing enforcement of a prohibited term.

On the other hand, if the landlord brings a no-cause eviction, you may lose possession even if you recover damages on your counterclaim.

To decide whether any counterclaim you are contemplating constitutes a defense, start by referring to Table #2 earlier in this chapter, which shows a chart of evictions and defenses, and read the relevant portions of this book carefully.

3. How to decide whether to counterclaim

If you have a basis for a counterclaim you should consider carefully whether you want to pursue your claim as a counterclaim in an eviction action or as a separate lawsuit against the landlord. Part of this consideration involves whether the counterclaim is based on facts that also constitute a defense to the eviction action.

As you will see, you don't have to file your claim as a counterclaim to use it as a defense to eviction, and you may want to file a counterclaim even if it has nothing to do with the landlord's right to evict you. Here are some important things to keep in mind.

If you counterclaim in a nonpayment of rent eviction, you will probably have to pay rent into court. The major disadvantage of this is that it puts your money beyond your reach until and unless the court releases it to you. You can avoid this burden by asserting the same facts that support your counterclaim as a recoupment instead, or simply as a defense to the landlord's claim for possession. See section **f.** of chapter 6 and the discussion of nonpayment of rent evictions earlier in this chapter. However, if you want an order that the landlord make repairs (or any other injunctive order) as a result of the eviction action, you will have to counterclaim.

If you don't counterclaim, you will lose the benefit of the "second chance" provision. Also, the only way in which you will be able to recover damages that exceed the amount of rent claimed by the landlord (or an order requiring the landlord to make repairs) is by filing a separate lawsuit.

On the other hand, you may have to pay rent into court anyway to delay the trial so that you have time to prepare your case.[60] Although this would only be current rent, while you may be required to pay back rent as well to support a counterclaim, you may decide that you might as well file a counterclaim to have the benefit of the "second chance" provision. In other words, if you're going to have to pay something into court anyway, any additional burden of counterclaiming may be relatively minimal. Besides, it will be clear to the court that you're not just trying to cover up an inability to pay the rent.

Another factor is that the counterclaims filed in an eviction action based on nonpayment of rent cannot exceed the monetary limits of the court in which the eviction is pending except, perhaps, for unlawful trade practice counterclaims. In district court, the limit is $10,000; in justice court, it is $2,500.[61] If you have a large claim for damages, it is usually best to file it separately in circuit court, which has no monetary limit.

According to the statutes and court of appeals decisions,[62] you should be able to counterclaim for any amount and have the case transferred to circuit court if your counterclaim exceeds the limits of the original court and if your eviction is not based on nonpayment of rent. It may be easier for your attorney to file a circuit court action before your landlord brings an eviction action. See section **g.** of chapter 6.

Also, you may want to file a counterclaim even when it does not involve facts that amount to a defense to the eviction action. It may be the quickest way to collect damages from your landlord even if you lose possession, and it may greatly improve your settlement possibilities. The court of appeals has held that if a tenant wins money on a counterclaim, the landlord cannot recover attorney fees against the tenant even if the landlord wins a judgment evicting the tenant.

It is impossible to reduce all of these competing considerations to a simple formula, but here are some general conclusions.

If your top priority is staying in your home, it is usually best to counterclaim in the eviction action unless you are unwilling to give up a good chance to collect damages in excess of the eviction court's monetary limits.

If your defenses to the eviction action are weak even with the counterclaim, or if your top priority is recovering damages which have little to do with your landlord's right to evict you, it is usually best to file your claim for damages separately.

Finally, note that counterclaims and recoupments may be used in an action for back rent after the tenant has moved, and the tenant cannot be required to pay rent into court in such a case.

e. WHETHER AND HOW TO DEFEND

A tenant faced with an eviction action must decide whether to defend it and, if so, whether to do so without an attorney.

1. Should the tenant defend?

Although the most obvious considerations in deciding whether to fight an eviction action are whether you want to stay and whether you have legitimate defenses, there are several other important considerations.

If you do not go to court to contest the landlord's eviction action, the result will be an eviction judgment by default. The judgment will award possession of your dwelling to the landlord and enough money to cover the cost of filing and serving the court papers. Your failure to contest the action will mean that attorney's fees cannot be awarded against you.[63] You should bear in mind that a record of a judgment against you may make it harder for you to rent in the future. Many landlords, as part of their tenant screening procedures, pay for lists of tenants who have been evicted through the courts. See chapter 3, section a.

On the other hand, a landlord may join an action for rent with the eviction action, although in such a case the summons must allow you 30 days in which to respond (7 days in justice court).[64] If you fail to contest this kind of action, the default judgment will also include a money judgment for unpaid rent. Also, the landlord may sue you separately for rent. Unless you win that action, it can result in a judgment for attorney's fees whether or not you contest it.

Another factor you should consider is that the "exemption statutes" make a lot of your income and property unavailable to your creditors, so that many low-income tenants are effectively "judgment-proof". In other words, their assets are all exempt from seizure to satisfy money judgments, so such judgments cannot be enforced against them. See Appendix #3 for most of the state exemption laws; other state and federal laws make all welfare benefits and most other government benefits exempt from execution.

On the other hand, the portion of the eviction judgment that awards the landlord possession ("restitution") can be enforced against anyone. If you let the eviction action go by default, you may find that you cannot move out before the judgment for possession is enforced — a situation to be avoided if at all possible.

By the way, there is nothing wrong with going to court at the time and place specified in the summons and simply asking the judge for some time in which to leave. If you do not contest the action, but simply explain your situation to the judge, you should not have to pay the landlord any attorney's fees, and the judge may give you a few days or a week or two to move out. This may be easier in counties with a mediation process attached to the FED (forcible entry and detainer) courts. Multnomah County usually requires mediation for all cases that would otherwise be sent to trial; only if the mediation fails is a court date set.

Whatever you decide, you must take the summons and complaint seriously. Remember that it is not always necessary that you receive these papers personally. Don't fail to appear in person or through an attorney at the time and place indicated on the summons unless you have decided to let the landlord take a judgment by default. If you don't show up, the landlord will probably recover a judgment evicting you as soon as the case is called. That judgment may be enforced very quickly.

Although there are devices by which an attorney can challenge technical deficiencies in the manner of service or in the form of the complaint, or attempt to convince a judge that your excuse for missing the first appearance was sufficient to warrant another chance, it is a serious mistake to ignore the papers because you think they have been improperly served or filled out. It is much harder to set aside a default judgment than it is to appear and to assert your rights at the time and place indicated on the summons.

If you elect to get an attorney, do everything you can to get the court papers to that attorney as soon as possible. Most courts will give you a day or so to do this if you show up at the time and place indicated on the summons and ask for an opportunity to find a lawyer. There is no guarantee that you will get this time, however, so try to get an attorney immediately.

2. Is an attorney necessary?

Before the act, contested eviction actions often ended with the tenant's negative reply to the question "did you pay the rent?" because there was no legally relevant excuse for non-payment. Today, however, eviction cases can be terribly complicated; it is not uncommon for trials to last a week or more. Accordingly, I recommend that you get the assistance of an attorney if at all possible.

On the other hand, legal fees for either side can run as high as $2,500 or more, although most cases will probably cost in the neighborhood of $800 to $1,500. If you win, you may be able to recover your attorney's fees from your opponent, but some landlords are accomplished at evading the enforcement of money judgments, just as many low-income tenants are "judgment proof," as discussed earlier.

There are some tenants who simply cannot afford an attorney, yet are not within legal aid's poverty income guidelines. It seems inevitable that some tenants will attempt to represent themselves, so I have provided some forms here that may be useful. Just remember that the law may have changed since this book was written, and that minor variations in the facts of your case may make a tremendous difference in the result.

3. How to do it yourself

(a) The forms

If you insist on representing yourself, the critical first step is to show up on time at the courtroom the summons identifies. This is the "first appearance." A party who is absent loses the case right then and there,65 and it is difficult to get a second chance to be heard. If both parties are present and do not reach a settlement (and if the tenant doesn't agree to get out or simply asks the court for more time), the case will be set for trial. The law now provides that an unrepresented defendant may proceed to trial by filing an answer in writing on a form available from the court clerk and by serving a copy on the plaintiff on the same day as first appearance.[66]

In practice, this means that the judge presiding at the first appearance (or the court clerk) will direct both parties to the clerk's office, the tenant will fill out the form answer, give a copy to the landlord on the spot, and both will be informed of the trial date on the spot. Filling out the form answer is relatively straightforward if you are not asserting a counterclaim. Note that if you fail to assert a defense that comes up at trial, the court cannot limit you to the answer (assuming you are not represented by a lawyer), but may give the landlord a continuance in which to prepare to meet that defense.[67] The idea is that the landlord is entitled to some notice before trial of what the issues will be.

Sample #27 assumes that the landlord's basis for eviction is nonpayment of rent, that the tenant does not wish to counterclaim, and that the defense is based on the disrepair of the premises. I have omitted the caption of the form, which contains blanks for the name of the court, the parties' names, and the court number, all of which you simply copy from the summons and complaint. (If you need a copy of the statutes, see page xiv of the Introduction.)

You should hand a copy to the landlord (or to whomever is representing the landlord) in the clerk's office, and there should be a form available for you to sign showing how, when, and where you served the copy of the answer on the landlord. (The original of the answer and the proof of service go to the clerk; you keep a copy of both.) If no form is available, you can make your own. Sample #28 is an example.

Note that in unusual circumstances you may have to serve the landlord with the answer or other court papers when you are not both in the courthouse. Service can be by first class mail to the address for the landlord reflected in the court papers on the summons. The proof of service would be

SAMPLE #27
FORM ANSWER TO EVICTION COMPLAINT

I (We) deny that the plaintiff(s) is (are) entitled to possession because:

___X___The landlord did not make the repairs.

List any repair problems: Toilet fills so slowly it can only be used once a day; no heat; no working lock and resulting loss of $400 property due to theft.

_____The landlord is attempting to evict me (us) because of my (our) complaints (or the eviction is otherwise retaliatory).

_____The eviction notice is wrong.

List any other defenses:_____

_____

_____

_____

I (We) ask that the plaintiff(s) take nothing by the complaint and that I (we) be awarded my (our) costs and disbursements.

July 18, 199-   *Leonard Tenant*

Date   Signature of defendant(s)

---

the same as above, except that you would recite "by mailing" the true copy of the answer "to the plaintiff addressed as follows" followed by the address.

The clerk of the court will charge a fee for filing the original of the answer, although this can be waived if you are too poor to pay it. The clerk may be able to assist you with this. Generally, you will have to see a judge to ask for a waiver.

The copy of your answer that you mail or hand to the plaintiff should have a certification that the copy is true

SAMPLE #28
PROOF OF SERVICE

I, Leonard Tenant, hereby say that on July 18, 199-, I handed a true, correct copy of the within Answer to the plaintiff in the clerk's office of this court.

Leonard Tenant
Leonard Tenant

Subscribed and sworn to this 18th day of July, 199-, at Portland, Oregon.

J. M. Notary

Notary Public
My commission expires 7/21/9-

written anywhere on it; all you need to write are the words "certified a true copy" and sign your name as defendant underneath.

If you have other defenses, state them in the appropriate places on the form; if you run out of room, attach a separate sheet and write "continued on attached sheet" on the form itself.

To counterclaim, you must modify the form answer. Sample #29 shows an example. These counterclaims are recoupment defenses as well because my sample assumes this is a nonpayment of rent eviction.

SAMPLE #29
COUNTERCLAIMS

List any other defenses: I COUNTERCLAIM for $400 because of the bad lock, $300 because of the defective toilet (lost rental value), and $800 because of no heat (lost rental value, discomfort). I ask that the court award me judgment against the plaintiff for $1,500.

As discussed in sections **c.** and **d.** of this chapter and in section **f.** of chapter 6, any claim for damages arising under the rental agreement or under the act can be used to defend a nonpayment of rent eviction by offsetting the rent claimed by the landlord.

Here are some rules to remember in writing up any answer:

(a) Make sure you don't admit anything you want to dispute. For example, if one of your defenses will be that the notice was improperly served because it was *only* mailed, don't say it was "served" in your answer; if anything, just say it was "mailed."

(b) Don't rely on these examples for your case. What you put in your answer must fit your case, and it must be true. It is unlawful to allege things you know to be false.

(c) Always date and sign your answer, and file the original in court. Unless you hand a copy to the landlord in open court, you will need a proof of service attached to the original.

(d) If you want a jury trial, you must write "jury trial demanded" somewhere on your answer.

(b) The judge

Perhaps the most unfortunate aspect of landlord and tenant law is that there are still a few judges who are so hostile to tenants' rights that a tenant is almost sure to lose an eviction action in their courtrooms. It is sad, but true, that the selection of the judge who tries your case may be the single most important factor in determining which side wins. Even assuming that you have a jury trial, the judge can decide not to let defenses go to the jury, and it is the judge who instructs the jury on the law. The strongest possible retaliatory eviction defense won't do you much good if the judge rules that retaliation is not a defense to eviction — and it has happened!

153

Although you don't get to select the judge who will hear your case, Oregon law gives all parties the right to file an affidavit and motion for change of judge on the grounds that the party (or attorney) believes that the judge cannot be impartial by reason of prejudice.[68] You do not need proof of prejudice, but only reasonable grounds to believe that the judge won't be fair in hearing your case.[69] You can disqualify up to two judges in one case.

To use this important right, it is of course necessary for you to find out whether there are any judges in your area you should avoid. Your best bet is to call a legal aid housing lawyer and simply ask. If he or she will give you an answer and advises you that certain judges cannot be fair in eviction cases, that's enough grounds to support a motion for change of judge. You must know the names of any judges you want to avoid by the time the case is assigned for trial, which may be the time indicated on the summons. This is because you waive your right to disqualify a judge unless you exercise that right as soon as you learn of the trial judge's identity. All you have to do is say, "Your Honor, I wish to file an affidavit for change of judge."

The law requires that you file a written motion and affidavit within 24 hours of your oral statement. Be aware, however, that some presiding judges insist that the affidavit be filed by the end of the day on which a party learns of the assignment and makes the oral motion. Sample #30 shows what the motion and affidavit should look like.

File the original with the clerk and keep a copy. If for some reason the judge you disqualify wants to dispute your challenge, there will be a short hearing in front of another judge, but the only question will be whether you had a good faith belief that the judge would not be impartial. The word of an attorney familiar with local practice is sufficient. It is extremely rare for a disqualified judge to challenge the moving party's good faith.

```
        In the District Court of the State of Oregon
                   County of Multnomah
J. Fullbird,    )
     Plaintiff,)                    No. 123456
     vs.        )              MOTION AND AFFIDAVIT
L. Tenant,      )              FOR CHANGE OF JUDGE
     Defendant.)
State of Oregon
County of Multnomah ss.


   I, Leonard Tenant, hereby say that I am the
defendant in the above-entitled matter, and that
I believe that I cannot have a fair and impartial
trial before the Honorable _____ who is
assigned to hear this case. I request that another
judge be assigned to hear this case.
   This motion and affidavit are filed in good
faith and not for the purpose of delay.

Leonard Tenant
Defendant
SUBSCRIBED AND SWORN TO before me this 14th day
of May, 199-, at Portland, Oregon.

                    I. M. Notary
                    Notary Public
                    My commission expires 7/21/9-
```

(c) The trial

When the parties appear at the time and place indicated on the summons, the judge will probably assign a time and place for trial or send the parties to another judge or a clerk to get a trial date. In some counties, the parties will be sent to a mediator to attempt to reach a settlement before the trial date is set, but this will probably happen, if at all, immediately after first appearance. If the mediation fails, the case will be set for trial without delay.

Either party may demand a jury trial, although this should be repeated in writing (on the form answer for the tenant; by a separate document filed with the court for the landlord). It is probably impractical for a lay person to attempt a jury trial without representation. Almost all trials without lawyers also have no jury.

If the tenant wants the trial delayed more than two days beyond the date set, the court will order the tenant to pay rent into court as it becomes due from the start of the action until final judgment.[70] The landlord is entitled to time in which to get an attorney.[71]

Once the trial date is set, both sides will have to decide whether all the witnesses they need will come to court voluntarily. If not, the clerk of the court should provide subpoenas. They must be served personally by a sheriff or anyone not a party to the lawsuit and at least 18 years old. The witness must be offered the witness fee and mileage reimbursement in cash or an equivalent at the time of service (ask the clerk for the current rates). Building inspectors typically require a subpoena for their records.

The most important rule to remember is that you can usually introduce evidence only through yourself or any other witness who has personal knowledge of the things being testified about. Generally, if a witness has to answer the question "how do you know?" by saying something like "so-and-so told me so" or "I read about it," you need another witness. A witness with personal knowledge can usually answer "because I saw it" or "because I heard it."

An important exception is that a witness can testify to a party's "admission against interest" or "prior inconsistent statement." For example, if another person heard a landlord say he or she brought the eviction action "to get rid of a troublemaker," that person can so testify if the landlord claims that the tenant's organizing activities had nothing to do with bringing the eviction action. In such a situation, the witness can testify to what the landlord said, even though the witness has no personal knowledge as to what was going on in the landlord's mind.

Practically, both sides will usually need a witness with personal knowledge of all the things that need to be proved. Sometimes, the parties can be the only witnesses because they have personal knowledge of all the relevant facts. Often, however, one or both sides will need several additional witnesses.

By the way, when the issue is the extent of any reduction in value caused by a landlord's violation of habitability obligations, it is important to understand that the question is not whether the dwelling is worth less than the agreed-upon rental.

The court of appeals has held that a landlord is obligated by law to provide "habitable" premises at the agreed rent and that the tenant can provide sufficient evidence to support an award of damages for habitability violations by bringing photographs and testifying, for example, that the repair problems reduced the rental value by 75%. Of course, the testimony of an inspector may help greatly.

Although courts usually allow people who are not lawyers some freedom from the rules of evidence, you may not be able to ask your witnesses leading questions that suggest the answer you want. For this reason, it is important (and entirely proper) to discuss in advance how the witness' testimony fits into your case and what you're trying to prove. Of course, it is unlawful to ask your witness to testify falsely.

The eviction statutes require that the court apply the provisions of the Landlord and Tenant Act to determine the rights of the parties, including —

(a) whether and in what amount rent is due;

157

(b) whether a tenancy or rental agreement has been validly terminated; and

(c) whether the tenant is entitled to remedies for retaliatory conduct by the landlord as provided in ORS 90.385 and 90.765.[72]

On the other hand, a judgment against a tenant should not include back rent or damages unless the landlord sued for rent or damages as well as for possession and used a 30-day summons.[73] Nonetheless, the court will release any rent paid into court to support a counterclaim according to the findings of the judge or jury. Although rent paid into court to support a delay in the trial date is in some doubt, it would probably be treated the same way.

4. How to settle

In chapter 5, I discussed settlement agreements appropriate before a repair controversy reaches the state of an eviction action. The agreement given in Sample #10 of that chapter is also useful if the landlord has served an eviction notice, but has not yet begun an eviction action in court. The only difference is that a paragraph should be added in which it is agreed that the landlord "rescinds" or "waives" any eviction notice served prior to the date of the agreement.

If an eviction action has been filed, however, the parties must deal with that action if they decide to settle their controversy without going to trial. You can agree on almost anything, but it is always safest to put it in writing. If the settlement is the result of a mediation process connected with the FED courts, the mediator will be able to tell the parties how to do the paperwork. Tenants should remember that a settlement that calls for a dismissal of the FED as part of the agreement may make it a lot easier to find a home to rent in the future, and should try to get the landlord to agree to a dismissal if possible. If a mediator is involved, he or she should be familiar with this interest; if not, and if the landlord will agree, insist on a resolution which will involve a dismissal.

If your settlement involves the tenant staying in the premises, you can use the sort of agreement given in Sample #10 in chapter 5, but add a clause agreeing that the eviction action will be dismissed (identify it by the names of the parties and the court and court number). Sample #31 shows an example of the form which the landlord files with the court to obtain the dismissal.

If, as is often the case, the tenant trades the right to fight the eviction for some time to get out and, perhaps, some waiver of unpaid rent, it is common for everyone to sign and file an agreement (a "stipulation") permitting the landlord to take a judgment that cannot be enforced until the agreed date. Tenants should never agree to a date earlier than they can be sure of being out, however, because the judgment can be enforced after the specified date just like any other judgment. (See the next section of this chapter.) Sample #32 shows an example of a stipulation for a judgment; this example becomes a judgment as soon as the judge signs it.

SAMPLE #31
DISMISSAL FORM

```
        In the District Court of the State of Oregon
                    County of Multnomah
J. Fullbird,)  Plaintiff,)      No. 123456
     vs.    )                   MOTION FOR
M. Petard,  )  Defendant.)      DISMISSAL


     J. Fullbird, plaintiff in the above-entitled
action, hereby requests an order of dismissal
judgment of nonsuit.
Dated: July 24, 199-
                              J. Fullbird
                              ─────────────
                              Plaintiff
```

SAMPLE #32
JUDGMENT BY STIPULATION

```
    In the District Court of the State of Oregon
              County of Multnomah
J. Fullbird,    )
      Plaintiff,)               No. 123456
      vs.                       JUDGMENT BY
M. Petard,      )               STIPULATION
      Defendant.)
```

Plaintiff and defendant hereby agree that judgment may be entered in this action as follows:

1. Plaintiff shall have restitution of the subject premises, with execution stayed through and including July 15, 199-;

2. Each party releases the other from any and all liability arising with respect to the subject tenancy;

3. Each party will bear its own costs.

June 10, 199- *J. Fullbird*   June 10, 199- *Marie Petard*
        Plaintiff   Defendant

IT IS SO ORDERED

               June 11, 199- *J.M. Judge*
                          District Judge

As with an answer, the names of the parties and of the court and the action number should agree with the summons and complaint. Also, the document should be typed and double spaced. Both parties should appear and ask the judge to sign the judgment. It may be necessary for a defendant who has not already filed an answer to pay a filing fee when the stipulation is filed, but this expense is worth it because the stipulation is the safest way to assure that execution will not occur before the date specified.

f. AFTER THE JUDGMENT

1. How a landlord enforces an eviction judgment

An eviction judgment does not authorize the landlord to lock out a tenant personally or to seize or remove the tenant's belongings. Although the abandoned property section covers situations in which a tenant is continuously absent from the premises for at least seven days after the eviction judgment (see chapter 11), in all other cases the landlord must have the sheriff (or the civil process office in Multnomah County) enforce the judgment if the tenant does not move.

The landlord must apply to the clerk of the court for an "execution of restitution" after obtaining the judgment. The statute directs that this writ be enforced by a two-step process.

First, the sheriff (or civil process deputy) must serve a notice on the tenant that states that the landlord is to have restitution of the premises and that unless the tenant gets out and takes his or her personal property (including motor vehicles) within three days, the sheriff will return to evict the tenant and remove the property to a safe place for storage. The "execution" and the notice are served much like the summons and complaint: the sheriff mails a copy of each and attempts personal service at the premises; if the tenant is absent, the sheriff must attach a copy of the notice to the tenant's door. This must all happen "by the end of the judicial day next following the payment of fees" for these services.[74]

The three-day period starts the day after mailing and service of the "execution" and sheriff's notice, and ends on the third calendar day following service, unless the third day is a Saturday, Sunday, or legal holiday, in which case the period ends on the next judicial day.[75]

Second, if the tenant fails to leave or to take the personal property away, the sheriff returns to lock out the tenant and to seize and store any personal property left on the premises.[76]

161

The landlord must pay a small fee to have the notice served. If the tenant must be removed by force, the landlord will have to deposit enough funds with the sheriff to cover the costs of removing the tenant, moving the belongings, and storing them, if the landlord wants the sheriff to be responsible for removing the tenant's belongings. A provision now exists in the eviction statutes that permits the landlord to save sheriff's moving costs by accepting responsibility for belongings left behind. Basically, this functions exactly like the abandoned property provisions, except that if the tenant claims the property on time, the landlord must release all of the property to the tenant without charge and without condition[77] (see chapter 11). In any event, expenses paid to the sheriff to enforce the judgment are added to the monetary part of the judgment for future enforcement against the assets of the tenant or for enforcement against any of the tenant's belongings that are left behind and not claimed as exempt by the tenant.

2. Can the tenant appeal?

If the tenant wishes to appeal the eviction judgment, he or she will have to file an "undertaking" or deposit a certain amount of money into court. An undertaking is a promise on the part of some third person that the tenant will pay whatever amounts that the undertaking covers if the appeal is unsuccessful. At present, the minimum amount of an undertaking is $500.

The person who signs the undertaking is usually an agent for a bonding company, but it may also be an individual who has sufficient nonexempt assets to cover the amount in question. The individual or company is known as a "surety." The court has the power to permit a tenant to deposit cash into court instead of an undertaking.[78]

If the tenant is appealing from a district court judgment and wants to stay in the premises during the appeal, the undertaking (or deposit) must be large enough to cover damages, costs, and disbursements that may be awarded on appeal, plus any damages arising from destruction or injury to the premises during the appeal and the value of the use and occupancy of the premises during the appeal.[79] Damages, costs, and disbursements usually include only the opponent's appellate court filing fees ($100), an $85 "prevailing fee," and the costs of duplicating briefs (the written arguments submitted to the appellate court).

If the tenant appeals and wins, the landlord will have to pay the tenant's filing fee ($60), plus the prevailing fee and costs of briefs.

The appeal will be to the court of appeals, which will consider the errors raised in the briefs by examining trial court papers and the testimony at the trial if it was recorded. If the judgment is affirmed (and the Supreme Court denies any requested further review), the tenant and any surety will be liable for all of these costs. If the tenant deposited money into court instead of an undertaking, the appropriate amount will be deducted and any balance will be returned to the tenant unless the landlord enforces any outstanding amount of the judgment against that balance. For example, the landlord may have an attorney's fee award, and this will not be covered by the undertaking.[80]

Note that attorney's fees on appeal are now recoverable against the losing party in addition to other costs.[81]

If the tenant wants to appeal from a district court judgment but wants to move out and needs no "stay" of the judgment during the appeal, the undertaking (or deposit) must cover only damages, costs, and disbursements that may be awarded on appeal.[82]

If the appeal is from a justice court eviction judgment, the entire process is different. The appeal is really just a new trial held in circuit court. To get a stay of the judgment, the tenant must file an undertaking (or deposit cash) to cover costs and disbursements and any judgment that might be awarded the landlord on appeal.[83] This includes a judgment for attorney's fees. If the tenant is moving and needs no stay, the undertaking or deposit need only cover costs and disbursements, which do not include any attorney's fee awarded to the landlord under the Landlord and Tenant Act.

Although a tenant of moderate means may find it financially impossible to appeal while staying in the premises, an important provision may help. The appeal statutes permit a court to "waive, reduce or limit the undertaking...upon a showing of good cause, including indigence, and on such terms as shall be just and equitable." This power now exists for appeals from district and justice courts,[84] but a judge who takes the landlord's interests into account may be unwilling to set the amount of the undertaking low enough for the tenant to afford.

Fortunately, there is a cheaper and quicker method of appeal known as a "writ of review." The writ is simply a written order signed by a circuit court judge and directed to the district or justice court. The writ requires that court to forward the case file and any record of testimony taken at trial to a circuit court judge.

The judge then reviews the case for any legal errors alleged in the petition by which the tenant asked for a writ of review. The court has discretion to issue a stay of the lower court judgment. The undertaking is limited by statute to $100 with or without a stay.

The writ of review may well be the only method of review that a tenant who wants to stay in the premises can afford.[85] If the writ of review is unsuccessful, the circuit court judgment denying relief can be appealed to the court of appeals. Any further stay, however, is discretionary, and will undoubtedly require a substantial undertaking.

9

EMERGENCIES, THE POLICE, AND TEMPORARY RESTRAINING ORDERS

The kind of circumstances for which the personal injury/property damage/outrageous conduct 24-hour notice was designed, the eviction process may seem very slow to a landlord when you add the time for service, first appearance, and, if the tenant defends the eviction action, the trial. However, this process is tremendously faster than most judicial proceedings. There are solutions if you want to speed up the process.

If the case is extreme, which it should be for this kind of eviction notice to be appropriate, the landlord should consider calling the police. The immediate objective is to remove a threat of violence, not necessarily to recover possession of the premises, and it is wise to keep those two objectives separate.

The police are trained to intervene in the most effective way to prevent further harm; circumstances under which they will make an arrest or leave with just a warning varies with the jurisdiction, the available jail space, and individual officers' discretion. A warning may be the most effective intervention; an arrested tenant is usually soon released and has every right to return "home" until possession is delivered to the landlord by the judicial process or intentional abandonment by the tenant. (A tenant who is in jail is rarely in a position to "abandon" merely by not returning to the premises, but there is no reason why summons and complaint cannot be served in jail in addition to the regular method.)

If the police won't help, there is still a device available — the same device that is available to a tenant who has been locked out by the landlord or whose utility services have been unlawfully shut off: the temporary restraining order.[1] The "TRO," as it is known among lawyers, is a form of injunctive court order designed to preserve the status quo until a full hearing can be had on a dispute. It is only available for extreme circumstances. The threatened loss or injury must be "irreparable" if the court doesn't grant the TRO, and legal remedies must be "inadequate" to compensate after the fact for the threatened harm or loss. This generally means that if money damages can make the party whole later, a TRO is not available.

A TRO is clearly unavailable just because the tenant has stopped paying the rent and has no money to pay a judgment, which is the major reason the eviction process is so quick compared to other judicial procedures and why landlords are free to extract deposits at the beginning of tenancies of an unlimited amount.

A landlord (or tenant) who thinks a TRO is appropriate should do everything possible to get a lawyer. Lawyers should know how serious something has to be to get a TRO before the local judges. They should also be familiar with the local practices (which judge do you go to and when) and be able to tell which judge is likely to decide the issue. A good lawyer may also have some suggestions about alternatives and should greatly increase the chances of success by drafting the supporting motion and affidavit and suggesting an appropriate form of relief (what, exactly, you want the court to order the tenant to do or not to do until the time of trial) with a view to the judge's sense of the proper role of a TRO in the circumstances.

The TRO has the advantage of directing a judge's discretion to the specific situation, such as enjoining the violent tenant from threatening behavior before trial, with the expectation that the resulting order will help to get police response if it is violated, without throwing the spouse and children in the street, too.

Again, you should have a lawyer for this. That's why, as a tenant's lawyer, I have essentially said "get a lawyer" to deal with lockouts and utility shutoffs (see chapter 7), even though the legal remedy is precisely the same as the one discussed here. Tenants who insist on handling a lockout or utility shutoff in court themselves (or who have no choice) may be able to adapt the procedures outlined here for landlords.

If you are a landlord who insists on representing yourself, take the following steps:[2]

(a) Make every effort to deal with the problem in some other way: talk to the tenant, call the police, find a social worker or probation officer if one is already assigned to a tenant with behavior problems.

(b) If convinced a TRO is necessary, call the courthouse, see which judge is handling eviction cases, talk to that judge's secretary or clerk (*not* to the judge directly), and try to arrange to present a motion for a TRO to the judge. If that proves unsuccessful, try to make similar arrangements to appear before the presiding judge (assuming you are unfamiliar with the practice in the county in question).

(c) Prepare and serve an appropriate 24-hour notice (if you haven't already done so), and make every effort to notify the tenant by telephone or by leaving a note at the premises (preferably both) exactly when and where you are asking the court to issue a TRO. The court should be very careful to make sure you did everything reasonably possible to notify the tenant of an opportunity to tell the tenant's side of the story before the court issues any order.

(d) Prepare and have served (after expiration of the 24-hour notice) an eviction summons and complaint, and, with the same caption (the name of the court, the parties, and the court number or a blank for that number to be entered at filing), an Application for Temporary Restraining Order (see Sample #33) and a Notice of Hearing (see Sample #34). The written Notice of Hearing is called a Praecipe, and you should be able to get one at the courthouse. If not, you can prepare your own following the sample shown here. In any event, make every effort to get written notice of the time and place to the tenant before the hearing. The proof of service is usually prepared by whomever serves the eviction summons and complaint. Make sure that person adds "Application for Temporary Restraining Order," "Affidavit in Support of Temporary Restraining Order," and "Praecipe" (or "Notice of Time and Place of Hearing") to the list of papers served.

(e) Prepare your witnesses and show up promptly for the court hearing.

The most critical document in this process is the Affidavit in Support of the Temporary Restraining Order (see Sample #35). Its function is to show the court that you have done everything reasonably possible to notify the opponent of the hearing, and that the circumstances really do call for extraordinary judicial intervention.

In particular, you must show why waiting for an FED judgment is not an adequate remedy. The affidavit (or affidavits) must be based on the personal knowledge of the person making the affidavit. This involves the law of evidence and the numerous exceptions to the hearsay rule — another good reason it helps to have a good lawyer. You will have to prepare your own form, as you can see from Sample #35 that the critical particulars will always vary.

SAMPLE #33
APPLICATION FOR TEMPORARY
RESTRAINING ORDER

In the District Court of the State of Oregon in and for the County of _____

GEORGE AND JENNIFER LANDLORD,)   No._____
          Plaintiffs,   )
           vs.   APPLICATION FOR
PAUL AND SHIRLEY TENANT,   )   TEMPORARY
         Defendants.   )   RESTRAINING
_____)   ORDER

George and Jennifer Landlord, plaintiffs in this pending forcible entry and wrongful detainer action, hereby move the court for an order restraining Paul Tenant, a defendant in this action, from committing any act that would damage the premises subject of this action, known as 123 S.W. Easy Street, Portland, Oregon, until further order of this court.

This application is based on the affidavit of George Landlord and the points and authorities cited below, and is made on the ground that the plaintiffs will suffer irreparable injury unless this court grants the relief sought in that the defendant will cause severe physical injury to the premises and will make good his threat to burn them down.

Date: August 13, 199-

George Landlord
George Landlord
plaintiff in pro per

Points and Authorities

ORS 90.400(5) provides for injunctive relief "for any noncompliance by the tenant with the rental agreement or ORS 90.325."

ORS 90.325(6) provides that a tenant shall "Not deliberately or negligently destroy, deface, damage, impair or remove any part of the premises or knowingly permit any person to do so."

SAMPLE #34
NOTICE OF HEARING

In the District Court of the State of Oregon
in and for the County of _____

GEORGE AND JENNIFER LANDLORD,)   No. _____
                Plaintiffs,) NOTICE OF TIME
     vs.   AND PLACE OF
PAUL AND SHIRLEY TENANT,   )   HEARING ON
             Defendants.)   PLAINTIFFS'
_____) APPLICATION FOR
                                    TEMPORARY
                      RESTRAINING ORDER

    TO DEFENDANTS PAUL AND SHIRLEY TENANT:

    Please take notice that the attached APPLICA-
TION FOR TEMPORARY RESTRAINING ORDER will be heard
on August 14, 199-, at 2:00 p.m. in Courtroom 399
of the _____ County Courthouse, 123 S.W. Main
Street, _____, Oregon, before the Honorable
James B. Just, District Judge.

Date: August 13, 199-

                      George Landlord
                      George Landlord
                      Plaintiff in pro per

In the example in Sample #35, the statements of Paul quoted by George are within an exception to the hearsay rule for "party admissions." This example should get George to a judge who will probably wonder what good it will do to issue a TRO. The answers are several: just getting the process rolling may impress Paul to back off; the police may respond more effectively at the next sign of trouble if they can see an order signed by the judge; the sanctions for contempt of court may serve as a deterrent to Paul. The remedies available in such circumstances are far from perfect.

SAMPLE #35
AFFIDAVIT IN SUPPORT OF TEMPORARY
RESTRAINING ORDER

In the District Court of the State of Oregon
in and for the County of _____

GEORGE AND JENNIFER LANDLORD,)   No._____
            Plaintiffs,) AFFIDAVIT OF
      vs.   GEORGE LANDLORD
PAUL AND SHIRLEY TENANT,   ) IN SUPPORT OF
           Defendants.) PLAINTIFFS'
_____) APPLICATION
                       FOR TEMPORARY
                       RESTRAINING ORDER

      State of Oregon   )
)ss.
      County of _____)

I, George Landlord, being first duly sworn, do hereby say:

I am a plaintiff in the above-entitled action, which is a forcible entry and detainer action pending in this court. I am the joint owner with my spouse, Jennifer Landlord, of the subject premises, 123 S.W. Easy Street, Portland, Oregon, and know the matters herein stated of my own personal knowledge.

I personally met the defendants, Paul and Shirley Tenant, on July 1, 199-, when they appeared at my door to discuss renting the subject premises. Paul Tenant told me he had recently been released from prison, having completed a term for arson. He insisted that he had been "framed" and that his probation officer would tell me that in any event he was employed and a good risk as a tenant. I overcame my natural reluctance to rent to these people only because I felt sorry for Shirley Tenant, who was holding an infant the couple told me was theirs. I rented to them after confirming Paul's employment; they paid the July rent and a small deposit in cash.

All went well until I failed to receive the August rent. I stopped by on August 5th, 199-, and talked to Shirley Tenant, who said that Paul had been fired and that he was out drinking with some of his old friends. I told her I was sorry, but that I had to have the rent and that I would be serving a 72-hour notice if I hadn't received the rent by August 8, 199-.

On August 8, 199-, I returned to the subject premises at 10:00 a.m., and handed a 72-hour non-payment of rent notice to Shirley Tenant at the front door. While we were talking, Paul Tenant appeared behind Shirley, violently threw her to one side, and confronted me. He said that he was not going to pay the rent because he'd lost his job, and that I had better not do anything to evict them because he'd "get even." When I told him I didn't appreciate being threatened, he stormed by me on the front porch, walked toward the garage, and yelled "C'mere, I'll show you what I mean."

His gait was uneven, his eyes bloodshot, and his speech slurred. I detected the odor of alcohol on his breath, and he appeared and behaved as if extremely intoxicated.

When I followed him to the garage, he struggled to open the garage door. He show me six gasoline cans and some rags. He said, "I'm experienced at this, you know" and gestured toward the cans. Then he picked up a sledge hammer and managed to strike several blows to the side of the garage, dislodging three pieces of siding. Then he staggered back to the house.

I immediately called the police. They arrived and cited Paul Tenant to appear to answer to the charge of criminal mischief. They said they couldn't arrest him because there was no jail space, but suggested that if I had a court order, it would help.

I spoke with Paul's parole officer, who offered no practical suggestions. I personally delivered a 24-hour notice to Shirley on August 9, 199-, at 10:00 a.m. On August 13, 199-, at 2:00 p.m., I notified Shirley on the phone, and told her to tell Paul of the time and place of this hearing; she said Paul was too drunk to come to the phone. I expect to file this action this day and will instruct the process server to serve this affidavit, the Notice of Time and Place of Hearing, and the Application for Temporary Restraining Order on the defendants.

George Landlord
George Landlord

Subscribed and sworn to before me this 13th day of August, 199-, at Portland, Oregon, by George Landlord, known by me to be the person whose signature above appears.

Adam Notable
Adam Notable, Notary Public
My commission expires: 9/15/9-

Although a bond or undertaking is normally required to make a temporary restraining order or preliminary (but not a permanent) injunction enforceable, no undertaking is required where the relief is sought to protect a person from violent or threatening behavior or to prevent unlawful conduct when the effect of the injunction is to restrict the enjoined party to available judicial remedies.[3] I had assaults and lockouts by landlords in mind when I suggested these exceptions, but the first one should work if and when a judge concludes that a tenant should be enjoined from threatening to beat up his or her landlord or other tenants. If the landlord wants more, however, such as an order that the violent member of the tenant's household stay away from the premises until trial, there is at least an argument that the normal undertaking is required.

10

HOW CAN TENANTS LEAVE?

A tenant who moves without properly terminating a tenancy may be liable for later rent. This chapter should help you avoid such problems and to defend an action for back rent if your landlord brings one against you. As always, keep copies of everything.

a. ENDING A MONTHLY OR WEEKLY TENANCY

Ending a month-to-month or week-to-week tenancy is usually quite simple. Section 90.900 of the Landlord and Tenant Act entitles either party to terminate a week-to-week tenancy with 10 days' notice and a month-to-month tenancy with 30 days' notice. In either situation, the notice must be in writing. It may be served personally or by mail, but if you choose this method you must add three days to the minimum effective date *and the notice must say so.* In other words, a 30-day notice effective September 1 could be served personally August 31, but if mailed would have to bear a postmark of August 28 or earlier.[1] The notice should specify the termination date and identify the premises. Sample #36 shows the basic form.

Note that the Landlord and Tenant Act makes the person who entered the rental agreement on behalf of the landlord, or the successor to that person, a proper addressee of the notice unless you have been informed in writing of the name and address of an owner or other person authorized to manage the premises.[2]

SAMPLE #36
TERMINATION NOTICE BY TENANT
(Month-to-month or week-to-week tenancy)

```
                                  March 27, 199-
Dear Mr. Fullbird:
     I am presently your tenant at 456 Rental Avenue,
Apt. 4. I hereby give notice that my tenancy will
end on April 30, 199-, and that I will be out of
possession by that date. The termination date of
April 30 represents an extension of three days from
this date because I am serving this notice by mail,
as required by ORS 90.910(2).
                                  Sincerely,
                                  Thomas Tenant
                                  Thomas Tenant
```

In the case of a month-to-month tenancy, the termination date need not coincide with the end of a rent period as long as you give at least 30 days' notice and, unless you have agreed otherwise, rent is apportioned day to day.[3] Under these circumstances, you might add a paragraph to your notice that reads something like the following:

> Because this termination date will occur 10 days after the next rent payment date, I will pay only one-third of next month's rent, or $50.

The following language is appropriate when you have paid the last month's rent in advance:

> As you will recall, I paid the last month's rent in advance at the beginning of my tenancy. Therefore, I will not pay rent for this month.

Things get a bit complicated if you paid the last month's rent in advance, but you want to terminate on a date that does not correspond with the end of a rental period. One approach is the following wording:

175

You will note that I am paying only one-third of this month's rent. This is because the termination date occurs 10 days after the next rent payment is due, and I have already paid a last month's rent at the beginning of the tenancy. By applying the last month's rent to the last 30 days of the tenancy, rent will be apportioned day to day, as required by ORS 90.900(2).

Of course, this approach only works if you give the landlord more than 30 days' notice. If you have paid a last month's rent in advance and you decide to terminate shortly after paying rent, something like this should work:

As you know, I have already paid the rent for this month, and I paid a last month's rent at the beginning of the tenancy. Because the termination date occurs after using up only one-third of that last month's rent, please return two-thirds ($100) to me now. ORS 90.300(8), 90.900(2).

If you expect trouble, you might point out that section 90.300(8) permits double damages if prepaid rent is wrongfully withheld (as in the case of all deposits).

If your landlord refuses to return the unused portion of the last month's rent, your remedies are the same as those available for wrongfully withheld deposits, as discussed in chapter 4.

If you have to leave with less than 30 days' notice, you should still let the landlord know as soon as you can so he or she will have an opportunity to find a new tenant quickly to decrease any possible loss. As the next section explains, the landlord must either make reasonable efforts to rent the premises again or accept immediate termination; your rent liability will continue only if the landlord makes reasonable efforts but fails to find a new tenant to pay rent before your liability ends. Your notice should limit the extent of liability for rent to 30 days from its service because the landlord has no complaint except that you failed to give a full 30 days' notice. In other words, since the most that the landlord could demand is 30 days' notice, you can be held responsible only for the period by which your notice falls short of 30 days, assuming, of course, that you are a month-to-month tenant.

If you have to leave with less than 30 days' notice, I suggest using the following language:

> I realize the termination date in this notice gives you less than 30 days' notice, and I am sorry that unforeseen personal circumstances prevented adequate notice. However, please note that unless you make reasonable efforts to re-rent the unit at a fair rental, my liability for rent will terminate as of the date of my "abandonment." ORS 90.410(3).

Particularly if you are giving less than full notice, but also whenever you feel disposed to extend the courtesy to your landlord, it may be a good idea to inform the landlord of your schedule and how he or she can get in touch with you to arrange to show the place to prospective tenants.

One word of caution: Once you serve a termination notice, at least where it complies with the statutory notice period and under at least one court of appeal's decision even if it doesn't, the landlord may use your notice as the basis of an eviction action if you decide not to move after all. Therefore, weigh carefully the advantages of prompt notice in compliance with the statute against the risks of committing yourself to leaving before you're really sure. Of course, your landlord may be willing to agree to let you stay if you change your mind.

Although it is unlawful for a landlord to keep a deposit (but not a nonrefundable fee) on the grounds that a tenant failed to stay for a certain length of time,[4] the parties can agree that the tenancy will last for a specific term or that more than 30 days' notice is required to terminate the tenancy.

Examine your rental agreement before proceeding as outlined above, and modify your notice to comply with any provision requiring more than the statutory notice. I suspect that a court might not enforce any agreement that required a greater period of notice by the tenant than that required by the landlord.

b. BREAKING A LEASE

If your rental agreement provides for a tenancy for a specific period of time, such as six months or a year, you have a term agreement rather than a month-to-month or week-to-week tenancy. This is commonly referred to as a lease, although that word can also refer to any kind of rental agreement.

If you have a typical term agreement, you cannot terminate your tenancy before the end of the term by simply serving a termination notice appropriate to a month-to-month or week-to-week tenancy. Unless the provisions of your agreement give you some other right of termination, you must have a cause to terminate your tenancy or you may be liable for the rent for the remainder of the term if you leave before it's over.

This section explains when you have a right to terminate before the term is up and how to minimize your risks if you are forced to terminate early without a right to do so. Although I discuss term agreements, the principles involved also apply to terminating month-to-month and week-to-week tenancies with less than the statutory notice.

1. When do you have the right to terminate?

The Landlord and Tenant Act gives tenants a right to terminate a tenancy for cause under several circumstances. Perhaps the most important is the right to serve a "fix it or I'm leaving" notice if the landlord violates the rental agreement or the habitability section of the act.[5]

This termination device is available only for violations of ORS 90.320 or "material" (serious) violations of the rental agreement. The right does not exist if the conditions were caused by the deliberate or negligent acts of the tenant or a guest.[6]

To exercise this right, you must deliver a notice to the landlord that states your complaint and advises the landlord that your tenancy will terminate unless the problem is corrected. The termination date stated must be at least 30 days from the landlord's receipt of the notice. The landlord has 30 days in which to correct the problem unless your complaint is that you are not receiving an essential service, in which case the landlord must correct the problem within seven days. To be safe, you should deliver the notice in person. If you do mail the notice, note that you must allow three extra days to the deadlines, and the notice must say so. If the landlord remedies the violation, the tenancy does not terminate. If the landlord fails to cure the problem within the specified time, or if the problem is of a sort that is not "remediable by repairs, the payment of damages or otherwise," the tenancy ends on the termination date stated in the notice.

Some landlords have the idea that this provision authorizes them to take seven days to fix any essential services or 30 days to fix anything else. It does no such thing; it merely places a limitation on the tenant's right to terminate a tenancy because of the problem. It has no effect on the right of the tenant to seek damages, withhold rent, use the repair and deduct remedy, or get a court order to deal with this problem. In other words, only the termination "remedy" is affected by these periods.[7]

I treat this device as a means to terminate rather than as a means of obtaining repairs because it almost never produces repairs. In fact, this remedy embodies a slogan that is still popular with some landlords: "If you don't like it, why don't you move?" This remedy is useful if you want to leave and need to get out of a rental agreement before its term expires.

Sample #37 is an example of a notice designed for a situation that does not involve an essential service.

If you state your intention to pursue damages more strongly, it may increase your landlord's unwillingness to comply, and thus ensure that you will end up with a right to terminate. Here's an alternative ending paragraph if you want to try this approach:

> Whether or not you remedy the breaches of your obligations set forth above, I am entitled to damages for the reduction in rental value they have caused to date. I estimate my total damages to date to be $150. Unless you pay that sum within 10 days, I will pursue my rights under ORS 90.360(2).

SAMPLE #37
"FIX IT OR I'M LEAVING" NOTICE

March 27, 199-

Dear Mr. Fullbird:

I am presently your tenant at 456 Rental Ave., Apt. 4. You have violated our rental agreement by failing to supply the paint you promised so I could paint the living room, and you have failed to supply habitable premises as required by ORS 90.320 in that the roof leaks and several windows are missing panes of glass.

Unless you remedy these problems by April 30, 199-, our rental agreement will terminate on that date. In addition, I am free to pursue my remedies for appropriate damages under ORS 90.360(2) and (3).

Sincerely,

Thomas Tenant
Thomas Tenant

If an essential service is involved, you must advise the landlord that he or she has seven days in which to cure that problem. Sample #38 covers both kinds of problems. One problem with this device is that you don't know whether the landlord will deprive you of your termination right by making repairs until the last minute except in the case of essential services.

If your landlord actually tells you that he or she will not remedy the breach, that should be enough to give you the right to terminate, at least if you rely upon the landlord's

SAMPLE #38
"FIX IT OR I'M LEAVING" NOTICE
(Including essential services)

```
                                    March 27, 199-
Dear Mr. Fullbird:
    I am presently your tenant at 456 Rental Ave.,
Apt. 4. You have violated our rental agreement by
failing to supply the paint you promised so I could
paint the living room. You have also failed to
supply habitable premises as required by ORS 90.320
in that the roof leaks, several windows are missing
panes of glass, and I have no hot water because
the water heater is broken.
    I consider the lack of hot water to be a lack
of an essential service. Unless you restore hot
water within seven days of your receipt of this
notice, this tenancy will terminate as of April
30, 199-. Whether or not you restore hot water
within seven days, this tenancy will terminate on
April 30, 199- unless you remedy the other problems
by that date. April 30 allows three days for mailing
this notice. ORS 90.910(2).

                              Sincerely,

                              Thomas Tenant
                              Thomas Tenant
```

word and rent another place. In such a case, you should be able to terminate safely on the date indicated in your notice even if the landlord does make repairs after you have relied on his or her word that no repairs would be made. It's safest to confirm it in writing as shown in Sample #39.

Of course, you and your landlord may find it advantageous to agree in writing that you can break your lease in return for releasing the landlord from any liability to you for the violations that led to the termination. Sample #40 shows one way of doing it.

If your landlord does remedy the breach and you stay, but the same breach occurs again within six months, you may terminate by serving a notice at least 14 days in advance of the termination date, and you needn't give the landlord a further opportunity to preserve the tenancy by making repairs (see Sample #41).[8]

The Landlord and Tenant Act recognizes that some violations cannot be remedied by repairs, the payment of damages, or otherwise. In such a case, the landlord cannot save the tenancy, and a notice something like the one in Sample #42 is appropriate.

In addition to the "fix it or I'm leaving" remedy for habitability violations, the act provides tenants with an immediate right of termination in four situations:

(a) When the landlord causes a lockout or utility shutoff[9]

(b) When the landlord abuses the right of access[10]

(c) When the landlord threatens eviction, decreases services, or raises rent in retaliation for a tenant's complaints or tenants' union activities[11]

(d) When conditions at the premises, not the fault of the tenant, pose a serious and imminent threat to the health or safety of occupants within one year from the beginning of the tenancy[12]

SAMPLE #39
CONFIRMATION OF REFUSAL TO REPAIR

April 5, 199-

Dear Mr. Fullbird:

This will confirm your representation to me of this date that you have no intention of remedying the problems specified in my notice of March 27, 199-. I am relying on your representation and will look for another place.

Sincerely,

Thomas Tenant

Thomas Tenant

SAMPLE #40
SETTLEMENT BREAKING LEASE

It is hereby agreed by and between J. Fullbird, landlord, and M. Petard, tenant, that their dispute concerning the condition of Apt. 4, 456 Rental Ave., shall be finally resolved as follows:

1. M. Petard will vacate those premises on or before April 30, 199-, and the tenancy shall end as of that date.

2. J. Fullbird hereby releases M. Petard of any and all liability that might exist concerning the subject tenancy.

3. M. Petard hereby releases J. Fullbird from any and all liability that might exist concerning the subject tenancy.

April 5, 199- _____*J. Fullbird*_____ (Landlord)

April 5, 199- _____*Marie Petard*_____ (Tenant)

March 27, 199-

Dear Mr. Fullbird:

I am presently your tenant at 456 Rental Ave., Apt. 4. Within the last six months, I gave you notice of the following breaches by you of our rental agreement and ORS 90.320:

> leaky roof
> missing panes of glass
> lack of hot water

Although you remedied those problems within the time allowed, the following breach has now recurred:

> leaky roof

Pursuant to ORS 91.360, I hereby notify you that our rental agreement shall terminate on April 14, 199-. That date allows three days for mailing this notice (ORS 91.910(2)).

Sincerely,

Thomas Tenant

Thomas Tenant

Although none of these grounds for termination expressly requires a written notice, and only the last requires "actual notice of the termination and the reason for the termination," it is safest to use one anyway to make a record of your position (see Sample #43).

If you use any of the devices outlined above to end your tenancy early and the landlord does not sue you for unpaid rent, you can pursue your remedies for damages by suing the landlord in district or circuit court (see chapter 6) or in small claims court (see chapter 4). Your bases for damages include those available if you were counterclaiming, as discussed in chapter 8.

SAMPLE #42
TERMINATION NOTICE
IRREMEDIAL VIOLATION

March 27, 199-

Dear Mr. Fullbird:

   I am your tenant at 456 Rental Ave., Apt. 4. The building inspector has informed me that the damage you did to the foundation of my house on March 26, 199-, cannot be repaired. Accordingly, I hereby give notice pursuant to ORS 90.360 that our rental agreement shall terminate of April 30, 199-. That date allows three days for mailing this notice (ORS 91.910(2)).

Sincerely,

Thomas Tenant

Thomas Tenant

SAMPLE #43
NOTICE OF TERMINATION FOR RETALIATION

March 27, 199-

Dear Mr. Fullbird:

   Because you have raised the rent and stopped paying for utilities in retaliation of my complaints to the building department, I hereby give notice that my tenancy at 456 Rental Ave., Apt. 4, will terminate on April 5, 199-, and I will pursue my other remedies for damages.

Sincerely,

Thomas Tenant

Thomas Tenant

If you terminate early and the landlord does sue you for unpaid rent, you should assert any claim for damages arising from the violation for which you terminated the tenancy (or from any other violations) as a recoupment and counterclaim. See chapter 6, section **f.**, and chapter 8, section **d.** In addition to defenses that are the same as those you might raise in a nonpayment of rent eviction, note that wrongful failure to refund a deposit can bring you twice the amount wrongfully withheld.[13] Note that if you had to move as a result of some legal proceeding the landlord was required to tell you about when you first rented the premises, you are entitled to twice the monthly rent or twice the actual damages (whichever is greater) and the return of all prepaid rent.[14] Note also that a landlord who wrongfully seizes and retains personal property of the tenant because of a rent dispute (or otherwise) forfeits the right to any unpaid rent and entitles the tenant to "up to twice the actual damages sustained by the tenant."[15]

In any event, you will not be required to pay rent into court.[16] In addition, the fact that you exercised a right of termination will constitute a defense to any rent claimed for a period after the termination date.

Finally, you may have additional defenses to rent claimed for periods after you left if your landlord failed to minimize his or her losses. These are discussed below because they are primarily useful to tenants who leave early with no right of termination.

2. Suppose you have no right to terminate?

Even if you must leave before the expiration of a term tenancy, there are several principles that may assist you in avoiding any liability for further rent.

(a) Your landlord must "mitigate" (minimize) losses.[17]

(b) Your landlord must make reasonable efforts to re-rent the premises at a fair rental; otherwise the rental agreement terminates as soon as he or she knows you've left.[18]

(c) You have the right to sublet or assign unless your rental agreement expressly provides to the contrary.

If you can find a new tenant willing to take over from you at the same rent and to stay for at least the unexpired portion of your term, you should be entirely free of any further rent liability unless the landlord has a good reason for not accepting the new tenant. A notice appropriate for such a situation is shown in Sample #44.

SAMPLE #44
NOTICE OF TERMINATION
AFTER FINDING NEW TENANT

March 31, 199-

Dear Mr. Fullbird:

I am presently your tenant at 456 Rental Ave., Apt. 4. Although I know my term does not expire before December 31, 199-, personal circumstances force me to break our rental agreement and to leave by April 30, 199-. I will do so.

The law requires that you either exercise reasonable efforts to re-rent the premises at a fair price or to accept a termination of the rental agreement as of the date of your notice of my "abandonment." ORS 90.410(3).

I have located a person who is willing to take over the remaining period of my tenancy at the same rent: Barry Roberts, who can be reached by telephone at 555-4567. I believe that you can have no reasonable basis for rejecting this tenant. If you fail to offer him a tenancy, my liability will terminate on April 30, 199-. If you accept him as a tenant, my liability will end as of the date on which his tenancy begins.

Sincerely,

Thomas Tenant

Thomas Tenant

If your landlord refuses to accept the new tenant, you should have a complete defense to rent for a period after you leave unless the landlord can convince a court that the refusal was reasonable. For example, a landlord who generally rents only to employed people can refuse to rent to the new tenant because that person has no job (this is not an unlawful basis of discrimination). If you fear that the landlord may have an argument that he or she had good reason to reject the new tenant, you can assign or sublet to the new tenant without the landlord's consent unless the rental agreement provides otherwise. With a sublease, the new tenant would pay rent to you, and you would pay the landlord. With an assignment, the new tenant would pay rent directly to the landlord. With both devices, however, you may be liable to the landlord for any rent the new tenant fails to pay during the rest of the term.

Finding a new tenant is the safest way to leave without a right of termination; it's even worth placing an ad if you have the time. Be sure that you are fair to the new tenant by disclosing the circumstances; you may even be liable in damages to that new tenant if there is trouble he or she could have avoided had you told the whole story.

Unfortunately, it may be impossible to find a new tenant on short notice. In such a situation, you should offer to make every possible accommodation to the landlord to help him or her to find a new tenant. For example, you might send a schedule of when you will be in to help show the property. You might replace the last paragraph in Sample #44 with something like this:

> Because we have a mutual interest in finding a new tenant, I will be glad to do everything possible to assist you. I will be happy to be available 9 a.m. to 9 p.m. Saturdays, Sundays, and Wednesdays to show the premises for the next few weeks. Please let me know if you want me to do this.

If you leave early without a right of termination and your landlord sues for unpaid rent, you may have a defense if you can show either that the landlord failed to make reasonable efforts to find a new tenant or that he or she unreasonably rejected a new tenant. Also, you may have the same remedies of recoupment and counterclaim available to a tenant who terminates with a right to do so, plus any of the additional defenses listed in the last section of this chapter.

Of course, you and your landlord may find a basis on which you can settle your claims against each other; but make sure you do it in writing.

11
WHAT TO DO WITH BELONGINGS LEFT BEHIND AND HOW TO GET THEM BACK

Because the Landlord and Tenant Act abolished the landlord's lien and distraint for rent, which used to permit landlords to seize a tenant's property until unpaid rent was paid, or to sell it to cover unpaid rent,[1] a landlord now has no claim for possession of the tenant's belongings except in three instances:[2]

(a) After an eviction judgment if the judgment has not been enforced and the tenant has been continuously absent for at least seven days after the judgment was signed

(b) After an eviction judgment has been enforced by a sheriff and the landlord has elected to be responsible for the belongings left by the tenant after the tenant has been put out of possession

(c) After an abandonment

This chapter discusses what a landlord should do with belongings under these circumstances and how a tenant can get them back. From the beginning, it is important to note that a landlord who cuts corners on the abandoned property procedures is taking a high risk. There is a chance that the tenant will sue for the "tort" known as "conversion" and recover punitive damages. One tenant recovered $6,000 in an Oregon case on this theory. The act also provides that a landlord who wrongfully seizes and retains a tenant's personal property (I won't give it back until you pay me the rent you owe) *forfeits* any right to unpaid rent and gives the tenant a claim for "up to twice the actual damages sustained by the tenant."[3]

a. WHAT LANDLORDS CAN DO

The legislature has made minor changes to the abandoned property section in all but one legislative session since its adoption in 1973. Each time, the objective was to make the procedures as practical as possible for landlords while preserving tenants' interests in retaining their belongings if at all possible. The general principle is that most possessions are going to be exempt under collection laws because there is a public interest in avoiding complete destitution on the part of the debtor. On the other hand, the landlord should generally be entitled to recover the costs of handling the property if that can be accomplished without depriving tenants of exempt property. The landlord must exercise due care to deal with the property for a prescribed period, must give notice to the tenant, and must allow the tenant to reclaim the goods within that period.

The landlord must make reasonable efforts to notify the tenant that unless the goods are reclaimed, they will be disposed of as provided for in ORS 90.425. The notice must be in writing, sent "by first class mail endorsed 'Please Forward' and addressed to the tenant's last-known address and to any alternate addresses known to the landlord."

The landlord must specify a date of disposal not less than 15 days after delivery of the notice to the tenant. If the tenant responds in writing on or before the date specified in the notice and indicates an intent to reclaim the goods, the landlord may not dispose of the goods until 15 days after the tenant's response or until the date specified in the landlord's notice, whichever is later.

After giving notice, the landlord must store the property in a safe place and exercise reasonable care for the property, except that the landlord may promptly dispose of rotting food and allow an animal control agency to remove any abandoned pets or livestock.[4]

191

With any of these versions of the abandoned property remedy, if the tenant fails to reclaim the goods during the required period, the landlord may sell them by private or public sale in the manner provided by ORS 79.5040(3). (If you need a copy of the statutes, see page xiv of the Introduction.) The landlord may deduct from the sale the costs of notice, storage, and sale, as well as any unpaid rent; the balance (if any) goes to the tenant with an accounting. If the tenant cannot "after due diligence" be found, the net proceeds must be paid to the county treasurer to be held for three years, and will revert to the general fund if unclaimed.[5]

If the landlord reasonably determines that the value of the goods is so low that the proceeds of any sale would probably not cover the costs of storage and public sale, the landlord may destroy or otherwise dispose of the goods if the tenant has failed to claim them in the permitted time.[6] It may be dangerous for a landlord to keep the goods for his or her own use, should there be a later dispute over their worth.

The landlord is liable to the tenant for any loss arising from the landlord's negligence during storage. If the landlord deliberately or maliciously violates the tenant's rights under the abandoned property section, he or she is liable for twice the tenant's actual damages.[7]

1. After judgment

A landlord who gets an eviction judgment must still have the sheriff enforce the judgment if the tenant does not leave voluntarily after the judgment is signed (see chapter 8, section f.). However, the act permits the landlord to use abandoned property remedies if the tenant has been continuously absent from the premises for seven days after termination of a tenancy by court order that has not been executed.[8]

The landlord does not have the right to sell the goods to cover the costs of the eviction action, damages, or other expenses arising from the tenancy, and the tenant cannot be required to pay these charges as the cost of getting the goods back from the landlord. Only a sheriff (or civil process deputy) can sell goods to cover costs, and then only to recover the landlord's costs of suit, costs of enforcing the eviction judgment, and costs of storage and sale — unless the landlord has obtained a judgment awarding back rent or damages, in which case these items may be recovered from the sheriff's sale as well.[9]

As with truly abandoned property, the tenant who claims the property within the time permitted may be required to pay the costs of storage and removal (if the goods have been moved for safekeeping) before being allowed to retrieve them.

If the sheriff actually evicts the tenant, the landlord must make a choice. In order to have the goods sold to cover court costs (or damages or attorney's fees if these are included in a judgment), the landlord will have to have the sheriff be responsible for them by paying an amount sufficient to cover commercial moving and storage. Because most goods will simply be reclaimed by a tenant who files a claim of exemption, and because goods left behind are usually worth less than the cost of having them removed and stored (at least in terms of what they will bring at a sheriff's sale) most landlords now use a new provision to save money.

This option allows landlords to deal with the property themselves and to use the abandoned property procedure for holding the goods, notifying the tenant, and disposing of them if they are not reclaimed.[10] Everything works exactly as described in the previous section with one very important exception: if the tenant reclaims the goods within the time allowed, *the landlord may not require the tenant to pay costs of storage, removal, or anything else as a condition of taking back the goods.*[11] The reason for this is that there is no longer a sheriff or a court available to adjudicate any claim of exemption; because of the landlord's choice, it is presumed that the goods are all exempt, and that the tenant should get them all back without paying anything, just as would happen if the sheriff had seized the goods and a claim of exemption been filed.

Note that this doesn't let the tenant off free. The costs of storage and notice can be added to the judgment to be enforced if and when the tenant has any nonexempt assets.[12]

2. After the tenant has abandoned belongings

If the tenant leaves without a judgment and leaves property behind, the landlord may treat the property as abandoned only if the landlord reasonably believes under all the circumstances that the tenant has left the property (including motor vehicles) with no intention of asserting any further claim to the premises or to such personal property.[13] This means a landlord may not treat the property as abandoned if the landlord suspects the tenant may intend to come back for the property (or to continue to reside on the premises). For example, if you have a tenant arrested and know he or she is in jail for a week or so, you also know the tenant has not abandoned the premises just because he or she is gone.

If the property is truly abandoned, follow the procedures outlined above carefully.

b. HOW TENANTS CAN GET THEIR BELONGINGS BACK

Whether the landlord gets your belongings after execution of an eviction judgment or an abandonment, or the sheriff takes them when enforcing an eviction judgment, you should try to get them back as soon as possible.

Of course, the best solution to this problem is prevention: don't leave your goods behind. If you find yourself in this situation, however, your remedies vary, depending on who has your goods and how they got them.

1. When the sheriff has your goods after enforcement of a judgment

This circumstance is much less likely to arise now that landlords have the option of being responsible for the belongings and saving commercial moving and storage costs. If the goods are valuable enough to bring a substantial recovery to the landlord, or the landlord is determined to minimize the risk of being responsible for the goods, the landlord may well still pay the sheriff to have the goods inventoried, removed, and stored by a commercial moving company that acts as the sheriff's agent.

If the sheriff or a storage company has the goods after a lawful eviction, you should immediately file a "claim of exemption" with the sheriff (or civil process office) and mail a copy to the landlord; take the court name and number from the eviction papers you should have received.

If you were around when the eviction judgment was enforced, you should have received a notice listing your exemption rights and advising you that the sheriff has forms on which you can file your claim. You can also make your own, as shown in Sample #45.

Examples of typical things for which you might wish to claim an exemption as follows:

(a) Books, pictures, and musical instruments to the value of $150

(b) Wearing apparel, jewelry, and personal items to the value of $500

(c) A vehicle to the value of $800

(d) Household goods and furniture, radios, television set, and utensils to the value of $800, plus 60 days' supply of food and fuel for the family

(e) One rifle or shotgun and one pistol for each person over 16 years old

Note: For more detailed and extensive listings of exempt property, consult the Oregon Exemption Statutes. If you need a copy of the statutes, see page xiv of the Introduction.

You should file the original with the court clerk, with a proof of service attached, as shown in Sample #46. It is no longer *required* that you serve anyone but the clerk with a

```
          In the District Court of Oregon
                County of Multnomah
Larry Landlord,        )     No. __1234__
              Plaintiff,)      Claim of
                 vs.   )      Exemption
Terry Tenant,          )
              Defendant.)
   I, Terry Tenant, hereby claim as exempt the
following items seized under this court's execu-
tion in the above entitled matter:
   (List everything conceivably within the limits
of the ORS Chapter 23 provisions, the Oregon
Exemption Statutes, plus anything you suspect may
be exempt under other provisions of the law listed
on the notice served with the writ.)

Dated: July 25, 199-          Terry Tenant
                              Defendant
```

copy of your claim, but sending a copy to the sheriff directly may prevent a sale of your goods while the copy the clerk sends is on its way to the sheriff.

Find out from the court clerk when and where the court will hear your claim, and be sure to show up on time.

You cannot be required to pay storage charges from the date of eviction or costs of removal if a commercial storage company has the goods and the court finds the goods exempt.

The exemption statutes are designed to protect certain kinds of belongings from collection of a money judgment. The landlord's storage and removal costs are added to the money portion of the eviction judgment. Requiring the tenant to pay such costs as the price of reclaiming exempt property would defeat the purpose of the exemption statutes.

SAMPLE #46
PROOF OF SERVICE

State of Oregon

ss.

County of Multnomah

I, Terry Tenant, hereby say I served a true copy of the within Claim of Exemption upon the Sheriff of Multnomah County (Civil Process Office of Multnomah County) by personally delivering the same to his or her place of business at the county courthouse, and that I served a true and correct copy of the Claim of Exemption upon the plaintiff by mailing the same to the Plaintiff addressed as follows:

123 Monied Heights
Portland, Oregon

(Take name and address from the eviction papers.)

Terry Tenant
Defendant

Subscribed and sworn to before me this 1st day of July, 199-

B. Humblespirit, Jr.
B. Humblespirit, Jr.
Notary Public
My commission expires: August 31, 199-

You need not pay any back rent or damages claimed by the landlord or even the costs of suit or expenses of enforcing the eviction judgment to be entitled to reclaim exempt property. This is so even if the landlord has obtained a judgment for rent or damages.

If the claim of exemption doesn't work, find a lawyer and refer him or her to ORS 105.155 (Forcible Entry and Wrongful Detainer), and ORS Chapter 23 (Exemption), if he or she doesn't know what you are up to.

197

How much you will have to pay to recover nonexempt goods depends on whether the sheriff is holding them for sale. If not, you will just have to pay any removal and storage costs. If the sheriff has seized the goods for sale, you will have to pay storage costs, the landlord's court costs, and costs of enforcing the eviction judgment, and any sheriff's fees already incurred. If the landlord has a judgment for back rent or damages this, too, may have to be paid before you can get your belongings back. If you cannot afford to pay all this, your remaining hope (assuming there have been no mistakes by the landlord or the sheriff) is that you can buy your belongings cheaply at the sheriff's sale. Bear in mind, however, that the landlord is free to "bid in" the value of the judgment, leaving the landlord the owner of the goods (unless the landlord is outbid). Your major strength at this point is that the landlord typically doesn't want your goods; your landlord wants to be paid.

Note that the claim of exemption procedure also works when your landlord or most other creditors are attempting to collect a money judgment (such as for back rent). If you file the exemption claim soon enough in the case of garnisheed wages or a bank account, whoever has the money must get it to the court by the time of the exemption hearing or face the threat of contempt proceedings. But also note that if you have no reasonable grounds for believing the money in question to be exempt, *you* may be sanctioned by a $100 fine and liability for your opponent's attorney's fees.

2. When the landlord has your goods and claims you have abandoned them

If the landlord claims that you abandoned your goods, there may be an issue as to whether you really have. If you have not, the landlord must let you take them without making you pay anything, because he or she has no right to them. If a landlord seizes and retains a tenant's personal property without complying with ORS 90.425, the tenant is relieved of any liability for unpaid rent and may recover up to twice the actual damages sustained by the tenant.[14]

Even if you abandoned the goods, the landlord must give them back to you if you claim them before they are disposed of and you pay the costs of storage only. If the landlord has not get given or attempted to give you written notice (see section **a.** of this chapter), there is a strong argument that the landlord is not even entitled to storage costs.[15]

If the landlord claims a right to your goods because of abandonment, and if the goods are not in commercial storage, here are the steps you should take immediately:

(a) Go to the landlord with a witness, a copy of section 90.425 of the act, and cash in an amount representing rent for the period from the time the landlord took control of your goods until the time of your demand for them.

(b) In the presence of the witness, offer cash in an amount representing rent from the time of the landlord's notice under 90.425(1) to the time of your demand, and demand release of the goods. (If there is not yet a notice, demand the return of the goods and argue that storage charges don't accrue until the notice is given.)

(c) If the landlord refuses to release the goods, repeat the demand after offering rent for the entire period from the time the landlord took possession to the time of the demand.

(d) If the landlord still refuses read section **4.** below or see a lawyer.

If the landlord has the goods and refuses to honor the offer of step (b), the landlord may be guilty of "conversion" (wrongfully appropriating goods that don't belong to him or her). The landlord is almost certainly guilty of "conversion" if the demand made in step (c) is refused. You should be able to recover your belongings and damages in court. If your only interest is in getting your goods back as soon as possible, see section **4.** below. It describes a new procedure for a quick and easy court determination of who is entitled to the goods. If you want money damages, you will probably have to see a lawyer, and it's best if you see a lawyer in any event.

If the goods are in the custody of a commercial storage company, its charges will have to be paid before it will release anything, and its charges include the costs of removal. A lawyer may help you to establish that the goods were never abandoned and may convince the landlord to settle by bailing out your goods for you. Otherwise, you will probably have to pay the storage company and seek recovery against the landlord in small claims court or through your lawyer in a civil action in district, justice, or circuit court. Your last hope is that you can bid in the sale when the storage company eventually sells the goods to satisfy its storage lien. Remember that the landlord has no right to keep the goods for ransom for overdue rent or damages. If you receive a notice concerning the storage and disposal of "abandoned goods" under section 90.425(1), which is only likely if you left a forwarding address, respond promptly in writing as shown in Sample #47.

SAMPLE #47
RESPONSE TO LANDLORD'S NOTICE
CONCERNING ABANDONED GOODS

June 30, 199-

Dear Mr. Landlord:

In response to your notice of June 20, 199-, I hereby declare my intention to remove my belongings from your custody by July 3, 199-. I do not concede these goods were ever abandoned by me and do not waive any rights I may have against you for your having taken them from my control.

Sincerely,

Thomas Tenant

Thomas Tenant

Of course, leave out the last sentence if you concede abandonment, but the mere fact that you did not remove all of your belongings at once does not prove that you abandoned what you left behind. The second date in your response should be either 15 days from the date on which you give your response to the landlord, or the same date as specified in the landlord's notice, whichever is later. If you have any trouble, see a lawyer.

If you and your landlord can reach an agreement, put it in writing. Sample #10 in chapter 5 should give you the idea.

3. When the landlord has your goods after enforcement of an eviction judgment

This is probably the most typical context for cases of landlords holding tenants' belongings, apart from low-rent residential hotels which use illegal lockouts as a normal course of business. A landlord who has exercised the option to be responsible for your belongings after enforcement of an eviction judgment has done so to avoid the greater expense of having the sheriff responsible through a commercial moving and storage company. Taking the sheriff (and the courthouse) out of the picture leaves no one to adjudicate a claim of exemption, so the trade-off is that the landlord must give the property back without *any* deductions for court costs, rent, or anything else. This is only true if you demand return within the same time periods as for abandoned property, and you, in fact, remove the property within those limits.

The procedure is exactly the same as for abandoned property with two exceptions:

(a) You do not have to offer any payment to get the goods back if you are on time.

(b) There is an *additional* statutory penalty for a landlord who refuses to return property after a timely demand: the tenant may recover, in addition to any other amount provided by law, twice the actual damages or twice the monthly rent, whichever is greater.[16]

Therefore, you can use the same demand and witness as suggested for abandoned property in the last section, except that you don't need to offer the landlord any money and you should have a copy of ORS 105.165 as well as ORS 90.425 to make your point. Note that the landlord is entitled to add the costs of execution, removal (if any), and sale (if any) to the money portion of the judgment against you whether or not you recover your belongings.[17]

If your landlord has taken or withheld your property unlawfully and will not return it, your choices are the same as with property taken without an eviction judgment, depending on whether your priority is getting the goods back or getting a money judgment against the landlord. Read the last section of this chapter and, as always, it's best if you can see a lawyer.

4. A simple court action to get property back

One of the paralegals in the legal aid office I worked in before I became a judge suggested that there ought to be a court proceeding like an FED, but for tenants who just wanted their belongings back from a landlord who had them unlawfully. The result was ORS 105.112, which creates just such a process. The whole procedure runs just like an FED, except that the only issue is whether the tenant will receive the belongings. Just as with an FED, damages are not available, but attorney fees are.[18] Form complaints (for tenants) and answers (for landlords) are available in the clerk's office, and their language is designed to guide the parties and the court to a correct analysis of who is entitled to the property.[19]

To use the procedure, study the complaint form in ORS 105.112(2)(a). Read the paragraphs carefully, and decide which one applies to your situation. If you cannot find a paragraph that applies, you probably are not entitled to an order compelling the landlord to give you your belongings back. If you can, go to the clerk's office, pay your filing fees (or ask that they be waived on grounds of indigency as with an eviction answer), check the right paragraph, and fill out the rest of the form.

A landlord who is served with a complaint for return of personal property should study the answer form in ORS 105.112(2)(c). A landlord who cannot find a paragraph that applies probably has no defense. Both forms have a paragraph designated "Other" in case your facts are unique, but the forms were an attempt to lay out all of the applicable law for everyone's benefit. If both parties find paragraphs to check, the issues will be identified for trial.

If the court finds that the property should be returned to the tenant, the court should enter an order compelling the sheriff to seize the property and return it to the tenant. The court may permit the landlord a period of time in which to deliver the property to the tenant to avoid further fees. The costs and fees may be added to the judgment in favor of the prevailing party, who may also seek attorney fees if represented by counsel.[20]

12
GETTING ASSISTANCE

a. FINDING AN ATTORNEY

If you read this book thoroughly, you may know more about landlord and tenant law than most Oregon attorneys, but you will still need their skills in legal procedure to maximize your chances of success if a dispute reaches the unfortunate stage of litigation. Yet it would be foolish to entrust your legal rights to a lawyer who cannot or will not adequately assert those rights.

The safest way to proceed is to ask a trusted friend for advice on attorneys. Although it is always nice to get a specialist, largely because a specialist is most likely to recognize your rights and assert them with a minimum of wasted time and effort, an attorney with a general knowledge who is willing to talk to you on a level of equality (again, you may know some law he or she does not) may be just as good or better.

If you don't have a trusted friend who has a solid recommendation to make, you might try to get a recommendation from your legal aid office even if you're not eligible. Ask to speak with the lawyer who handles evictions. If that person is willing to give you the name of an attorney in private practice who is accomplished at representing tenants, you will probably have a hot tip. Understand, however, that your local legal aid attorneys are caught in something of a contradiction: local bar associations have often tried to restrict referrals for fear many private attorneys would be left out. On the other hand, there is no good reason why a legal aid lawyer should have less freedom to give you an honest answer to your question than does a private attorney.

Of course, if you are eligible for legal aid, you will have the mixed blessing of access to that legal aid lawyer yourself. The blessing is mixed because, although the legal aid lawyer is likely to be the most experienced attorney available for representing tenants, he or she may be too overworked to pay much attention to your case before it reaches the critical stage of an eviction action. The more preparatory work you can do yourself, the better.

A few legal aid programs sponsor volunteer lawyer panels; in Multnomah County, the Volunteer Lawyers Project (224-1606) can sometimes find a low-income tenant a lawyer. Some localities now also have low-cost legal clinics, such as the White Bird Clinic in Lane County (342-8255). Law schools sometimes provide client representation as a teaching device, and the Lewis and Clark Legal Clinic (affiliated with Northwestern School of Law in Portland) does some landlord and tenant work (222-6429).

Still no luck? Thanks to recent changes in rules governing attorney advertising, lawyers are now permitted to list their specialties in the Yellow Pages. This change was the product of a fairly recent United States Supreme Court opinion that required that state bars stop prohibiting advertising.

So far, those who advertise have not told the public whether they represent tenants. The most help you will get from the Yellow Pages now is that some attorneys list "landlord/tenant" among their specialties. Whether such a lawyer represents tenants can only be determined by asking. As lawyers get used to advertising, and as more and more of them become active in this field, those who represent tenants should start saying so in the telephone book.

The Oregon State Bar does offer some assistance. You can reach the bar's Lawyer Referral Service toll-free from anywhere in the state by calling 800-452-7636 (224-6580 in the Portland area). Ask for a landlord/tenant specialist. You will find that most of the attorneys listed this way represent landlords. I suggest that you find out right away whether the lawyer represents tenants. Although there are attorneys who can do a good job for either side, I would hesitate to entrust a case to an attorney who had never actually handled my side of a dispute. If you find a listed attorney who seems worth talking to, the first visit will cost you $35 at present, but once you get the lawyer's telephone number you may be able to arrange a visit for free if you have a good case for damages (and a contingent fee arrangement). You should know at the end of the appointment whether you want to hire that attorney, give up, or keep looking.

There are a few private lawyer referral agencies springing up. Their ads may imply that they guarantee a qualified attorney, but the only qualification they require is paying a fee to be listed and surviving as a lawyer for a few years. In common with the bar itself, these agencies don't guarantee you will see a more qualified lawyer than if you picked up the Yellow Pages and selected one without their help.

Finally, a nonprofit organization, Oregon Prepaid Legal Insurance, Incorporated, is now selling legal insurance which, in many ways, is very much like medical insurance. In return for a monthly premium, insured people are entitled to limited amounts of certain kinds of legal services, including several hours per year of advice and consultation and several hundred dollars' worth of civil defense services, including eviction defense.

So far, the insurance is available only on a group basis and must be purchased by employees, unions, or other groups of at least 10 members. Larger groups can buy it on a voluntary basis (not all members of the group have to buy it), and there is some room for modifying benefits to suit the needs of your group. You can get information by calling 227-2501 (they will accept collect calls).

There are places you can call for landlord/tenant legal information even if they can't provide you with a lawyer.

Legal aid offices commonly provide this service to low-income people. The Multifamily Housing Council runs a landlord/tenant hotline for tenants and landlords. (They are a landlord's organization, but their advice has been sound for both sides. They may even suggest rent withholding before legal aid would!) You can reach them at 378-1912.

The bar association sponsors a "Tel-Law" program that plays you the tape of your choice over the telephone — not bad for a general overview, but unlikely to answer a specific question except by accident. That program can be reached at 1-800-452-4776 state-wide, or at 248-0705 in the Portland area.

b. TENANTS' UNIONS

Typically, a tenants' union is organized on a neighborhood, city, or other geographical basis, or with respect to a common landlord. The objectives of a tenants' union may be to improve tenants' rights generally through legislation or regulations, or to use combined economic power to demand collective bargaining from a common landlord. A tenants' union is likely to be the most effective means of enforcing any rights of tenants and most of the remedies discussed in this book may be used by tenants working together. This kind of organization is likely to seek such goals as —

(a) security of possession,

(b) tenant participation in rule-making,

(c) limitations on rent increases, and

(d) repairs.

You should know that tenants' unions are perfectly legal and have the sanction of section 90.385:

> Except as provided in this section, a landlord may not retaliate by increasing rent or decreasing services, by serving a notice to terminate the tenancy or by bringing or threatening to bring an action for possession after: ...

(c) The tenant has organized or become a member of a tenants' union or similar organization.

Subject to the limitations discussed in section **b.** of chapter 8, a landlord should not win an eviction action if the tenant establishes that the motive for the eviction was to retaliate against the tenant for tenants' union activities.

Tenants' unions are becoming common among college students. Public housing tenants are entitled to assistance in forming a tenants' association if one does not already exist (see section **a.** of chapter 13). A state-wide organization for mobile home tenants, the Oregon State Tenants' Association, has successfully sponsored mobile home bills in every session of the legislature since 1977. (OSTA can be reached at 3791-B River Road North, Salem, Oregon, 97303, telephone 393-7737.) Starting with the 1985 session, OSTA was joined in its efforts by the Mobile Home Owners' Association, another state-wide advocacy group for mobile home tenants. (MHOA can be reached at P.O. Box 325, Tualatin, Oregon, 97026, telephone 682-1659.)

The materials listed in Appendix #1 should help you find out more about tenants' unions.

Although the services of an attorney can be invaluable for achieving some sense of power as an organizational aid, you should never allow your organization to depend too heavily on your lawyer. It cannot survive for any substantial length of time unless its members achieve and preserve their own sense of direction and purpose. Besides, lawyers are inherently conservative about tactics because they are trained to foresee the worst possible risks and to avoid them as completely as possible. Ask your organization's lawyer about the risks, but make sure he or she doesn't take part in deciding whether those risks are worth taking.

c. ELDERLY RENTAL ASSISTANCE

As predicted in the last edition of this book, the legislature ended the Home Owner and Renter Refund Program in response to the 1989 Proposition 5 tax limitation measure. The Elderly Rental Assistance Program remains, however, and its benefits have been somewhat improved. You are entitled to this assistance if you meet all of the following criteria:[1]

(a) You are 58 or older by the end of the year immediately preceding the year in which assistance is claimed.

(b) Your annual income is less than $10,000.

(c) Your total rent for the year (not including deposits) plus fuel and utility payments (except for telephone bills) is more than 20% of your household income.

(d) You file an appropriate claim with the Department of Revenue.

The amount of the rental assistance payment is the difference between your rent and 20% of your income *unless* you would receive a greater payment under the schedule modified for the last year of the HARP program. Now that the HARP program has been terminated, the schedule is relevant only for Elderly Rental Assistance purposes.[2] It provides for a payment of $500 for persons whose annual household income does not exceed $499, with smaller payments for higher incomes ending with $18 for persons whose household income does not exceed $9,999.[3] If you are eligible, you should receive the amount determined under the HARP schedule if it is the greater amount.

Contact the Department of Revenue for more information on the Elderly Rental Assistance program.

13

FEDERAL HOUSING PROGRAMS

Although there are many types of federally supported housing, for convenience, in this chapter I have divided them into public housing, subsidized housing, and leased housing. Before treating them separately, here are features they have in common.

Most important, the federal government seems to have abandoned the objective of ensuring an adequate supply of decent housing for low-income people. Instead of allotting more money to expand the inadequate supply of federal housing, Congress adopted legislation designed to reduce the cost of operating existing programs by keeping poor people out! Congress has allowed wealthier low-income tenants to displace the poorest people on waiting lists, raised maximum income limits for eligibility, and permitted rent increases.

This regressive legislation is called the Housing and Community Development Act of 1974. It hurts federal housing tenants who must now pay a larger portion of their incomes as rent, and it hurts those who will be excluded from federal housing by the new eligibility standards. It also hurts all tenants, because it increases competition for a dwindling supply of low-rent housing in the private sector.

This trend has continued since 1974, and the federal government has drastically reduced the amounts it spends to subsidize private developers who wish to build new (or rehabilitate existing) housing for low-income people. Congress has also started to create "voucher" programs that may altogether evade traditional limits on the proportion of income poor people have to pay as rent.

A second feature that these types of federal housing have in common is that many of the rights of tenants are codified in constantly changing regulations published in the Code of Federal Regulations (CFR) or, in the case of the most recent regulations, the Federal Register (FR). The rights of these tenants exist primarily as a result of many cases brought against the Department of Housing and Urban Development (HUD) in which federal courts found that HUD was violating its duties under federal statutes. The lesson here is that the rights of federal tenants, like the rights of all tenants, will be honored, enforced, or improved only to the extent that tenants are willing to assert their rights vigorously. Do not assume that federal landlords of any description know the law or that they will obey the law when compliance is expensive unless someone makes a meaningful request.

The third feature these programs share is that the most comprehensive and comprehensible source of information about them is available in a publication of the National Housing Law Project, 1950 Addison Street, Berkeley, California 94704. The publication is "HUD Housing Programs, Tenants' Rights." It has occasional supplements, and is an essential tool for anyone seriously interested in exploring or enforcing federal housing tenants' rights.

In general, federal programs have substantial limitations on the amount a tenant must pay as rent, they limit the grounds on which a tenant can be evicted, and they impose additional obligations on participating landlords. All of these attributes may provide a defense to an eviction that would be unavailable without federal involvement.

a. PUBLIC HOUSING[1]

Public housing projects are constructed and managed by a "local housing agency" organized under state law with obligations

211

under both state and federal law. The Landlord and Tenant Act applies to housing authorities, but authorities are also bound by an "annual contributions contract" with HUD as well as by HUD circulars, directives, and regulations, not to mention the Housing Act itself.

For some reason, housing authorities are not listed in the telephone book under government listings, perhaps because they don't fit into the city/county/state hierarchy. (A local government body may make itself a housing authority or create an independent agency.) They are listed in the white pages under "Housing Authority of _____."

Public housing gives people with incomes of up to 80% of the median income in a particular area an opportunity to rent inexpensive units. The rents of these units are limited by federal law and based on income. The low-income housing market is so tight that there are almost always waiting lists that are months or even years long for "family" projects. If you are offered a place at all, it is likely to be the least desirable public housing around. Find out if you lose your place in line, or even your eligibility, by turning down one or more units.

Public housing designed for senior citizens tends to be considerably more desirable than that available to families, and it may be easier to come by if you're eligible.

Public housing tenants are entitled to have a written lease listing many of the rights given in the Landlord and Tenant Act, and adding certain other rights:

(a) Regular redetermination of rent to assure that a tenant will not pay more (or less) than that permitted by federal law (generally 30% of adjusted income)[2]

(b) Rent abatement in case the housing authority fails to make major repairs under certain circumstances[3]

(c) An informal conference and an administrative hearing before most kinds of eviction (although HUD has repeatedly proposed rules that would undercut this right)[4]

(d) Security of possession: a tenant cannot be evicted, or denied a lease renewal, without good cause[5]

All of these rights can help many public housing tenants who are threatened with eviction. The right to an informal conference and to a grievance hearing means that the tenant will have two opportunities to win before going to court. The housing authority may require that the tenant continue to pay rent in order to have a grievance hearing; if rent is in dispute, it will be paid into a special account until after the hearing determines how much is due. Also, a housing authority may exclude from its grievance procedures an eviction based on a tenant's "creation or maintenance of a threat to the health or safety of other tenants or housing authority employees."

For example, a tenant who receives an eviction notice for holding loud parties should find that the notice advises him or her of rights to an informal conference and to a formal grievance hearing, if the tenant requests them promptly. At the conference, the tenant may convince the housing authority representative that the parties were not loud enough to justify an eviction. Although the conference may end the matter with a warning to avoid loud parties in the future, the tenant may also simply lose. If so, and if the tenant continues to pay the rent, he or she can make the same argument at a formal grievance hearing. If the tenant loses again, the housing authority will still have to go through a court eviction action to evict him or her, just as if the tenant had ignored the right to a conference and an administrative hearing. If a hearing was held, the housing authority must serve a new eviction notice before going to court.[6] In court, the tenant will be able to make the same arguments that he or she may have made earlier.

A tenant who is unable or unwilling to continue paying rent to be entitled to a grievance hearing, or who simply fails to request one within the short time allowed, may still defend the eviction action in court. In fact, the rights of public housing tenants may create defenses to eviction that are unavailable to most private tenants.

In any kind of eviction action, a public housing tenant may find that any of the following circumstances will constitute a defense:

(a) The eviction notice failed to state a reason for the eviction, the reason stated was improper, or the reason was not stated with specificity (it is not enough merely to restate the lease provision in question).

(b) The eviction notice failed to advise the tenant of a right to an informal conference and to a grievance hearing.

(c) The housing authority failed to afford the tenant an informal conference or, unless the tenant refused to pay rent pending the hearing, a grievance hearing (if the tenant made a prompt request for this), or the eviction is based on the tenant's threat to the health or safety of other tenants or housing authority employees.

In addition, a public housing tenant may have the following defenses to a nonpayment of rent eviction:

(a) The rent claimed exceeds the permissible maximum under federal law according to the tenant's income.

(b) The rent claimed was abated because of the authority's refusal to make repairs, as provided by the tenant's lease.

In an eviction for cause, the tenant may find provisions of the lease give rise to a defense. If the reason for the eviction doesn't fit those given by the Landlord and Tenant Act, it cannot support an eviction unless it constitutes a material (i.e., serious) violation of the tenant's obligations under the lease.

Finally, a public housing tenant cannot be evicted without cause, and this should be a complete defense to any no-cause eviction.

Remember that these rights and defenses are in addition to those that the tenant has under state law, as discussed in the rest of this book.

Public housing tenants also have some rights that may be useful even if they don't help in defending evictions. Under Oregon law, public housing tenants are entitled to at least one position on a housing authority board or commission, unless the governing body of a city or county has taken on the powers of a housing authority without creating a separate entity, or unless the authority has neither 75% nor 25 of its units occupied.[7]

Another important privilege of public housing tenants is that housing authorities are supposed to encourage and support tenant's associations, and the concept of tenant *management* has even become accepted.[8] Authorities are authorized to assist such associations financially. In some localities, public housing tenants' associations wield some real power in negotiating leases and in influencing the spending of "modernization" funds.

Another project that a public housing tenants' association might undertake is to enforce federal limitations on how much a housing authority can charge for utilities. Because of the expense involved, housing authorities tend to ignore those limits or to evade them by charging tenants for "excessive" utility usage that is really not excessive at all. The United States Supreme Court has recognized that tenants can sue for relief under federal law limiting utility charges by housing authorities.[9]

Generally speaking, public housing tenants have greater security of possession and rights of participation than any other tenants, but many of the units are undesirable, and it's hard to get in. This is not just because of the long waiting lists.

Applicants for public housing are now screened according to criteria suggested by HUD regulations. Although a housing authority's admission policy shall not "automatically deny admission to a particular group or category of otherwise eligible applicants" (e.g., unwed mothers or families with children born out of wedlock), the regulations are otherwise obviously designed to give local housing authorities ample excuses for denying public housing to precisely those applicants who most desperately need low-rent housing. An applicant's past performance in meeting financial obligations, especially rent, is the first suggested criterion. It is obvious that some people have no idea what poverty is all about!

An applicant who is denied eligibility for public housing is entitled to be told and to be given the opportunity to have an informal hearing on the denial.[10]

Projects designed for elderly or handicapped tenants (in whole or in part) must permit pets, subject to reasonable regulation.[11]

b. SUBSIDIZED HOUSING

I use "subsidized housing" to include multi-family low-rent housing constructed or operated with the assistance of a federal subsidy, direct or through a state agency, in the form of low-interest construction loans, mortgage assistance payments and/or payments supplementing the rent paid by tenants.[12] Most of these projects are privately owned by nonprofit or limited profit corporations or similar organizations, but these are frequently really tax shelters for wealthy investors. Some projects are owned by HUD, usually after tax considerations have led private investors to default.

Like public housing authorities, owners of subsidized projects have obligations under federal law and under their contracts. Local projects can be found by contacting the nearest area office of HUD, which is listed in the phone book under "U.S. Government."

216

Although subsidized housing tenants don't have a right to a full administrative grievance procedure, many have the right at least to a less formal procedure before having to face a court.[13] Most are entitled to detailed eviction notices and security of possession, as well as the right to insist on good cause for eviction (or nonrenewal) along lines very similar to the rights of public housing tenants.[14] Many also enjoy minimal participation rights when the project owner seeks HUD concurrence in rent schedule adjustments.[15] Note that tenants often want the "fair market rents" to go *up*, because this gives the owner more to work with without necessarily affecting the amount paid by tenants as their share of the rent.

Again, tenants in subsidized housing enjoy all the rights and defenses of private tenants. In addition, they often have defenses to eviction if their subsidized landlord fails to comply with procedural or substantive provisions of federal law.

Finally, there is also great potential for organized subsidized housing tenants to have some control over the management of their projects.

c. LEASED HOUSING[16]

Leased housing programs have varied over the years, but they have always involved private landlords willing to rent to eligible tenants. The tenant pays a limited rent calculated on the basis of income, and the federal government makes up the difference.

Leased housing programs are administered by public housing authorities in areas that have such an authority; otherwise the programs are administered directly by HUD.

To qualify for this kind of housing, a tenant's family income must not exceed 80% of the median for the locality. If you are eligible, you must apply to your local housing authority or to HUD for a Section 8 Certificate. These are distributed to eligible applicants in limited numbers, depending on the amount of money available at the time in your area.

Once you have the certificate, you have a limited amount of time in which to find a willing landlord and a dwelling that meets HUD's criteria.

The landlord must be willing to sign a lease with substantially limited powers of termination. Generally, the landlord must have good cause to terminate (the lease has no definite term; that is, there is no fixed expiration date). After the first year, however, the landlord can terminate for a wider range of "good cause," such as a business or economic reason or the desire to use the unit for personal or family use or for a purpose other than use as a residential rental unit.[17] The dwelling must have an amount of space HUD deems adequate for a family of your size, and it must comply with applicable federal regulations. Those regulations amount to a simplified federal housing code, covering most of the same requirements as Oregon's habitability statute plus such details as adequate lighting and the absence of lead-based paint.[18] Finally, the total rent must be within the limits established by a HUD schedule for your area.[19]

A landlord who wants to evict a Section 8 tenant must notify the public housing authority (or HUD, if there is no housing authority). The tenant has no right to a hearing with the housing authority, unless it is the housing authority that is proposing to deny or terminate the tenant's subsidy.[20] On the other hand, if the tenant notifies the housing authority and there was no serious damage to the premises, the tenant should be able to keep the certificate to use at a new rental unit.

The tenant has a limited period to find new housing following an eviction (or if the tenant decides to move on his or her own) because the Section 8 certificate applies to the tenant, not the house.

Legal aid attorneys convinced the Portland Housing Authority that it must give hearing rights to leased housing tenants before approving eviction or revoking a Section 8 certificate. Litigation may further expand the rights of leased housing tenants.

These procedures for eviction and moving do not apply to "Section 8 New Construction" or "Section 8 Substantial Rehabilitation" projects. As their names imply, these projects were built or rehabilitated with federal assistance. They are a form of subsidized housing; the rights of tenants in these projects are the same as those in other subsidized housing, as discussed in the previous section.

A landlord's failure to comply with the notice requirements of the regulations may provide a leased housing tenant with additional defenses to an eviction of any kind. A tenant cannot be evicted without cause. If you show that a non-renewal was retaliatory (see chapter 8), you should be able to defeat an eviction even if the landlord claimed a cause that could be sufficient without a retaliatory motive.

You should be able to defend a nonpayment of rent eviction if you can show that you are being charged an amount that exceeds permissible limits. If HUD isn't paying its share, an attorney may be able to bring them into the eviction action. You may have a defense if the rent was raised by HUD without giving you at least an opportunity to object in writing.

Newer "voucher" programs may ultimately replace existing approaches to leased housing subsidies. In essence, these programs involve an income supplement to assist tenants to pay for housing, but will probably cost tenants more for rent while assuring them less procedural and substantive protection than the Section 8 Existing Housing program.[21]

14

MOBILE HOME TENANCIES

Some provisions of the Landlord and Tenant Act (ORS 90.500 to 90.840) apply only to mobile and floating homes owned by the tenant and located in a space rented in a "manufactured dwelling" "facility" (what used to be called a mobile home park) or a moorage "facility." In addition, mobile and floating home owners are entitled to the benefits of all of the provisions of the Landlord and Tenant Act except those "which reasonably apply only to the structure that is used as a home, residence or sleeping place..."[1] In other words, the landlord is not responsible for the mobile or floating home that you own.[2]

If you need a copy of the act, see page xiv of the Introduction.

All mobile home tenants should know of two state-wide organizations devoted solely to the rights of mobile home tenants:

Oregon State Tenants' Association
3791-B River Road North
Salem, Oregon 97303

Mobile Home Owners' Association
P.O. Box 325
Tualatin, Oregon 97026

OSTA has a full-time staff working on legislation, a monthly newsletter, and local chapters in many areas of the state. MHOA grew out of the closure of three mobile home parks in Washington County.

a. THE RENTAL AGREEMENT

The law requires that mobile and floating home tenants be provided with a written rental agreement that specifies the following:[3]

(a) The location and size of the rented space

(b) Whether the facility is "older person housing" for purposes of the federal Fair Housing Act (see chapter 15)

(c) The rent per month

(d) All personal property, services, and facilities to be provided by the landlord

(e) All rules and regulations which, if violated, may be cause for eviction

(f) All refundable deposits, nonrefundable fees, and installation charges imposed by the landlord or governmental agencies

(g) Improvements that the tenant may make to the rental space, including plant materials and landscaping

(h) Provisions for dealing with improvements to the rental space at the termination of the tenancy

(i) Any limitations the landlord applies in approving a purchaser of a mobile home as a tenant in the event the tenant elects to sell the mobile home. Such limitations may include, but are not limited to, pets, number of occupants, credit references, character references, and criminal records

(j) That the tenant shall not sell the tenant's mobile or floating home to a person who intends to leave the mobile home on the rental space until the landlord has accepted the person as a tenant

(k) The term of the tenancy

(l) The process by which the rental agreement or rules can be changed

(m) The process by which notices shall be given by either the landlord or the tenant

Conversion form oral to written agreements continues to create many disputes between mobile home tenants and park operators. The problem arises when the operator (often a new owner or manager) presents tenants with a proposed rental agreement that seems to give the management more rights and the tenants fewer rights than the tenants thought they had under the previous arrangement — typically in the area of rent increases, sales of mobile homes, and park rules. When this occurs in the context of recent rent increases and outstanding maintenance complaints, trouble is common.

The 1987 legislature directed the Housing Division to study the need for an alternative dispute resolution device for mobile home controversies and report to the 1989 legislature. The 1989 legislature responded with a law that created a "Mobile Home Park Ombudsman" within the state's Housing Agency. The position is funded by a periodic assessment on mobile home spaces. The Ombudsman is to assist mobile home parks to establish an informal dispute resolution procedure (parks are directed to adopt such a procedure), and requires the inclusion of arbitration or mediation clauses in mobile home rental agreements.[4] Neither side, however, can be compelled to submit to arbitration or mediation of disputes concerning park closure, sale of a park, or rent disputes — precisely the disputes that are most typically troublesome. The law also modifies the FED statutes to provide for enforcement of an arbitration clause in the context of an eviction action, but this cannot result in a delay of more than 30 days without the parties' agreement.[5]

The 1991 legislature added some language which retroactively legitimizes "month-to-month" mobile home tenancies. I say retroactively because the concept of "good cause eviction" connected to mobile home tenancies since 1977 is really inconsistent with a month-to-month tenancy, because

222

the essence of a month-to-month tenancy is that either side can terminate without cause on 30 days' notice. When the legislature first passed the mobile home portions of the Landlord and Tenant Act, it left landlords with no way to modify or terminate a rental agreement unless there was cause for termination or the rental agreement itself had an expiration date. "Month-to-month" agreements were left in limbo. The 1991 legislation requires landlords to adopt a written policy, covering essentially the same ground as the required rental agreement plus "facility policy" covering rent "adjustments," zoning, sale of the facility, and dispute resolution.[6] The written rental agreement and facility rules must be attached to the policy and given to new tenants as they enter. Existing tenants "who are on month-to-month rental agreements" shall get the policy with the next 90-day rent increase notice.[7]

This change may be intended to allow mobile home landlords with "month-to-month" tenancies to change their provisions unilaterally by announcing the change with a rent increase notice. If so, this provision greatly undermines the security of possession won by mobile home tenants in 1977 — at least for those whose landlords continued to call tenancies "month-to-month." Perhaps the legislature simply did not foresee the possibility of a landlord using this provision to make such a basic modification of the tenant's agreement as to make the tenant unable to remain.

b. CONDITIONS OF OCCUPANCY

No mobile home landlord may impose conditions of rental or occupancy that unreasonably restrict the tenant or prospective tenant in his or her choice of mobile or floating home dealers, fuel suppliers, furnishings, goods, services, or accessories. A landlord may not give preference to a tenant who purchased a mobile or floating home from a particular dealer, and a dealer cannot require a purchaser to rent space at a particular facility or group of facilities.[8]

c. TERMINATION

A tenant may terminate a mobile or floating home agreement by giving at least 30 days' written notice, and a rental agreement may not set a termination date of less than 30 days after the parties enter into the agreement. Also, a tenant may not be required to give more than 30 days' notice.[9]

A landlord may terminate a mobile or floating home space rental prior to any termination date provided in the agreement only for cause. This can occur in the three following situations:[10]

(a) If the tenant violates a law or ordinance that relates to the tenant's conduct as a tenant, or if the tenant violates a valid rule, the landlord may serve a written notice specifying a termination date at least 30 days from the service of the notice. If termination is based on violation of a rule, it must be one that the rental agreement specifies as a rule that, if violated, may be cause for eviction. In any event, the notice must set forth facts sufficient to notify the tenant of the reasons for termination. The tenant can avoid termination by curing the violation within the 30-day period. However, if the violation recurs within 6 months, the landlord may terminate by serving at least 20 days' written notice specifying the violation and the termination date.[11]

(b) A landlord of a mobile home park or moorage facility who wants to close the facility or a part of it which includes a mobile or floating home space and convert the land or moorage to another use may terminate the rental agreement by giving the tenant at least 365 days' notice in writing.[12] The landlord may terminate on 180 days' notice (only to close the park for a different use) if the landlord finds a space acceptable to the tenant to which the tenant can move the mobile home, and the landlord pays the cost of moving and setup expenses not exceeding $3,500.[13] In practice, this will probably mean only that the landlord is free to make a deal with a tenant who is willing to accept cash to move more quickly; if the tenant *agrees* to move more quickly than 365 days (or 180 days), the agreement is not illegal (as long as the right to extended notice wasn't purportedly waived in advance).

A landlord may not increase rent to offset payments to be made to get a tenant to move more quickly, and a landlord may not increase the rent for any reason after giving a park-closure notice under this section. Note, however, that none of this applies to land taken by the government through eminent domain.[14]

(c) If the tenant fails to pay the rent, or the landlord has other *cause* to evict under the Landlord and Tenant Act, the landlord may use the same procedures available to all landlords under the Landlord and Tenant Act and the eviction statutes.[15] The whole point of all this is to free mobile home tenants of evictions without cause (typically on a 30-day notice), not to remove the right of landlords to evict for a reason that the law and the rental agreement recognize as sufficient grounds for termination. Of course, the same defenses are available (see chapter 8). Remember that the written rental agreement must specify all rules and regulations that, if violated, may be cause for eviction.[16]

The upshot is that a mobile home tenant has security of possession prior to any termination date specified in the rental agreement unless the tenant gives the landlord some cause to evict or the landlord wants to go out of business. At the same time, the tenant is always free to terminate on 30 days' written notice.

The 1991 legislature completed the task of renaming all mobile homes "manufactured dwellings." In fact the words "mobile home" and "mobile home park" do not appear in the

225

mobile home provisions at all — everything is a "manufactured home" or "manufactured dwelling" and "parks" are now "facilities."[17] From the perspective of tenants, this brought with it some good news and some bad news. The good news is that the same legislation cured any prior mistaken omission of "floating homes" from the protections of the mobile home provisions of the Act. [Maybe by the next edition I can bring myself to calling mobile homes "manufactured dwellings," but I haven't quite adjusted yet.] It is clear that floating homes are protected by the good cause eviction provisions of ORS 90.630. The bad news, at least from the perspective of some tenants, is that landlords may be free to modify so-called "month-to-month" agreements as discussed in subpart **a.** of this section; the special protections are now limited to tenants of mobile or floating homes in facilities; and people living in converted school busses or recreational vehicles (or any "do-it-yourself" conversion) are expressly excluded from the mobile home provisions of the Act. For a mobile home to be covered by the "manufactured dwelling" provisions, it must be one of the following: (1) a residential trailer constructed before 1962 for movement on public highways with sleeping, cooking and plumbing facilities, intended for human occupancy, and used for residential purposes; (2) a mobile home constructed between January 1, 1962, and June 15, 1976, in accordance with Oregon mobile home law in effect at the time of its construction; or (3) a manufactured home constructed in accordance with federal manufactured housing construction and safety standards in effect at the time of its construction.[18]

So what happens to the mobile home owner who rents space outside a "facility" or a tenant who rents a space (whether or not in a facility)? Both continue to be covered by the portions of the Act which apply to all tenants. The only remaining special protection for any of these tenants is a new provision which requires a 180-day notice for a landlord to terminate a month-to-month rental agreement for a manufactured dwelling or floating home space not located in a facility.[19] This doesn't do anything for people renting a space for a converted school bus (for example), and both sets of tenants excluded from the mobile home provisions by the 1991 legislature must look to general landlord tenant law (described in other chapters in this book) to determine when and how landlords can terminate.

d. RENT INCREASES

As noted above, a mobile home rental agreement must specify the amount of rent. A general section of the Landlord and Tenant Act provides that rent may not be increased without a 30-day written notice.[20] I think it's clear that this general provision is only a limitation on the power of landlords to raise rent *if they are otherwise free to do so.*

The usual basis for the right to raise rent is a provision of a rental agreement or the fact that a landlord may end a month-to-month (or other periodic tenancy) without a reason or for almost any reason at all. In a month-to-month tenancy, the 30-day written rent increase notice is the equivalent of notice that if the tenant does not agree, the tenancy will be terminated. In other words, a landlord cannot increase the rent at all if the parties have a *term* tenancy unless the rental agreement permits the landlord to do so. Although there may be some room for argument, mobile home tenancies should be treated like any other extended rental agreements in this respect.

Accordingly, a mobile home landlord must provide for rent increases in the rental agreement to be sure he or she has the power to raise rent at all during the tenancy. Also, a mobile home tenant who wants to be free of all doubt might ask for a provision specifying that rent will not be increased during the tenancy. In either event, the result might well be a formula permitting increases only to cover the landlord's increases in taxes and operating expenses, as discussed in chapter 3, section **b.**

As a practical matter, a landlord must be able to raise rent over time to cover increasing costs because only in this way can it remain economically possible for the landlord to continue to provide maintenance, services, and management critical to the tenants' interests. A legitimate policy objective, should the legislature seek to clarify this area, is to ensure that a tenant will understand from the outset (i.e., when making the decision whether to place a home in a mobile home park or floating home facility) whether and to what extent rent can be raised. It would be a simple matter to require such a clause in the rental agreement.

Assuming that the landlord has the right to raise rent (which is clearly the case if the rental agreement says something like "the lessor reserves the right to raise rent by giving written notice as provided by law"), there are still special procedures that must be followed in mobile and floating home tenancies. These are spelled out in detail in the statute,[21] but I will outline the procedure here:

(a) The landlord must serve written notice showing the amount of the increase, the new rent, and its effective date, which must be at least 90 days from the notice.

(b) The tenants must receive notice of an opportunity to meet with a representative of the landlord "for discussion," and the representative must be available at the time and place specified in the notice.

(c) The notice of an opportunity to "discuss" must be given with or after the notice of rent increase (but not less than 10 days before the time and place of the opportunity) *unless* the time and place is a regular office hour or regularly scheduled meeting (in which case the notice may be given in the rental agreement or at any other time from or after the inception of the rental agreement).

(d) If a tenants' association demands a meeting in writing within 10 days of the rent increase notice, a representative of the landlord must attend a meeting open at least to all tenants of the park, with written notice of

228

the time and place of the meeting (if such a meeting is held, the landlord need not also have individual "discussions").

All this means that tenants have at least the right to confront someone for an explanation or at least to hear their concerns. As expressly provided in the section, however, this requirement does not give a landlord a right to raise rent if that right doesn't already exist, and it does not require a landlord who has the right to raise the rent to compromise or reduce the rent increase.[22]

The 1991 legislature provided that unless the rental agreement provides otherwise, a facility landlord may bill separately for utility service fees and charges assessed "by the utility for services to or for spaces in the facility." If the landlord does so, the utility charges and fees are not considered part of the rent, and increases in these amounts are not subject to the rent raise provisions. Also, the legislature provided that the landlord's written statement of policy cannot be the basis for a challenge to a rent increase.[23]

e. RETALIATION

The language I proposed to the 1975 legislature to increase protection against retaliation for all tenants ended up instead in a section that applies only to mobile and floating home tenants.[24] That section provides that, in addition to the prohibitions of the general retaliation statute, a mobile or floating home landlord may not retaliate by increasing rent, decreasing services, or by bringing or threatening to bring an action for possession after —

(a) the tenant has expressed an intention to complain to a code enforcement agency,

(b) the tenant has made any complaint to the landlord in good faith,

229

(c) the tenant has filed or expressed an intention to file a complaint alleging unlawful discrimination with the Civil Rights Division of the Bureau of Labor, or

(d) the tenant has performed or expressed intent to perform any other act for the purpose of asserting, protecting, or invoking the protection of any right secured to tenants under any federal, state, or local law.

There is no good reason why the protection of this statute should not extend to all tenants, but for the present it is limited to mobile home tenants.

f. SALES OF MOBILE HOMES

A landlord cannot limit a tenant's right to sell a mobile home or forbid a tenant to place a "for sale" sign on or in the mobile home (within reasonable regulations). The landlord may require not more than 30 days' written notice before a sale and a written application from the buyer if the buyer wants to keep the mobile home on the rented space and become a tenant. The landlord may reject the buyer as a tenant, but only for a reason specified in the written rental agreement. The landlord must furnish both the buyer and the seller with a written statement of the reasons for any rejection.[25]

If the landlord accepts the tenant as a purchaser, the landlord must inform the purchaser at that time what conditions will be applied should the purchaser later sell the mobile home, and the conditions need not be the same as those reserved in the present lease, although they must be part of the buyer's rental agreement to be enforceable.[26]

This provision for gradual change is intentional; it balances the right of a tenant moving into a park to rely on the conditions disclosed at that time in selling the mobile home to a new tenant against the needs of park management to make changes over time. This comes up a lot in "upgrade" policies where owners try to weed out older homes, although it is not at all clear that an owner can rely on characteristics of the mobile home rather than those of the purchaser to screen a new tenant. Tenants are somewhat divided on this; I've met as many who want to protect older tenants living on a fixed income (if your buyer can't sell the home, it may not be worth much) as I have those who want to keep up the image of their communities.

If the landlord fails to require an application from a buyer who wants to stay on as a tenant or fails to act on an application within 20 days (or longer, if the landlord and prospective purchaser agree) —

(a) the landlord cannot recover damages based on the selling tenant's breach of the landlord's right to screen buyers as tenants;

(b) the buyer can occupy as a tenant under the same conditions and terms as applied to the seller; and

(c) the landlord cannot impose terms or conditions that are inconsistent with those applicable to the old tenant without the written consent of the buyer.[27]

Note that a buyer has a claim for damages or $100, whichever is greater, if the seller sells the home before the landlord has accepted the buyer as a new tenant or if the landlord rejects the buyer as a tenant and the seller knew the buyer wanted to stay on as a tenant.[28]

g. POLITICAL RIGHTS

Primarily as a result of disputes over tenant organizing rights, several laws have been adopted over the years to protect tenants' political rights in a mobile home park or floating home facilities. Essentially, these provisions echo constitutional rights to free speech and assembly, subject to reasonable regulation concerning time, place, and manner. Tenants are permitted to use common areas for meetings, go door-to-door to talk to other tenants, and invite tenant association representatives, public officials, and candidates for office to speak. A landlord need not permit solicitation of money (except by a tenants' association member seeking payment of delinquent dues from another "existing" member) and may enforce a tenant's request not to be canvassed.[29]

h. LAND USE REGULATION PARTICIPATION

Several park closures led to considerable public interest and a task force to study ways to avoid wholesale displacement of mobile home tenants as land found its way into a "higher and better" (i.e., more profitable) use than as a mobile home park. The study was turned over to an interim legislative committee, and many bills were generated. Two thoughts were contained in these bills:

(a) Tenants ought to be relieved of the financial hardship of park closures, particularly where the costs of moving a home represented a large proportion of its value or when there was no park willing to accept the mobile home.

(b) Park owners ought to be relieved of land use regulation pressures to make it easier to develop new parks and to maintain existing parks.

Part of this concern was felt in the 1985 legislature, which created a right of a mobile home tenants' association to demand that it be notified should a park become subject to a listing agreement[30] (the demand must be renewed annually to remain effective) and required local governments to notify tenants (at each mailing address) of zone change applications.[31]

The 1987 legislature went further by requiring that cities and counties affirmatively provide for mobile home parks as an "allowed use" in their land use planning and regulation process. (Mobile home parks have typically had a more tenuous status as a "conditional use," which made opening a new park quite burdensome.)

A 1987 bill would have required local governments to make provision for manufactured housing in their land use regulations, but the Governor vetoed the bill.[32] The 1989 legislature tried again. It directed the new Mobile Home Ombudsman to monitor local government actions related to applications for permits to expand or create new mobile home parks, to maintain a list of parks and vacancies, and to maintain an inventory of lots or parcels of five or more acres within urban growth boundaries that are zoned for mobile home parks. (Another 1989 law requires the maintenance of a "clearinghouse" of information concerning the availability of mobile home spaces in the state.)

Another successful 1989 bill directs the Housing Agency to assist tenants who wish to buy their mobile home park, and gives a duly constituted tenants' association the right to demand notice and good faith negotiation from a park owner who is attempting to sell a mobile home park.[33] To be entitled to this procedure, the association must be organized as a corporation or association under the appropriate state statutes,[34] so this is not a last minute project. An association that follows the statutes correctly will have the right to be treated like any other potential buyer, plus the potential for technical and financial assistance from the Housing Agency — funded by a one-time $5 assessment on every mobile home park space in Oregon. A 1987 bill amended the condominium statutes (now in ORS chapter 100) to make it possible for tenants to form a condominium association to try to get financing for buying a park.

i. WHEN A TENANT DIES

Two competing interests conflict when a mobile or floating home tenant who lives alone dies. The park management has an interest in collecting rent for the space and may also want to get rid of an older mobile home as part of an ongoing "upgrade" of the park. The tenant's heirs, on the other hand, have the often tedious process of probating an estate, getting

233

affairs in order, and disposing of the assets of the estate. In a small estate, typical of lower-income, older tenants, the Oregon Small Estate Act[35] makes probate less cumbersome, but the mobile home is probably the major asset of the estate, and this still takes time.

With these interests in mind, the following solution was negotiated. If a mobile home tenant residing alone dies, the landlord may be able to follow the abandoned property procedures (see chapter 11, part a.), with some important differences.

To use this procedure, at least one of two conditions must be satisfied:

(a) a personal representative has been appointed for the deceased tenant, or

(b) the landlord requested in writing within two years before the tenant's death that the tenant designate someone to be notified in the event of the tenant's death.[36]

If the landlord has made an effort to get the tenant to appoint someone, the fact that the tenant has failed to do so shouldn't impede the landlord's rights to dispose of the mobile home. If there is a personal representative, then there is an appropriate person to notify anyway. Therefore, assuming one of those conditions is satisfied, the landlord may use the abandoned property procedures, providing the notice required by ORS 90.425(2) is sent to all of the following people:

(a) any personal representative of the tenant;

(b) any person previously designated by the tenant for this purpose; and,

(c) if there is no personal representative and the tenant failed to designate a person in response to the landlord's request, all living relatives of the tenant for whom the landlord has an address if any.

The notice must state —

(a) that any person entitled to possession of the mobile home may remove it within 90 days of the notice after paying storage costs and costs incidental to storage under ORS 90.425(4);

(b) that the mobile home may remain on the space beyond 90 days pending the conclusion of probate proceedings (i.e., if the reason is to accommodate the conclusion of probate proceedings that have not been concluded) if storage charges not exceeding the monthly rent are kept current;

(c) any terms or conditions under which anyone entitled to possession of the mobile home may stay on as a tenant;

(d) that if the mobile home is neither removed or storage costs brought current within 90 days, it will be disposed of as abandoned unless a person entitled to possession has been accepted as a tenant.[37]

The landlord is entitled to screen anyone entitled to possession of the mobile home (someone taking possession under the will, by intestate succession (inheritance without a will), or a purchaser from the estate) under the same limits as apply when a tenant sells a mobile home (see section **f.** above).[38]

j. STATUTORY DAMAGES

As mentioned earlier in this book, various provisions of the Landlord and Tenant Act carry statutory damages designed to assure a tenant of recovering at least a minimum amount if the tenant goes to court to enforce a right. The mobile home provisions of the act also carry statutory damages for some violations. I have already mentioned the $100 minimum penalty for a landlord who fails to give the tenant a copy of a written rental agreement; in addition, a tenant aggrieved by a violation of any of the following mobile home protections is entitled to at least $200:[39]

(a) The mobile home retaliation section

(b) The section requiring cause for evictions

(c) The section restricting limitations on sales of mobile homes

(d) The section limiting conditions of occupancy

A tenant whose landlord has violated the right to a written rental agreement (and to a copy) has a claim for $100 or actual damages, whichever is greater. The landlord can reduce the risk for this violation in two ways:

(a) The landlord can avoid liability to the tenant who complains by offering within 10 days of the tenant's request to enter into a written rental agreement if the agreement is consistent with the act and does not substantially alter the tenant's existing oral agreement.

(b) The landlord can avoid all further liability to all *other* tenants by offering to enter into written rental agreements with each of the other tenants of the landlord within 10 days of being served with a complaint (the first paper filed to start a lawsuit) by the first tenant provided that the offered written agreement is consistent with the act and not a substantial modification.[40]

A buyer of a mobile home is entitled to recover damages of at least $100 from a seller if the sale is made before the landlord approved the buyer as a tenant if the seller knew the buyer wanted to stay and the seller's landlord rejects the buyer.[41]

In common with all tenants, a mobile home tenant who successfully brings an action for damages is entitled to recover court costs and attorney's fees at the trial level and on appeal (if any) in addition to any statutory damages.[42]

15

USE THE LAW TO PROTECT YOURSELF

a. WHAT DO YOU DO ABOUT DISCRIMINATION?

There are three major sources of protection against discrimination in the rental or sale of housing. The City of Eugene, Oregon has created its own additional remedies. All provide remedies by way of damages and other relief to someone denied housing as a result of unlawful discrimination, and each may provide a defense to an unlawfully discriminatory eviction. You may need a lawyer quickly to use any of these protections as a defense to an eviction.

1. The Civil Rights Act of 1866

The oldest source of protection against discrimination is the Civil Rights Act of 1866.[1] It prohibits racial discrimination only, and permits a victim of such discrimination in housing to bring an action in state or federal court for appropriate relief. The Civil Rights Act can support a defense to an eviction action, but it is safest to get to court before the eviction action is commenced. As a plaintiff, you can seek an order preventing the eviction action (an injunction) as well as damages.

2. The Fair Housing Act of 1968 and the Fair Housing Amendments of 1988

The next major federal legislation was the Fair Housing Act of 1968, which prohibits discrimination on grounds of race, color, religion, sex, or national origin in the sale or rental of housing.[2] There were two separate bureaucracies — one state and one federal — charged with the responsibility of enforcing your

237

rights, although you could also obtain an attorney and proceed immediately to court in lieu of or in addition to bureaucratic enforcement. The most recent federal anti-discrimination legislation was the Fair Housing Amendments of 1988, which added handicap and, with important but limited exceptions, "familial status" (essentially having children) as unlawful bases of discrimination.[3]

"Handicap" includes a physical or mental impairment that substantially limits a major life activity, having a record of having such an impairment, or being regarded as having such an impairment. It includes alcoholics (but does not prohibit discrimination on the basis of behavior). It does not include transvesticism, or current use of or addiction to illegal drugs. It does not prohibit discrimination against a person whose tenancy would constitute a direct threat to health or safety, or substantial physical damages to property. AIDS victims are protected. It is permissible under the act to discriminate on the basis that a person has been convicted of illegal manufacture or distribution of drugs.[4]

Owners and managers must allow reasonable modifications, at a tenant's expense, to make a rental unit appropriate for a handicapped person, although modifications that affect the usability of the premises to other tenants must be removed at the end of the tenancy. The tenant can be required to open an escrow account (i.e., interest belongs to the tenant) to ensure restoration, but cannot be required to pay a deposit.

New residential projects, of four or more units, completed under building permits issued on or after January 13, 1990, must provide an "accessible route" to and through "adaptable" units. "Accessible" means a wheelchair can navigate; "adaptable" means reachable faucets, knobs, and switches; walls reinforced for grab bars; and kitchens and bathrooms big enough for wheelchair use. If there is an elevator, all units must be adaptable; otherwise, all on the ground floor must be adaptable.

"Familial status" protections prohibit discrimination against tenants who have children, both in accepting new tenants and in establishing rules and conditions of occupancy. This is a fundamental change in landlord/tenant law; with important but narrow exceptions, *it is now illegal to decline to rent to people because they have children.*

Technically, the new familial status protections apply to a household that includes a person under 18 and a parent, legal guardian, or "designee" of a legal guardian. The important exception is for "Housing for Older Persons" which avoids familial status protections for housing where —

(a) the project is publicly funded for seniors;

(b) the persons are 62 or older; or

(c) at least 80% of the households are headed by someone 55 or older and there are significant facilities or services for older persons and published policies and procedures demonstrate an intent to provide housing for persons over 55.

Nondiscriminatory occupancy limits, such as so many persons per bedroom can be legal. There is some chance that a person excluded by such a limit could show that the effect of the occupancy limit is to discriminate against them because of some protected characteristic — for example, because of a cultural preference for living in large, extended families. Some courts have recognized this kind of "disparate impact" theory — a limit which doesn't bother most people has the effect of excluding Hispanics or Asians, for example. Landlords have tried to create some legislative protection by providing that "if adopted, an occupancy guideline for a dwelling unit shall not be more restrictive than two people per bedroom and shall be reasonable."[5] This 1991 amendment lists some factors to be considered in determining reasonableness, such as the size of the bedrooms and of the dwelling unit, and "[a]ny discriminatory impact" on persons protected by the anti-discrimination laws. Unfortunately, this doesn't really give anyone any useful guidance, but the language reminds landlords considering an occupancy limit to think about the possibility of disparate impact.

The Fair Housing Amendments retain the exclusion for small landlords which was recognized in the Civil Rights Act of 1968, but this is of little significance because Oregon has expanded its anti-discrimination statutes, which have no "mom and pop" exclusion, to cover all of the new federally protected classes.

The Fair Housing Amendments greatly increase the remedies for discrimination in housing by lengthening statutes of limitations, allowing attorney fees in administrative as well as court proceedings, providing for substantial civil penalties and unlimited punitive damages, and allowing both court and administrative proceedings to continue until either reaches an actual hearing. The amendments prescribe fairly strict time guidelines for enforcement agencies.

The Civil Rights Act of 1968 permitted states to create agencies to enforce its provisions and thereby to avoid federal agency enforcement (by HUD) as long as the state agency was doing its job and was "substantially equivalent" to the federal law in its laws and its procedures. That is why the Civil Rights Division (CRD) has been the enforcement agency in Oregon.

The 1988 amendments greatly expand the scope of the federal anti-discrimination laws and also tighten the time frames in which the agency must perform. The amendments give state agencies until January 13, 1992,[6] to achieve "equivalency," on pain of losing their jurisdiction (and some federal funding) over *all* discrimination complaints under the federal law.

As of this writing, there is real doubt whether the Civil Rights Division (CRD) will even try to achieve "equivalency," let alone receive the necessary funding if it does try. So there is real doubt whether CRD will be the agency to enforce civil rights in Oregon in the future. For the time being, CRD is continuing to handle most discrimination complaints, both because Oregon law has prohibited discrimination on the basis of handicap before the Fair Housing Amendments of 1988, and because HUD has contracted with CRD to perform the *investigation* of familial status complaints in this interim period. HUD is responsible for post-investigation administrative enforcement of familial status cases and, presumably, for enforcing new construction adaptability requirements.

This much is clear: Neither HUD nor CRD will ever have the resources to enforce vigorously all legitimate fair housing complaints. The most effective remedy is the private one of finding a good attorney willing to take a case on a contingent fee basis, and to go directly to court. This should be easier now that there is no limit to punitive damages that are available.

To get an agency involved, you may file a complaint either with the nearest office of the Department of Housing and Urban Development (HUD) or with the Civil Rights Division of the Oregon Bureau of Labor. Wherever you file, unless CRD loses its jurisdiction, CRD will investigate and recommend disposition. It can ask the state attorney general to assist you as your lawyer, and it can refer the case to HUD, which can ask the United States attorney general to file a case in court for you. The agencies have power to obtain relief for you without going to court in many circumstances, but you will generally need your own lawyer to use the fair housing laws to defend an eviction.

3. State law

State law has also prohibited housing discrimination on grounds of race, color, religion, sex, and national origin, as well as physical or mental condition.[7] The 1989 legislature brought the substantive requirements into full conformity with the Fair Housing Act Amendments of 1988. Because Oregon law has no exception for small ("mom and pop") landlords, the full range of federal protections are available to all Oregon tenants as a matter of state law. The 1989 Oregon legislation removed the former limitation of punitive damages — there is now no limit.

Oregon law also protects against discrimination on the basis of "marital status."[8] A separate provision, ORS 346.630, makes it unlawful to deny rental housing to a blind person because the person has a seeing-eye dog (even if pets are otherwise prohibited). ORS 346.660 provides similar protection for deaf persons with a "hearing ear dog." And ORS 346.690 protects people who need "assistance animals" generally, while ORS 90.930 expressly applies this protection to landlord/tenant relationships.

There is some doubt as to the kinds of discrimination that are unlawful under state law. The statute allows landlords to discriminate on the basis of sex if the landlord wants to avoid a situation in which unrelated persons of the opposite sex share bath or bedroom facilities.[9] An attorney general once concluded that this exception permits a landlord to refuse to rent to unmarried couples. On the other hand, the statute makes no similar exception to the prohibition against discriminating on the basis of *marital status*, a proscription that is almost meaningless if subject to the exception. Besides, when a landlord refuses to rent to an unmarried couple, it's not their gender that bothers the landlord, but their marital status.

Another area of doubt under state (and federal) law is whether the prohibition against discrimination on grounds of sex proscribes discrimination on the basis of sexual preference. Clearly, the exception for unrelated people of opposite sexes sharing sleeping or bathroom facilities won't help the landlord here. The question is which of the two dictionary definitions of "sex" the legislature had in mind:

(a) One of the two divisions of organisms formed on the distinction of male or female; males or females collectively, or

(b) The character of being male or female, or of pertaining to the distinctive function of the male or female in reproduction.

In short, is it discrimination on the basis of gender or on the basis of character and behavior that is prohibited? Of course, the more progressive and enlightened approach is to prohibit discrimination on the basis of sexual preference as well as discrimination on the basis of gender, but don't hold your breath. Achieving this interpretation is a possible objective, but, like convincing a court to protect unmarried couples against housing discrimination, it is an uphill struggle.

As noted above, which agency enforces which protections is not yet settled. If you want an agency to try to enforce your rights, call the Civil Rights Division of the Bureau of Labor (229-6600). However, your best bet is usually to get an attorney to take your case to court. A court may award punitive damages in any amount it deems appropriate, as well as actual damages.

The court may also award you appropriate equitable relief such as an injunction directing the landlord to allow you to rent the next available unit if you were wrongfully excluded, or an injunction restraining your landlord from proceeding further with an unlawfully discriminatory eviction action.[10]

If you have a defense to a threatened or pending eviction action because of evidence that the eviction is unlawfully discriminatory, get an attorney or file a complaint with the Civil Rights Division immediately. If you file with the division, ask them whether they are willing to appear in the eviction action to ask that it be delayed pending the outcome of your civil rights complaint. If you have filed an administrative complaint, you may be able to make use of the statute that says your opponent cannot deprive you of "any services" or "real property" with the intention of defeating the purposes of the anti-discrimination laws.[11]

4.   Local laws

As of this writing, the cities of Eugene, Portland, Salem, and Springfield have enacted their own fair housing ordinances, and Lane County has an Affirmative Action Committee which provides some investigation of civil rights complaints in housing. All cover at least the same ground as the state and federal protections. Portland's ordinance, which is the newest, adds protection against discrimination based on sexual orientation or source of income; Salem prohibits discrimination based on receiving public assistance benefits. As of this writing, Portland's protection for discrimination on the basis of sexual orientation is under fire through litigation and a proposed ballot measure. Both are the work of the Oregon Citizen's Alliance, a group of people whose abnormal abhorrence of what they consider to be deviant sexuality, coupled with their bizarre notion of the role of government in a free society, have also led them to sponsor a state wide ballot measure which would declare homosexuality to be evil and would prohibit any protections against discrimination based on sexual orientation.

Although Eugene's Human Rights Council and Lane County's Affirmative Action Committee have some capacity to respond to a complaint, none of the local schemes provide any direct enforcement beyond attempting to talk the parties into a settlement. If you want to get someone to make a landlord rent you the vacant rental that the landlord has unlawfully refused to rent to you, you will need an attorney, or an agency with an attorney, who can help right away. See the next section.

5.   Fair Housing Council of Oregon

It has long been established that it is entirely lawful to investigate allegedly unlawful discrimination by using "testers." Testers are trained investigators who pose as renters (or buyers) of homes. They are selected to test for the suspected basis of discrimination. For example, if an Hispanic family with an $800 monthly income and two pre-teen children suspect a landlord is discriminating when they are told the advertised vacancy has "just been rented," non-minority testers are sent to present the landlord with essentially the same prospective tenants except for their ethnicity: $800 monthly income and two pre-teen children. If the tester's application is accepted, the result is strong evidence of discrimination. Some testing projects send two sets of testers which are as nearly identical as possible except for their ethnicity (or familial status if the question is familial status discrimination).

The Oregon Fair Housing Council is a state-wide project funded by a federal grant. It is able to respond to complaints of discrimination in violation of state or federal law (it does not yet cover income or sexual orientation discrimination), typically within 24 hours. If the investigation supports the discrimination charge, the Council can refer you to Legal Aid if you are eligible, or to a private attorney willing to take such cases in your area. The Council is presently considering offering its own conciliation services. At present, the Oregon Fair Housing Council is probably the most effective avenue for a quick and effective remedy for discrimination in rental housing. You can reach them at 1-800-424-FAIR [1-800-424-3247].

b. THE UNLAWFUL TRADE PRACTICES ACT AND UNLAWFUL DEBT COLLECTION PRACTICES ACT

Subject to one major limitation, Oregon's Unlawful Trade Practices Act has important consumer protection provisions that extend to certain behavior by landlords. If you have rights under the act, it can be extremely useful.

(a) It expressly permits a private right of action in which you are entitled to a minimum recovery of $200 plus attorney's fees upon showing that you have suffered any ascertainable loss as a result of a prohibited practice.[12]

245

(b) You may obtain punitive damages and injunctive relief in appropriate cases.[13]

(c) You may assert rights arising under the act as a counterclaim in any action brought by your landlord.[14]

(d) There is an enforcement agency: the Consumer Protection Division of the Oregon Department of Justice, and any local district attorney.[15]

Here are some of the practices the act deems unlawful:[16]

(a) Passing off real estate as being owned by another

(b) Representing that real estate has characteristics, uses, benefits, or qualities that it does not have

(c) Representing that real estate is new if it is deteriorated, altered, or reconditioned

(d) Representing that real estate is of a particular standard or quality if it is of another standard or quality

(e) Advertising real estate with the intent not to provide it as advertised

(f) Making false or misleading representations concerning the existence of, reasons for, or amount of price reductions

(g) Promising to deliver real estate within a certain period of time with intent not to deliver as promised

(h) Making false or misleading representations concerning the landlord's cost for real estate or services

(i) Failing to disclose any known material defect concurrently with the delivery of real estate

The one major limitation on the usefulness of these provisions for tenants is the amendment to the act providing that "real estate does not cover conduct covered by" the Landlord and Tenant Act.[17] Although it is impossible to make sense out of a literal reading of this change, the legislature apparently intended only to avoid giving a tenant remedies under both the Landlord and Tenant Act and the Unlawful Trade Practices Act for the same conduct of the landlord. Reduced to written and tape recorded form, the comments and testimony of witnesses that constitute the "legislative history" of the change show that the people from the attorney general's office who supported the change thought it would not exclude a landlord who engaged in false advertising.

Assuming that the legislature intended only to avoid giving tenants remedies under both acts for the same conduct, here is how to determine whether you have a remedy under the Unlawful Trade Practices Act:

(a) If the landlord's conduct is permitted or prohibited by the Landlord and Tenant Act, that conduct cannot give you a right to relief under the Unlawful Trade Practices Act.

(b) If the conduct is neither permitted nor prohibited by the Landlord and Tenant Act, but it does violate the Unlawful Trade Practices Act, then you have a right to relief under the latter act.

Example

Assume that at the time you enter a rental agreement and move into your new home, your landlord —

(a) fails to tell you that the house will be demolished in two months to make room for a new highway;

(b) promises that you will have the use of a washer and dryer; and

(c) represents that your new neighborhood is quiet.

Assume further that your landlord knew better at the time, that you have to move in two months because of the highway, that you never get to use a washer and dryer, and that the neighborhood turns out to be the noisiest in the city. You have a Landlord and Tenant Act claim for the failure to provide a washer and dryer because that act entitles you to damages for any material violation of the rental agreement.

You do not have an Unlawful Trade Practices claim because the broken promise is covered by the Landlord and Tenant Act. The other two problems are not covered by the Landlord and Tenant Act; they will be covered by the Unlawful Trade Practices Act if a court agrees that impending demolition is a "defect" or that impending demolition or noisy neighborhoods have to do with the benefits or qualities of real estate. (A failure to disclose a fact can constitute a misrepresentation.)

In addition to the conduct listed above, the Unlawful Trade Practices Act contains some prohibitions that only the Consumer Protection Division can enforce. In other words, if you have a problem that is covered by the following list, and if the conduct does not also violate the Landlord and Tenant Act, you may get some help by complaining to the Consumer Protection Division, but you can't get help from a court yourself or with a private attorney. The Unlawful Trade Practices Act prohibits the use of "any unconscionable tactic" in connection with the rental of real estate. Unconscionable tactics include, but are not limited to, the following:

(a) Knowingly taking advantage of a tenant's physical infirmity, ignorance, illiteracy, or inability to understand the language of an agreement

(b) Permitting a tenant to enter into a rental agreement with knowledge that there is no reasonable probability that the tenant can pay the rent in full when due

A similar provision is the Unlawful Collection Practices Act, which is designed to prohibit abuses in the course of debt collection. Although other issues may well arise, it seems clear that a residential rental agreement qualifies as a "consumer transaction" under these statutes,[18] and that a landlord who violates their provisions may be liable to an offended tenant.

To the extent that a tenant seeks to assert an unlawful collection practice as a counterclaim in an eviction action (see chapter 8, part **d.**), the tenant *may* be limited to the same test as a tenant seeking to assert an unlawful trade practice in or out of an eviction: if it's covered by the Residential Landlord and Tenant Act, it isn't also covered by the Unlawful Debt Collection Practices Act. This is because the statute giving the right to counterclaim in any action by a "lessee of real estate" may incorporate the definition of "real estate" as excluding "conduct covered by" the landlord and tenant act.[19]

Note, however, that unlike the Unlawful Trade Practices Act, which has provisions that often define the violation in terms of "real estate," the provisions of the Unlawful Debt Collection Practices Act do not depend on "real estate" for their definitions of prohibited conduct. The upshot is that at least outside an eviction action (i.e., if the landlord is suing for rent or the tenant is suing the landlord), there is no basis for avoiding an unlawful debt collection practice charge just because the conduct may also be covered by the Landlord and Tenant Act.

In any event, the same remedies of a minimum of $200, plus attorney fees, injunction, and punitive damages are available as for unlawful trade practices. A tenant may seek those remedies against a landlord who does any of the following to try to collect rent or other debts:[20]

(a) Use or threaten force or violence

(b) Threaten arrest or criminal prosecution

(c) Threaten to seize belongings

(d) Use profane, obscene, or abusive language

(e) Communicate with the debtor repeatedly or continuously or at times known to be inconvenient with intent to harass or annoy the debtor or a member of the debtor's family

(f) Communicate or threaten to communicate with the debtor's employer concerning the nature or existence of the debt

(g) Contact the debtor at work[21]

(h) Fail in a written communication to identify the debt collector and the collector's address or the creditor (if different from the debt collector)

(i) Fail in any oral communication to identify the caller and the nature of the contact within 30 seconds

(j) Cause any expense for long distance calls or the like by concealing the true purposes of the debt collector's communication

(k) Attempt or threaten to enforce a right or remedy knowing that the right or remedy doesn't exist or threatening action that the collector doesn't take in the regular course of business

(l) Use any form of communication that simulates legal process or pretends governmental authorization

(m) Represent that a debt may be increased by fees or charges that may not legally be added (Remember that attorney fees and court costs to the prevailing party are available under the Landlord and Tenant Act.)

(n) Attempt to collect interest not permitted by law or the contract between the parties (the legal rate is presently 9%)

(o) Threaten to assign or sell the debtor's account with a misrepresentation or implication that the debtor would lose defenses or be subjected to harsh, vindictive, or abusive collection practices

If it looks like there's nothing left you can do to collect a debt, you're missing the point. The law permits a written demand or a courteous phone call; the law then expects that a dissatisfied creditor with a legitimate claim will decide whether or not it is worth going to court to recover the debt.

c. LOBBYING FOR NEW LEGISLATION

There are many areas of landlord and tenant relations that could use some legislative adjustment. Tenants can try to influence legislators individually, but concerted action is usually the most effective. If you are interested in working on legislation, try to contact a tenants' union. The Oregon State Tenants' Association, and the Oregon Mobile Home Owners' Association, which represents the interests of mobile home tenants, have been very active in legislative work and have contributed to the development of landlord tenant law in Oregon.

Here are their addresses:

Oregon State Tenants' Association
3791-B River Road North
Salem, Oregon 97303
Phone: 393-7737

Mobile Home Owners' Association
P.O. Box 325
Tualatin, Oregon 97026
Phone: 682-1659

As of this writing, there is a newly forming organization that is focused on the principle that all tenants should be free of evictions for no cause:

Oregon Renters Equality Union
P.O. Box 33127
Portland, Oregon 97233

Of course, you may find other tenants' associations that are active in your area; see chapter 12, section **b.** If you are eligible for legal aid, you should know that legal aid attorneys can provide you with representation before the legislature as well as the courts.[22] In fact, legal aid lobbyists were largely responsible for the passage of the Landlord and Tenant Act in 1973, and have successfully represented tenants' interests in each subsequent legislative session.

Even if you are not eligible for legal aid and have no other access to a lobbyist, your testimony may be important when the legislature considers landlord/tenant bills in the future. If you have encountered a problem that you think merits legislative attention, get in touch with your local tenants' association, the closest legal aid housing specialist, or the Oregon State and Student Public Interest Research Group. O.S.P.I.R.G. has regularly published a *Renter's Handbook* and is collecting tenants' comments between legislative sessions. Here is their address:

O.S.P.I.R.G.
1536 S.E. 11th Avenue
Portland, Oregon 97214
Phone: 231-4181

Here are a few ideas that could win legislative approval. Some of them were considered in prior sessions and some may be a long time coming, but remember that the Landlord and Tenant Act itself took three legislative sessions (six years of struggle) before it was passed.

(a) Expand good cause eviction to all tenants.

(b) Expand the mobile home version of the retaliatory eviction statute to protect all tenants.

(c) Require that all deposits bear interest.

(d) Prohibit rental discrimination against welfare recipients and families with children.

d. RENT CONTROL

Unless you have a term tenancy or your tenancy is somehow involved with a federal, state, or locally funded program that limits rent increases, your rent can be raised on 30 days' written notice by any amount and for no reason at all and for any reason that is not prohibited (the prohibited reasons are the same as the defenses to termination of a month-to-month tenancy: retaliation or unlawful discrimination, and possible "inequity"). Whether and to what extent rent can be raised for tenants with a term agreement or other security of possession (such as mobile home tenants) is determined by the rental agreement.

Tenants have frequently asked that the legislature pass a law limiting rent raises; the legislature has repeatedly refused. In fact, the legislature adopted a law forbidding local rent control (with exceptions for publicly funded or subsidized rentals).[23] The Oregon Homebuilders, real estate interests, and a host of other constituencies convinced lawmakers that rent control by local jurisdictions would deter new investment in the state, increase "deferred maintenance," lead to abandonment of existing units, and increase the property tax burden on owner-occupied housing.

I think the rent control debate is greatly inflated in importance. To have any hope of political feasibility, and to withstand constitutional attack, any rent control scheme must allow rent increases to accommodate increased taxes and other costs and must allow a "reasonable return" on the owner's investment. As a practical matter, except when housing is in extremely short supply, this means that the vast majority of tenants will not pay a lower rent with rent control than without it. In fact, if a rent control scheme allows a certain maximum increase per year, many landlords may increase rents to the allowable ceiling just *because* there is rent control and they fear they would be unable to raise the rent to meet unforeseen future expenses. At the same time, owners needn't fear rent control quite so anxiously; they would be permitted to pay increased costs and taxes and to make a reasonable profit under any rent control scheme that would ever have a reasonable chance of passage in the foreseeable future.

Of course, the real objection to rent control from most who oppose it is an ideological concern — the idea that government has no business regulating this aspect of business decision making. Whatever the reason, the emotional response to rent control is real even if it is not based in fact, and the emotional

253

response might well have the impact on investors that the opponents of rent control predict for legislators.

In any event, as a political matter it seems out of the question that the Oregon Legislature would consider any form of rent control until and unless there is an extreme housing shortage, a pattern of abuses by landlords who raise the rent way beyond economic justification just because the market will bear it, and demonstrable hardship to popular groups such as the fixed-income elderly.

APPENDIX 1
A SELECTIVE BIBLIOGRAPHY OF
MATERIALS ON TENANTS' UNIONS

a. BOOKS

Burghardt, Stephen, ed., *Tenants and the Urban Housing Crisis*. Dexter, Michigan: New Press, 1972.

Goodman, Emily Jane. *Tenant Survival Book*. New York: Bobbs Merrill Co., 1974.

Hawley, Peter K. *Housing in the Public Domain: The Only Solution*. New York: Metropolitan Council on Housing, 1978.

Kahn, Si. *How People Get Power — Organizing Oppressed Communities for Action*. New York: McGraw-Hill, Inc., 1972.

Lipsky, Michael. *Protest in City Politics: Rent Strikes, Housing and the Power of the Poor*. Chicago: Rand McNally, 1970.

Matthews, Douglas. *Sue the Bastards*. New York: Arbor House, 1973.

Moskovitz, Myron, and Ralph E. Warner. *California Tenants Handbook*. 7th ed. Berkeley: Nolo Press, 1986.

Oregon State and Student Public Interest Research Group. *OSPIRG Renter's Handbook*. 8th ed. Portland, Oregon: OSPIRG, 1990.

b. VIDEOTAPES

Pushed Out for Profit. Ideas in Motion. 141 10th Street, San Francisco, California, 94103

c. NEWSLETTERS

OSTA Review. Oregon State Tenants' Association.
P.O. Box 7224, Salem, Oregon, 97303

Shelterforce. National Housing Institute, 439 Main Street
Orange, New Jersey, 07050

d. OTHER SOURCES OF INFORMATION

The following organizations publish information from time
to time. Contact them directly for current lists of materials.

National Housing Law Project
1950 Addison Street
Berkeley, California, 94704

Tenants' Action Project
2022 Blake Street
Berkeley, California, 94704

The Tenants' Union
(formerly Seattle Tenants' Union)
3902 S. Ferdinand
Seattle, Washington, 98118

NOTES

Chapter 2

1. ORS 90.320(1)(f)
2. ORS 90.320(1)(g). The requirement that the landlord provide removal service in Portland was added in 1987.
3. ORS 90.315
4. ORS 90.335(5), 90.410
5. ORS 90.305
6. ORS 90.310(1)
7. ORS 90.310(2)
8. ORS 90.310(3)
9. ORS 90.310(4)
10. ORS 90.325
11. ORS 90.900(1), (2)
12. ORS 90.340, 90.410(1)
13. ORS 90.100(14), 90.110(4)
14. See also ORS 90.115, 90.120

Chapter 3

1. 15 USC 1681, et. seq.
2. ORS 90.380
3. ORS 90.240(2), 90.305(4)
4. ORS 90.305(1)
5. ORS 90.315
6. ORS 90.330
7. ORS 90.240(4)
8. ORS 90.135, 90.245
9. ORS 90.245(2)
10. ORS 90.300
11. ORS 105.120(3). There are important exceptions. See chapter 8.
12. ORS 90.320(2)
13. ORS 90.320(1)(g)
14. ORS 90.240(4)
15. ORS 90.340
16. ORS 90.260
17. Note that the federal Fair Housing Amendments of 1988, which prevent discrimination on the basis of "familial status," impose

limits on a landlord's ability to adopt occupancy limits. See chapter 15.
18. ORS 90.330(2)
19. ORS 90.245(2)
20. ORS 90.240(2)
21. ORS 90.305(4)

Chapter 4

1. ORS 90.300 (6)-(8)
2. ORS 90.300 (1), (7)
3. ORS 90.300(8)
4. ORS 90.300(3)-(4)
5. ORS 90.300(5); *Zemp v. Roland,* 31 Or App 1105 (1977). The difference is that a "fee" limits the tenants' liability to the amount of the fee, while a deposit does not.
6. ORS 90.125(1)
7. ORS 90.360(4)
8. ORS 90.375, 90.385(2)
9. ORS 90.920(2)
10. ORS 90.380(3)
11. ORS 90.900(2)
12. ORS 105.120(3)
13. ORS 90.900(2)
14. ORS 90.900(1)
15. ORS 90.300(1), (6)-(8)
16. ORS 46.455, 46.461 [district court, small claims court]; ORS 55.011, 55.095 [justice court, small claims court]. Note that, like the old procedure in regular court, if the defendant fails to file an appropriate motion, the excessive counterclaim is ignored (district, small claims) or stricken (justice, small claims).
17. ORS 55.110 et seq.
18. ORS 90.305(3)(b). A nondisclosing manager also becomes the agent of the landlord for "expending or making available . . . all rent collected from the premises" as necessary to perform the landlord's obligations under the act or the rental agreement. This means that such a manager may be compelled by a court to divert rent still held or yet to be collected from tenants. This provision may or may not limit the manager's financial exposure to the tenant, probably depending on the manager's actual role in the breach of the landlord's obligation. For example, a manager hired when habitability problems already existed will probably not be personally liable for damages caused to the tenant by those problems (but may be compelled to use rent collected from the premises to fix them); a manager who locks out a

tenant may well be personally liable to the tenant, perhaps even if the manager *has* complied with the disclosure requirements.

19. ORS 90.100(5)-(8)
20. ORS 90.300(10)
21. ORS 90.300(6)-(8)

Chapter 5

1. Actually, proof that the defendant knew of the risks of special damages is usually required only in contract actions — where the plaintiff is basing the claim for special damages on the defendant's breach of a promise. For example, breach of a promise to deliver equipment at a certain time would normally require payment of general damages measured by the lost use of the equipment during any delay in delivery. To recover for lost profits on a job that depended on the early receipt of the equipment, the plaintiff would normally have to show that the defendant knew enough of the circumstances to expect lost profits to exist as a "special damage." In tort law (the collection of legal principles, such as negligence, which govern the liability of parties for non contractual, non-criminal wrongs), actual notice is unnecessary.

   Because the habitability requirements of the act were intended by the legislature to arise independently of the agreement of the parties, as a matter of the state's "police power," actual notice should not be necessary to the recovery of special damages. It is always safest, however, to give notice so as to remove any doubts.

2. *Brewer v. Erwin*, 287 OR 435 (1979)
3. ORS 90.360(2)
4. ORS 90.385(3)(c)

Chapter 6

1. If you have received an eviction notice, see chapter 8, Evictions and Defenses.
2. ORS 90.325(6), 90.400(5), 90.430
3. In Portland, the landlord must be responsible for garbage removal service. See footnote 19.
4. Compare ORS 90.365(4) with ORS 90.375
5. ORS 90.365(1)(a)
6. ORS 90.365(1)(c), (2)
7. ORS 90.365(3), (3)(c), (d)
8. ORS 90.365(3)
9. ORS 90.365(5)(a)
10. ORS 90.365(3)(b); see section **a.** of this chapter
11. ORS 90.365(3)(c)
12. ORS 90.365(3)(a)

13. ORS 90.385(2), 90.375; see also 90.245(2), 90.425(6), 90.900(3), 90.920(2), 90.710
14. ORS 90.125, 90.360(2)
15. ORS 90.100(1)
16. If a recoupment is used that does not involve the same transaction, it is called a "setoff." One way in which a setoff based on the act or the rental agreement might exist in an eviction action (or action for back rent or damages) is if the claim for damages related to a prior tenancy between the same parties.
17. ORS 90.125(1), 90.130
18. Oregon has abolished the old distinction between equitable and legal forms of action, under which a defendant's request for injunctive relief would have been a "countersuit" rather than a "counterclaim."
19. If you counterclaim and pay rent into court, the redemption provision means that you may not have to show that your damages were as great as the unpaid rent.
20. ORS 46.040, 51.080, 90.370(1)
21. As noted elsewhere, the retaliation defense is unavailable if the tenant is in default in rent. Yet any available recoupment (or counterclaim) may offset any default if the amount of damages involved is equal to or greater than the unpaid rent. One exception is that a tenant cannot use damages for retaliatory eviction (as opposed to a retaliatory reduction in services) to offset a default in rent in the same eviction.
22. "Redemption," outside the landlord/tenant world, is most often encountered as the right of a judgment debtor whose real property has been sold under a money judgment to buy back the property within a statutory period of redemption, typically one year.
23. ORS 90.370
24. ORS 90.370(1). The Oregon Supreme Court and the Court of Appeals have recognized that this is the way the statute works. *Napolski v. Champney*, 295 Or 408 (1983), *Eddy v. Parazoo*, 77 Or App 120 (1985), *Amatisto v. Paz*, 82 Or App 341 (1986). The 1987 legislature amended ORS 90.370(1) only to the extent that a tenant who wins by paying rent into court but has to make up a balance between the amount paid into court and the rent found due, will not recover attorney fees.
25. ORS 22.010, 22.070

Chapter 7
1. ORS 90.375, 90.335(5), 90.435
2. ORS 90.375
3. OAR 860-21-305 to 860-21-420 apply to residential electric and gas service, OAR 860-21-505 applies to others, such as telephone.
4. OAR 860-21-405(2)(c); 860-21-415

5. OAR 860-21-410
6. OAR 860-21-405(5), (6)
7. ORS 90.315
8. ORS 90.920(2)
9. ORS 90.420
10. ORS 90.425(11)

Chapter 8

1. ORS 46.221 [district court]; 51.310 [justice court except FEDs]; 105.130 [FEDs in district or justice court]
2. ORS 105.135. These provisions apply to commercial as well as residential tenancies.
3. ORS 105.135(2)
4. ORS 52.110; ORCP 7C., 24B.
5. ORS 105.137(3)
6. ORS 90.385(2), 90.375
7. ORS 90.385(2)
8. ORS 90.385(3)(c). Note that the appellate courts agree that "require" means require — it is not enough that the landlord wants to demolish the property, or to make changes that can only be made to code if the premises are empty; for this exception to defeat the defense, vacating the premises must be required to achieve code compliance. Of course, the landlord is free to evict to demolish or remodel an empty unit as long as the eviction is not in response to tenant's behavior that is protected by the retaliation statute and as long as the landlord is otherwise entitled to evict.
9. ORS 90.415(1)
10. ORS 90.240(5)
11. ORS 105.120(3)
12. ORS 90.910(1), (2)
13. ORS 105.115(2)(b)
14. Compare *id.* with ORS 90.920(1)
15. ORS 90.400 specifies notice procedures for evictions based on a tenant's breach of the obligations of ORS 90.325 (reasonable use of the premises), a violation of the rental agreement, nonpayment of rent, and irreparable injury. The only situation that would give a landlord a right to evict but which is not covered by ORS 90.400 or 91.900 (the no-cause eviction section) is when the right to terminate is based on the tenant's refusal to allow lawful access (ORS 90.920(1)). Arguably, this situation is one in which the tenant is "holding contrary" to the act within the meaning of ORS 105.115(2)(b), so that no notice is necessary. On the other hand, ORS 105.120(2) seems to require notices for all kinds of evictions. Again, giving a notice is always safest.

16. ORS 90.335(3)
17. ORS 91.900(1), (2)
18. Compare ORS 91.900(1) with ORS 91.900(2)
19. ORS 90.240(1)
20. ORS 90.400(1)(a), (c)
21. ORS 90.400(1)(d)
22. ORS 90.135
23. ORS 90.245(1)(a)
24. ORS 90.245(1)(b)
25. ORS 90.245(1)(c)
26. ORS 90.330
27. ORS 346.630 (seeing-eye dogs); ORS 346.660 (hearing-ear dogs); ORS 346.690 (assistance animals); ORS 90.930. ORS 346.690 provides a right to minimum damages of $200 plus attorney fees for violations; ORS 346.991 makes a violator subject to criminal prosecution.
28. ORS 90.400(2)
29. ORS 90.910(2), (3)
30. ORS 90.385(3)(b)
31. ORS 90.415(3), (4)
32. ORS 90.415(5), (6)
33. ORS 90.250; see chapter 6, section e.
34. ORS 90.240(4)(a)
35. See chapter 14, section d.
36. ORS 90.385(1)
37. 1989 Or Laws ch 791 [forfeiture], ch 846 [nuisance abatement], ch 915 [decontamination of "meth labs"]. Property managers should note that 1989 Or Laws ch 1062 entitles them to record with the county recorder a request for notice of any forfeiture or nuisance abatement proceedings concerning property for which they are responsible.
38. ORS 90.400(3)(c)
39. ORS 90.100(13)
40. ORS 105.139
41. ORS 91.120. This rather awkward wording reflects land-lords' concern that the requirement of an eviction notice not convert an employee into a tenant — a concern that led to the final sentence of the new section: "This section does not create the relationship of landlord and tenant between a landlord and such employee." For the same reason, this section was not among those renumbered and moved to ORS Chapter 90 when the residential landlord/tenant provisions were moved to make more room in 1989.
42. In addition to counterclaims in nonpayment of rent evictions permitted by ORS 90.370(1), the following statutes together give a

tenant the right to counterclaim in any kind of eviction action:
ORS 90.125 (remedies of the act shall be administered so that
an aggrieved party can recover appropriate damages; any right
declared by the act is enforceable by "action" unless the act
specified a different and limited effect); ORS 90.100(1) ("action"
includes counterclaim); ORS 90.360(2) (a tenant may seek damages for any noncompliance with the rental agreement or ORS
90.320). When the legislature adopted ORS 105.132 in 1985, the
proponents of that section (which prohibits counterclaims in
eviction actions unless the right to counterclaim is "provided
by statute") agreed that these sections of the Landlord and Tenant Act do provide for counterclaims.

43. ORS 90.330
44. ORS 90.130
45. ORS 90.245(2)
46. ORS 90.360(2)
47. ORS 90.125, 90.360(2)
48. ORS 90.315
49. ORS 90.365(1)(b)
50. ORS 90.375. Note that the 1987 legislature clarified that a tenant
    need not terminate the tenancy, obtain injunctive relief, or re-
    cover possession of the premises to be entitled to money dam-
    ages, and that the statute affords all of these kinds of relief to
    the tenant.
51. ORS 90.920(2)
52. ORS 90.385(2), 90.375
53. ORS 90.425(11)
54. ORS 646.638(1), (6); see chapter 15, section **b**.
55. ORS 646.641(1), 646.638(6); see chapter 15, section **b**.
56. ORS 91.755. The Unlawful Trade Practices Act permits a court to
    award attorney's fees and costs to a successful defendant only
    if it finds the claim "frivolous." ORS 646-638(3)
57. ORS 90.370(1)
58. *Napolski v. Champney*, 295 Or 408 (1983); *Eddy v. Parazoo*,
    77 Or App 120 (1985); *Amatisto v. Paz*, 82 Or App 341 (1986)
59. ORS 90.370(4)
60. ORS 105.140(2)
61. ORS 51.080, 90.370(1). While the 1985 legislature expressly
    recognized that nonpayment of rent evictions were an exception
    to the rule that a district court case (including other evictions)
    with a counterclaim in excess of district court jurisdiction can be
    transferred to circuit court, the 1987 legislature repealed the stat-
    ute in question (ORS 91.070(2)), and revamped the motion to
    transfer procedure completely. It used to be that a party who
    failed to file a motion to transfer to circuit court with the exces-
    sive counterclaim would have the counterclaim stricken and stay
    in district court. Now, the sanction is simply that either party

may move to transfer the case or the court can do so on its own motion. ORS 46.060-46.080. The new revision makes no exception for nonpayment evictions governed by ORS 90.370(1), which limits counterclaims to the jurisdiction of the initial court. I expect that appellate courts will continue to recognize that nonpayment of rent evictions cannot be transferred because counterclaims are so limited.

62. Compare *Ingersoll v. Mattson*, 47 Or App 471 (1980) [FED may not be transferred to circuit court when it is based on nonpayment of rent] with *LFC v. Burtchaell*, 47 Or App 471 (1980) [transfer should be granted if right to possession is *not* based on nonpayment and counterclaim exceeds district court jurisdiction]. See ORS 46.060-46.080.

63. ORS 105.137(3)

64. ORS 52.110, ORCP 7 C., 24B.

65. ORS 105.137(1), (2)

66. ORS 105.137(6)(a)

67. ORS 105.137(7)

68. ORS 14.210-.270, 46.141, 52.530(1)(b)

69. In 1987, the Supreme Court interpreted the earlier statutes to make it a bit harder to disqualify judges, and the legislature promptly responded by making it easier. The party seeking a change merely has to swear that the party does not believe a fair trial can be had in front of the judge; the judge can dispute the request, but has the burden of proving that the request was filed in bad faith. I testified in favor of this result as one who has been on both sides of such motions, but who believes that a party's belief in the fairness of the process is of tremendous importance — and that judges shouldn't take this personally. 1987 HB 2183. Now that I am a full-time judge myself, I still endorse this "peremptory challenge" as important to the legitimacy of the judicial process.

70. ORS 105.140(2)

71. ORS 105.137(4). The tenant does not have to pay rent into court when it is the landlord who wants a continuance for more than two days.

72. ORS 105.115(3)

73. ORS 52.110; ORCP 7 C., 24 B.

74. ORS 105.155(2)

75. ORS 105.155(3)

76. ORS 105.155(1), (3)

77. ORS 105.165, 90.425

78. ORS 22.010-22.070

79. 46.250(4), (6), 19.040(1)(b)

80. ORCP 68 A.(2); *Northwest Acceptance Corp. v. Bles Studs, Inc.*, 74 Or App 248 (1985)

81. ORS 90.255
82. ORS 46.250(4)(a)
83. ORS 55.030, 55.040
84. ORS 46.250(4)(b), 53.040
85. Bills have been introduced in at least three legislative sessions to abolish the writ of review as a device by which to appeal a district court judgment. On all three occasions, I testified against the bill, and argued that this provides the only financially feasible method of reviewing errors in cases involving the nonwealthy. So far, the legislature seems convinced.

Chapter 9

1. ORCP 79, 82
2. Note that *in an eviction action* involving a tenancy covered by the Landlord and Tenant Act, a plaintiff may appear in person, through an attorney, or through a nonattorney who is an agent or employee of the plaintiff, or an agent or employee of an agent of the plaintiff — in other words, property managers (ORS 105.130(4)). This is probably not enough to allow a property manager to act on behalf of an owner (or an officer or employee of a corporate owner to act for that corporate owner) in bringing an action for a restraining order; this would probably constitute the unlawful practice of law, unless the manager, officer or employee happened to be a lawyer.
3. The language is now in ORCP 82 A.(1).

Chapter 10

1. ORS 90.910
2. ORS 90.305
3. ORS 91.900(2)
4. ORS 90.300(5)
5. ORS 90.360(1)
6. ORS 90.360(1)(d)
7. ORS 90.360(2), (3)
8. ORS 90.360(1)(c)
9. ORS 90.375; see chapter 7.
10. ORS 90.920(2); see chapter 7.
11. ORS 90.385(1), (2), 90.375; see chapter 8, section **b.**
12. ORS 90.380(3). This provision was primarily intended for tenants who find they have moved into a former "meth lab," but also extends to all serious threats to health — toxins, radiation, imminent structural failure, etc.
13. ORS 90.300(8); see chapter 4.
14. ORS 90.310; see chapter 2, section **a.4.**

15. ORS 90.425(11); see chapter 11.
16. ORS 90.370(2)
17. ORS 90.125(1)
18. ORS 90.410(3)

Chapter 11

1. ORS 90.420
2. ORS 90.425(1)
3. ORS 90.425(11)
4. ORS 90.425(5)
5. ORS 90.425(9)
6. ORS 90.425(4)(b)
7. ORS 90.425(7)
8. ORS 90.425(1)(b)
9. ORS 105.155 prescribes a form of writ of restitution that commands the sheriff to recover "costs and disbursements...and all accruing costs" by levying on the goods. See chapter 8, section f.
10. ORS 105.165
11. ORS 105.165(1)(b); ORS 90.425(6)
12. ORS 105.165(2)
13. ORS 90.425(1)(a)
14. ORS 90.425(11)
15. ORS 90.425(5) provides, "*After notifying the tenant* as required by subsections (1) and (2) of this section *the landlord shall store* all goods, chattels, motor vehicles and other personal property of the tenant in a place of safekeeping and shall exercise reasonable care for the property..." (emphasis added). Because the duty to use reasonable care for the property exists independent of the act, this language may well mean that the landlord may not recover storage costs incurred before giving or attempting to give the required notice.
16. ORS 105.165(3)
17. ORS 105.165(2)
18. ORS 105.112(2)(d)-(h)
19. ORS 105.112(2)(a)-(c)
20. ORS 105.112(2)(g)

Chapter 12

1. ORS 310.635
2. 1991 Or Laws ch 786, 2
3. ORS 310.640

Chapter 13

1. Public housing projects were initiated by the Housing Act of 1937, which is codified in the United States Code at 42 USC. 1437, et seq. Most of the important regulations are presently at 24 CFR Parts 913-999.

2. Rent is the greater of 30% of adjusted income, 10% of actual monthly income, or the full amount of any shelter allowance in a family's welfare grant. 42 USC 1437a; 24 CFR Part 913

3. 24 CFR 966.4(h)(4)

4. 24 CFR Part 966, Subpart B

5. 42 USC 1437d(k), (l); 24 CFR 966.4(l)(1)

6. 24 CFR 966.58

7. ORS 456.095(4)

8. 24 CFR Part 964

9. *Wright v. Roanoke Redevelopment and Housing Authority*, 479 U.S. 418, 107 S.Ct. 766 (1987)

10. 24 CFR 960.207

11. 24 CFR Part 942

12. I include here Section 8 New Construction (24 CFR Part 880); Section 8 Substantial Rehabilitation (24 CFR Part 881); Section 8 Housing Assistance (24 CFR Part 883); Section 202 Elderly and Handicapped (24 CRF Part 885); Section 236 (24 CFR Part 236); and Section 221(d)(3) Housing (24 CRF Part 221).

13. 24 CFR 880.607(c) (Section 8 New Construction); 24 CFR 881.607(c) (Section 8 Substantial Rehabilitation); 24 CFR 883.708(c) (Section 8 Housing Assistance)

14. 24 CFR Part 880 (Section 8 New Construction); 24 CFR Part 881 (Section 8 Substantial Rehabilitation); 24 CFR 883.708 (Section 8 Housing Assistance); 24 CFR Part 247 (Section 202, 236, and 221(d)(3))

15. 24 CFR Part 245 requires notice to tenants for section 236, 221(d)(3), and 202 projects. The procedure for the various section 8 projects only requires publication of proposed "fair market rents" in the Federal Register. 24 CFR Part 888.

16. The most common form is Section 8 Existing Housing (24 CFR Part 882).

17. 24 CFR 882.215(a), (c)

18. 24 CFR 882.109

19. 24 CFR 882.106

20. 24 CFR 882.215(c), 882.216(b)

21. See 42 USC 1437f(o)

Chapter 14

1. ORS 90.120

2. If the landlord owns the mobile or floating home, the tenant probably has just those rights available to all residential tenants.

3. ORS 90.510
4. ORS 446.537
5. ORS 105.138
6. ORS 90.510(1)
7. ORS 90.510(3)
8. ORS 90.525
9. ORS 90.620
10. ORS 90.630
11. ORS 90.630(3)
12. ORS 90.630(4)
13. ORS 90.630(4)(b)
14. ORS 90.630(4)
15. ORS 90.630(5): "Nothing in this section shall limit a landlord's right to terminate a tenancy for nonpayment of rent or any other cause stated in ORS 90.100 to 90.940 by complying with ORS 105.105 to 105.165." "Cause," of course, is a reference to the distinction between eviction without cause and eviction for cause — see chapter 8.
16. ORS 90.510(5)(e)
17. 1991 Or Laws ch 844
18. 1991 Or Laws ch 844; 2; ORS 90.500(3); 446.003(20).
19. 1991 Or Laws ch 844; 31.
20. ORS 90.240(4)(a)
21. ORS 90.600
22. ORS 90.600(5), (6)
23. ORS 90.510(6); 90.600(7)
24. ORS 90.765
25. ORS 90.680(1), (3), (5)(b)
26. ORS 90.680(5)(b), (c); 90.510(2)(h)
27. ORS 90.680(6)
28. ORS 91.710(2)(d)
29. ORS 90.750, 90.755
30. ORS 90.760
31. OS 215.223 [counties], 227.175 [cities]
32. 1987 HB 2260
33. ORS 90.800 – 90.840
34. ORS 90.815 requires organization under ORS Chapter 60 (corporations), 62 (cooperatives), or 65 (non-profit corporations).
35. ORS 114.505, et seq.
36. ORS 90.690(1)
37. ORS 90.690(2)
38. ORS 90.690(3)

39. ORS 91.710
40. ORS 91.710(2)
41. ORS 91.710(2)(d)
42. ORS 91.710(3); ORS 90.255

Chapter 15

1. 42 USC 1981, 1982
2. 42 USC 3601, et seq.
3. Public Law 100-430, 102 Stat 1619, signed September 3, 1988. The act amends many provisions of the Civil Rights Act of 1968 and adds several provisions. Most of its terms became effective March 12, 1989. The deadline beyond which most multifamily new construction will have to be "adaptable" for handicapped persons is March 13, 1991, although HUD regulations exempt buildings for which a permit was issued on or before January 13, 1990.
4. 42 USC 1364(f), 3602, 3604. Although the handicap protections do not require "that a dwelling be made available to an individual whose tenancy would constitute a direct threat to the health or safety of other individuals or whose tenancy would result in substantial physical damage to the property of others (42 USC 3604(9)), the legislative and regulatory history establishes that this exception does not deprive AIDS victims of the protections of the handicap protections. 134 Cong Rec S10557 (August 2, 1988); 54 Fed Reg 3245 (January 23, 1989).
5. ORS 90.330(3)
6. This date can be pushed as far as September 13, 1992, by the Secretary of HUD. 42 USC 3610(f)(4)
7. ORS 659.033, 659.430
8. ORS 659.033
9. ORS 659.033(3)
10. ORS 659.121(2)
11. ORS 659.055
12. ORS 646.638(1)
13. id.
14. ORS 646.638(6)
15. ORS 646.605(5), 646.618-.632
16. ORS 646.608(1)
17. ORS 646.605(7)
18. The prohibitions of the statute are applicable to "a debt collector, while collecting or attempting to collect a debt." ORS 646.639(2). "Consumer transaction" includes "a transaction between a consumer and a person who sells, leases or provides property, services or credit to consumers"; "Consumer" means a "natural person who purchases or acquires property, services or

credit for personal, family or household purposes"; "Debt" means "any obligation or alleged obligation arising out of consumer transaction"; "Debt collector" means "any person who...attempts to enforce an obligation that is owed or due to any commercial creditor, or alleged to be owed or due to any commercial creditor, by a consumer as a result of a consumer transaction" except bad checks; and "Commercial creditor" means "a person who in the ordinary course of business engages in consumer transactions." ORS 646.639(1)

19. ORS 646.638(6)

20. ORS 646.639(2), 646.641

21. This is a bit complicated: The collector may contact the debtor by mail if the envelope does not reveal that the communication is not from a debt collector (other than a provider of goods, credit, or services). The collector may telephone no more than once a week to the debtor's place of employment, provided the collector has made a good faith effort to reach the debtor at home between 6:00 p.m. and 9:00 p.m., and provided further that the debtor has not requested not to be contacted at work and the collector has no notice that the employer prohibits such calls.

22. Although the national Legal Services Corporation was increasingly restrictive of legislative work under the Reagan Administration, legal aid programs in Oregon receive money from other sources as well. Legislative work is financed with non-Legal Services money in those programs which engage in lobbying.

23. ORS 91.225

INDEX

A